CG125BR—
1985 MODE

C000272667

Honda CG125
Service and Repair Manual

by Pete Shoemark and Jeremy Churchill

(433-7AG12-168)

Models covered
CG125. 124cc. June 1976 to May 1978
CG125 K1. 124cc. May 1978 to March 1981
CG125-B. 124cc. March 1981 to March 1982
CG125-C. 124cc. March 1982 to November 1984
CG125-E. 124cc. November 1984 to April 1985
CG125 BR-E/F. 124cc. April 1985 to April 1988
CG125 BR-J. 124cc. April 1988 to September 1991
CG125 BR-K. 124cc. September 1991 to April 1995
CG125 BR-S/T. 124cc. April 1995 to November 1997
CG125-W. 124cc. November 1997 to 2000
CG125M-1. 124cc. 2001 to 2003
CG125ES-4. 124cc. 2004 to 2006
CG125ES-7. 124cc. 2007

© Haynes Publishing 2007

A book in the **Haynes Service and Repair Manual Series**

ISBN 978 1 84425 753 9

British Library Cataloguing in Publication Data
A catalogue record for this book is available from the British Library

Printed in the USA

ABCDE
FGHIJ
KLMNO
PQ
3

Haynes Publishing
Sparkford, Yeovil, Somerset BA22 7JJ, England

Haynes North America, Inc
861 Lawrence Drive, Newbury Park, California 91320, USA

Haynes Publishing Nordiska AB
Box 1504, 751 45 UPPSALA, Sweden

Printed using 33-lb Resolute Book 65 4.0 from Resolute Forest P oducts Calhoun, TN mill. Resolute is a member of World Wildlife Fund's Climate Savers programme committed to significantly reducing GHG emissions. This paper uses 50% less wood fibre than traditional offset. The Calhoun Mill is certified to the following sustainable forest management and chain of custody standards: SFI, PEFC and FSC Controlled Wood.

Acknowledgements

Our thanks are due to APS Motorcycles of Wells (formerly Fran Ridewood & Co), Paul Branson Motorcycles of Yeovil, and CSM of Taunton, who supplied the machines featured in this manual.

We would also like to thank the Avon Rubber Company, who kindly supplied information and technical assistance on tyre fitting; NGK Spark Plugs (UK) Ltd for information on spark plug maintenance and electrode conditions and Renold Limited for advice on chain care and renewal.

About this manual

The author of this manual has the conviction that the only way in which a meaningful and easy to follow text can be written is first to do the work himself, under conditions similar to those found in the average household. As a result, the hands seen in the photographs are those of the author. Even the machines are not new: examples that have covered a considerable mileage were selected so that the conditions encountered would be typical of those found by the average owner.

Unless specially mentioned, and therefore considered essential, Honda service tools have not been used. There is invariably some alternative means of slackening or removing some vital component when service tools are not available and risk of damage has to be avoided at all costs.

Each of the six Chapters is divided into numbered Sections. Within the Sections are numbered paragraphs. In consequence, cross reference throughout this manual is both straightforward and logical. When a reference is made 'See Section 5.12' it means Section 5, paragraph 12 in the same Chapter. If another Chapter were meant, the text would read 'See Chapter 2,

Section 5.12'. All photographs are captioned with a Section/paragraph number to which they refer and are always relevant to the Chapter text adjacent.

Figure numbers (usually line illustrations) appear in numerical order, within a given Chapter. Fig. 1.1 therefore refers to the first figure in Chapter 1. Left-hand and right-hand descriptions of the machines and their component parts refer to the right and left of a given machine when the rider is seated normally.

Motorcycle manufacturers continually make changes to specifications and recommendations, and these, when notified, are incorporated into our manuals at the earliest opportunity.

We take great pride in the accuracy of information given in this manual, but motorcycle manufacturers make alterations and design changes during the production run of a particular motorcycle of which they do not inform us. No liability can be accepted by the authors or publishers for loss, damage or injury caused by any errors in, or omissions from, the information given.

Contents

The Honda CG125 model

The Honda CG125-C model

Introduction to the Honda CG125

The CG125 model first appeared in the UK in June 1976. It can be regarded in many ways as a utility version of the popular CB125 with which it shares many features. The basic difference between the two models is the CG125's use of pushrod operated overhead valves in place of the more popular overhead camshaft arrangement. The unit provides surprisingly brisk performance coupled with good fuel economy. The machine in general is functional and sensibly equipped, and does not suffer the surfeit of gadgetry so often found on its contemporaries. Its inherent simplicity makes it an ideal learner's or commuter's mount, both in terms of ease of riding and in its ease of maintenance. A noteworthy feature is the adoption of a full rear chain enclosure. Although this is by no means a new idea, having appeared and disappeared many times over the years with the changing dictates of fashion, it is, nevertheless, an eminently sensible feature, greatly extending chain life.

Despite remaining basically unchanged, the CG125 has received several modifications and has been altered slightly in appearance to keep up with its rivals. Five distinct versions have appeared, with differences of varying significance, which are identified (where applicable) in this Manual by their Honda model code suffixes. Identification details, as available, are given below with the approximate dates of import; note that the latter need not necessarily coincide with the machine's date of registration.

The CG125 model (no identifying suffix) has the frame numbers CG125-1023061 to 1111090. Engine numbers are not available. Identified by its shrouded, external spring, front forks, this model was imported from June 1976 to May 1978.

The CG125 K1 model has the frame numbers CG125-1114636 to 1162518. Engine numbers not available. It differed most noticeably from the CG125 model in having front forks with internal springs and exposed stanchions, and was imported from May 1978 to March 1981.

The CG125-B model has the frame numbers CG125-1202755 to 1223689; its engine numbers start at CG125E-1374586. It can be distinguished from the K1 model only by its different paintwork and graphics and was imported from March 1981 to March 1982.

The CG125-C model has the frame numbers CG125-1272831 to 1286692; its engine numbers start at CG125E-1513928 on. Fitted with revised tail lamp, flashing indicator lamps, handlebar switches and the usual detail changes to paintwork and graphics. This model is also fitted with a higher compression engine and the (T)PFC carburettor for greater fuel economy. Note also that the ignition switch is combined in a new warning lamp cluster, mounted next to the speedometer. Imported from March 1982 to November 1984.

The CG125-E model has the frame number CG125-1288790 to 1293380 and the engine numbers CG125E-1689761 to 1694851. Identical to the C model except for detail changes to the graphics, this model was imported from November 1984 to April 1985.

All the aforementioned models are of Japanese manufacture and are covered in Chapters 1 to 6. Later models were manufactured in Brazil and Turkey; refer to Chapter 7 for further information.

Model dimensions and weight

Overall length	1840 mm (72.4 in)
Overall width	735 mm (28.9 in)
Overall height	1025 mm (40.4 in)
Wheelbase	1200 mm (47.2 in)
Seat height	755 mm (29.7 in)
Ground clearance	135 mm (5.3 in)
Dry weight	95 kg (209 lb)

Ordering spare parts

When ordering spare parts for the CG125 models, it is advisable to deal direct with an official Honda agent, who will be able to supply many of the items required ex-stock. It is advisable to get acquainted with the local Honda agent, and to rely on his advice when purchasing spares. He is in a better position to specify exactly the parts required and to identify the relevant spare part numbers so that there is less chance of the wrong part being supplied by the manufacturer due to a vague or incomplete description.

When ordering spares, always quote the frame and engine numbers in full, together with any prefixes or suffixes in the form of letters. The frame number is found stamped on the right-hand side of the steering head, in line with the forks. The engine number is stamped on the left-hand side of the crankcase, immediately behind the oil strainer cap.

Use only parts of genuine Honda manufacture. A few pattern parts are available, sometimes at a cheaper price, but there is no guarantee that they will give such good service as the originals they replace. Retain any worn or broken parts until the replacements have been obtained; they are sometimes needed as a pattern to help identify the correct replacement when design changes have been made during a production run.

Some of the more expendable parts such as spark plugs, bulbs, tyres, oils and greases etc., can be obtained from accessory shops and motor factors, who have convenient opening hours and can often be found not far from home. It is also possible to obtain them on a Mail Order basis from a number of specialists who advertise regularly in the motorcycle magazines.

Frame number location

Engine number location

Safety first!

Professional motor mechanics are trained in safe working procedures. However enthusiastic you may be about getting on with the job in hand, do take the time to ensure that your safety is not put at risk. A moment's lack of attention can result in an accident, as can failure to observe certain elementary precautions.

There will always be new ways of having accidents, and the following points do not pretend to be a comprehensive list of all dangers; they are intended rather to make you aware of the risks and to encourage a safety-conscious approach to all work you carry out on your vehicle.

Essential DOs and DON'Ts

DON'T start the engine without first ascertaining that the transmission is in neutral.

DON'T suddenly remove the filler cap from a hot cooling system – cover it with a cloth and release the pressure gradually first, or you may get scalded by escaping coolant.

DON'T attempt to drain oil until you are sure it has cooled sufficiently to avoid scalding you.

DON'T grasp any part of the engine, exhaust or silencer without first ascertaining that it is sufficiently cool to avoid burning you.

DON'T allow brake fluid or antifreeze to contact the machine's paintwork or plastic components.

DON'T syphon toxic liquids such as fuel, brake fluid or antifreeze by mouth, or allow them to remain on your skin.

DON'T inhale dust – it may be injurious to health (see *Asbestos* heading).

DON'T allow any spilt oil or grease to remain on the floor – wipe it up straight away, before someone slips on it.

DON'T use ill-fitting spanners or other tools which may slip and cause injury.

DON'T attempt to lift a heavy component which may be beyond your capability – get assistance.

DON'T rush to finish a job, or take unverified short cuts.

DON'T allow children or animals in or around an unattended vehicle.

DON'T inflate a tyre to a pressure above the recommended maximum. Apart from overstressing the carcase and wheel rim, in extreme cases the tyre may blow off forcibly.

DO ensure that the machine is supported securely at all times. This is especially important when the machine is blocked up to aid wheel or fork removal.

DO take care when attempting to slacken a stubborn nut or bolt. It is generally better to pull on a spanner, rather than push, so that if slippage occurs you fall away from the machine rather than on to it.

DO wear eye protection when using power tools such as drill, sander, bench grinder etc.

DO use a barrier cream on your hands prior to undertaking dirty jobs – it will protect your skin from infection as well as making the dirt easier to remove afterwards; but make sure your hands aren't left slippery. Note that long-term contact with used engine oil can be a health hazard.

DO keep loose clothing (cuffs, tie etc) and long hair well out of the way of moving mechanical parts.

DO remove rings, wristwatch etc, before working on the vehicle – especially the electrical system.

DO keep your work area tidy – it is only too easy to fall over articles left lying around.

DO exercise caution when compressing springs for removal or installation. Ensure that the tension is applied and released in a controlled manner, using suitable tools which preclude the possibility of the spring escaping violently.

DO ensure that any lifting tackle used has a safe working load rating adequate for the job.

DO get someone to check periodically that all is well, when working alone on the vehicle.

DO carry out work in a logical sequence and check that everything is correctly assembled and tightened afterwards.

DO remember that your vehicle's safety affects that of yourself and others. If in doubt on any point, get specialist advice.

IF, in spite of following these precautions, you are unfortunate enough to injure yourself, seek medical attention as soon as possible.

Asbestos

Certain friction, insulating, sealing, and other products – such as brake linings, clutch linings, gaskets, etc – contain asbestos. *Extreme care must be taken to avoid inhalation of dust from such products since it is hazardous to health.* If in doubt, assume that they *do* contain asbestos.

Fire

Remember at all times that petrol (gasoline) is highly flammable. Never smoke, or have any kind of naked flame around, when working on the vehicle. But the risk does not end there – a spark caused by an electrical short-circuit, by two metal surfaces contacting each other, by careless use of tools, or even by static electricity built up in your body under certain conditions, can ignite petrol vapour, which in a confined space is highly explosive.

Always disconnect the battery earth (ground) terminal before working on any part of the fuel or electrical system, and never risk spilling fuel on to a hot engine or exhaust.

It is recommended that a fire extinguisher of a type suitable for fuel and electrical fires is kept handy in the garage or workplace at all times. Never try to extinguish a fuel or electrical fire with water.

Note: *Any reference to a 'torch' appearing in this manual should always be taken to mean a hand-held battery-operated electric lamp or flashlight. It does **not** mean a welding/gas torch or blowlamp.*

Fumes

Certain fumes are highly toxic and can quickly cause unconsciousness and even death if inhaled to any extent. Petrol (gasoline) vapour comes into this category, as do the vapours from certain solvents such as trichloroethylene. Any draining or pouring of such volatile fluids should be done in a well ventilated area.

When using cleaning fluids and solvents, read the instructions carefully. Never use materials from unmarked containers – they may give off poisonous vapours.

Never run the engine of a motor vehicle in an enclosed space such as a garage. Exhaust fumes contain carbon monoxide which is extremely poisonous; if you need to run the engine, always do so in the open air or at least have the rear of the vehicle outside the workplace.

The battery

Never cause a spark, or allow a naked light, near the vehicle's battery. It will normally be giving off a certain amount of hydrogen gas, which is highly explosive.

Always disconnect the battery earth (ground) terminal before working on the fuel or electrical systems.

If possible, loosen the filler plugs or cover when charging the battery from an external source. Do not charge at an excessive rate or the battery may burst.

Take care when topping up and when carrying the battery. The acid electrolyte, even when diluted, is very corrosive and should not be allowed to contact the eyes or skin.

If you ever need to prepare electrolyte yourself, always add the acid slowly to the water, and never the other way round. Protect against splashes by wearing rubber gloves and goggles.

Mains electricity and electrical equipment

When using an electric power tool, inspection light etc, always ensure that the appliance is correctly connected to its plug and that, where necessary, it is properly earthed (grounded). Do not use such appliances in damp conditions and, again, beware of creating a spark or applying excessive heat in the vicinity of fuel or fuel vapour. Also ensure that the appliances meet the relevant national safety standards.

Ignition HT voltage

A severe electric shock can result from touching certain parts of the ignition system, such as the HT leads, when the engine is running or being cranked, particularly if components are damp or the insulation is defective. Where an electronic ignition system is fitted, the HT voltage is much higher and could prove fatal.

Routine maintenance

Refer to Chapter 7 for information relating to 1985-on models

Introduction

Periodic routine maintenance is a continuous process that commences immediately the machine is used. It must be carried out at specified mileage recordings, or on a calendar basis if the machine is not used frequently, whichever is the sooner. Maintenance should be regarded as an insurance policy, to help keep the machine in the peak of condition and to ensure long, trouble-free service. It has the additional benefit of giving early warning of any faults that may develop and will act as a regular safety check, to the obvious advantage of both rider and machine alike.

The various maintenance tasks are described under their respective mileage and calendar headings. Accompanying diagrams are provided, where necessary. It should be remembered that the interval between the various maintenance tasks serves only as a guide. As the machine gets older or is used under particularly adverse conditions, it would be advisable to reduce the period between each check.

For ease of reference each service operation is described in detail under the relevant heading. However, if further general information is required, it can be found within the manual under the pertinent section heading in the relevant Chapter.

In order that the routine maintenance tasks are carried out with as much ease as possible, it is essential that a good selection of general workshop tools is available.

Included in the kit must be a range of metric ring or combination spanners, a selection of crosshead screwdrivers and at least one pair of circlip pliers.

Additionally, owing to the extreme tightness of most casing screws on Japanese machines, an impact screwdriver, together with a choice of large and small crosshead screw bits, is absolutely indispensable. This is particularly so if the engine has not been dismantled since leaving the factory.

Daily (pre-ride check)

It is recommended that the following items are checked whenever the machine is about to be used. This is important to prevent the risk of unexpected failure of any component while riding the machine and, with experience, can be reduced to a simple checklist which will only take a few moments to complete. For those owners who are not inclined to check all items with such frequency, it is suggested that the best course is to carry out the checks in the form of a service which can be undertaken each week or before any long journey. It is essential that all items are checked and serviced with reasonable frequency.

1   Check the engine oil level

With the machine standing upright on its centre stand on level ground, start the engine and allow it to idle for a few seconds so that the oil can circulate, then stop the engine. Wait one or two minutes for the level to settle and unscrew the dipstick/filler plug from the rear of the crankcase right-hand cover. Wipe it clean and insert it into the filler orifice; **do not screw** it in, but allow it to rest. Withdraw the dipstick; the oil level should be between the maximum and minimum level lines, ie in the cross-hatched area.

If topping up is necessary use only good quality SAE10W/40 engine oil of the specified type. Do not allow the level to rise above the top of the cross-hatched area on the dipstick, and never use the machine if the level is found to be in the plain area below the cross-hatching; top up immediately.

Tighten the dipstick securely and wash off any spilt oil.

2   Check the fuel level

Checking the petrol level may seem obvious, but it is all too easy to forget. Ensure that you have enough petrol to complete your journey, or at least to get you to the nearest petrol station.

3   Check the brakes

Check the front and rear brakes work effectively and without binding. Ensure that the cable or rod linkage is lubricated and properly adjusted.

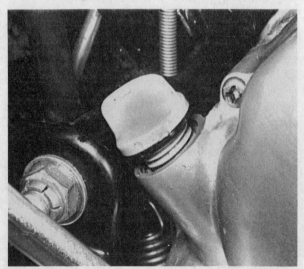
Rest dipstick in position to obtain correct reading

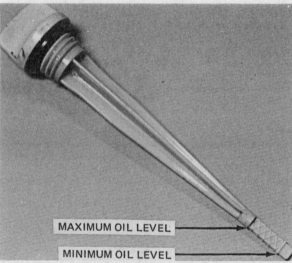
MAXIMUM OIL LEVEL

MINIMUM OIL LEVEL

Dipstick shows allowable oil level range

4 Check the tyre pressures and tread wear

Check the tyre pressures with a gauge that is known to be accurate. It is worthwhile purchasing a pocket gauge for this purpose because the gauges on garage forecourt airlines are notoriously inaccurate. The pressures, which should be checked with the tyres cold, are specified at the end of Routine maintenance and in Chapter 5.

At the same time as the tyre pressures are checked, examine the tyres themselves. Check them for damage, especially splitting of the sidewalls. Remove any small stones or other road debris caught between the treads. When checking the tyres for damage, they should be examined for tread depth in view of both the legal and safety aspects. It is vital to keep the tread depth within the UK legal limits of 1 mm of depth over three-quarters of the tread breadth around the entire circumference with no bald patches. Many riders, however, consider nearer 2 mm to be the limit for secure roadholding, traction, and braking, especially in adverse weather conditions, and it should be noted that Honda recommend minimum tread depths of 1.5 mm (0.06 in) for the front tyre and 2.0 mm (0.08 in) for the rear; these measurements to be taken at the centre of the tread. Renew any tyre that is found to be damaged or excessively worn.

5 Safety check

Check that the front and rear suspension is operating correctly, that the chain is lubricated and adjusted correctly and that the battery is in good condition. Check the throttle and clutch cables and levers, the gear lever and the footrests and stand to ensure that they are adjusted correctly, functioning correctly, and that all nuts and bolts are securely fastened.

6 Legal check

Check that all lights, turn signals, horn and speedometer are working correctly to make sure that the machine complies with all legal requirements in this respect. Check also that the headlamp is correctly aimed to comply with local legislation.

Monthly or every 600 miles (1000 km)

1 Check the battery

The battery should be checked regularly to ensure that the electrolyte level is maintained between the level lines on the casing, that the terminals are clean and securely fastened and that the vent tube is correctly routed and free from blockages. Refer to Chapter 6.5 for details.

2 Check the final drive chain

Despite its full enclosure, the final drive chain requires regular attention to ensure maximum chain life. Remove the rubber plug from the chaincase inspection aperture to check the tension and carry out temporary lubrication. The best lubricant is commercial chain lubricant, contained in an aerosol can; engine oil or gear oil are better than nothing but are flung off too quickly to be of any real use. Best of all are the special chain greases described in Chapter 5.14.

Adjust the chain after lubrication, so that there is approximately 20 mm ($\frac{3}{4}$ in) slack in the middle of the lower run. Always check with the chain at the tightest point as a chain rarely wears evenly during service.

Adjustment is accomplished after placing the machine on the centre stand and slackening the spindle nut, so that the wheel can be drawn backwards by means of the drawbolt adjusters in the swinging arm fork ends.

The torque arm nut and the rear brake adjuster must also be slackened during this operation. Adjust the drawbolts an equal amount to preserve wheel alignment. The fork ends are clearly marked with a series of parallel lines above the adjusters, to provide a simple visual check.

3 Additional engine oil change

Since the engine relies so heavily on the quantity and quality of its oil, and since the oil in any motorcycle engine is worked far harder than in other vehicles, it is recommended that the engine oil is changed at more frequent intervals than those specified by the manufacturer. This is particularly important if the machine is used at very high speeds for long periods of time, and even more important if the machine is used only at very slow speed or for very short journeys. The oil should be changed at approximate intervals of every month or every 1000 miles, depending on usage. Honda specify that the oil should be changed at least once annually or every 1800 miles (3000 km), whichever comes first.

Three-monthly, or every 1850 miles (3000 km)

1 Change the engine oil and clean the filter gauze

This is the specified interval at which the engine/gearbox oil should be changed; in normal use it should be regarded as the maximum permissible.

It is recommended that the oil be changed after a run to ensure that the engine is warm. This helps the oil to drain thoroughly. Obtain a container of at least 1 litre (1.76 pints)

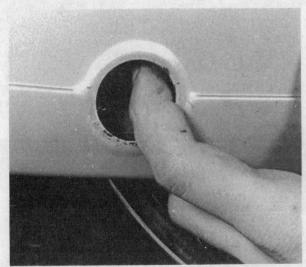

Free play can be felt via the inspection hole

Move each adjuster by an equal amount

capacity and place it beneath the engine unit to catch the old oil. Unscrew the drain plug on the underside of the crankcase and allow the oil to drain.

Remove the large hexagon-headed plug which is located just below the left-hand engine casing. Remove the plug, followed by the spring and gauze element, and then wash all these components carefully in a suitable solvent. Wipe out any residual oil from the housing with a clean lint-free rag prior to reassembly. Refit the drain plug, tightening it to a torque setting of 2.0 – 3.5 kgf m (14.5 – 25 lbf ft), and refill the engine with the correct quantity and grade of oil.

Six-monthly, or every 3700 miles (6000 km)

Repeat all service operations listed under previous headings, then carry out the following:

1   Clean the air filter

Pull off the right-hand side panel and remove the two nuts which secure the air filter cover. Withdraw the cover, checking that the sealing gasket is in good condition, pull out the retaining spring and withdraw the element assembly. Peel off the inner and outer foam sleeves. Wash all components in white spirit (Stoddard solvent) or in warm water and detergent and dry them thoroughly. Soak the foam sleeves in the specified oil, then squeeze them gently (do not wring them out or they will be damaged) to expel all surplus oil. Refit the sleeves to the element frame. On reassembly ensure that all components are correctly fitted so that unfiltered air cannot bypass the element.

2   Check the spark plug

Remove the spark plug cap, unscrew the plug and check its condition, comparing it with the colour photographs on page 65. If it is badly worn or fouled it must be renewed. If it is fit for further service check the gap and reset it if necessary, as described in Chapter 3.8.

3   Check the valve clearances

It is important that the correct valve clearance is maintained. A small amount of free play is designed into the valve train to allow for expansion of the various components. If the setting deviates greatly from that specified, a marked drop in performance will be evident. In the case of the clearance becoming too great, it will be found that valve operation will be noisy, and performance will drop off as a result of the valves not opening fully. If on the other hand, the clearance is too small, the valves may not close completely. This will not only cause loss of compression, but will also cause the valves to burn out very quickly. In extreme cases, a valve head may strike the piston crown, causing extensive damage to the engine. The clearances should be checked and adjusted with a **cold** engine.

Place the machine on its centre stand and remove the rocker cover, taking care not to damage the O ring. Remove the gearchange pedal and the left-hand outer cover to expose the generator rotor.

Remove plug and allow old oil to drain

Remove the spark plug, then slowly rotate the engine anti-clockwise by way of the generator rotor, watching the inlet valve. When it has opened and closed again (sunk down and risen up to its original position), rotate the engine further until the 'T' mark on the rotor periphery aligns exactly with the raised index mark which is positioned between 12 and 1 o'clock (from the crankshaft) on the generator stator. The engine will then be in the correct position for checking the valve clearances, namely at Top Dead Centre (TDC) on the compression stroke; check that there is free play at both rockers.

Using a 0.08 mm (0.003 in) feeler gauge, check the clearance between the top of each valve stem and its corresponding rocker. The feeler gauge must be a light sliding fit, with the rocker and valve stem **just** nipping it. If necessary, slacken the locknut, and turn the small square-headed adjuster to obtain the correct setting. Tighten the locknut, holding the adjuster at the same time to prevent it from moving. Finally, recheck the setting and then repeat the procedure on the other rocker.

4   Check the contact breaker points and ignition timing

Note: since the generator stator plate is located by its countersunk retaining screws, the ignition timing can only be altered by opening or closing the contact breaker gap; therefore both operations are described as one. The full procedure is given here for ease of reference, but if the points are found to be in good condition and if the gap has not altered or is within the tolerance, then the ignition timing will be sufficiently accurate and there will be no need to carry out the full check. First remove the gearchange pedal, the left-hand outer cover, the spark plug and the left-hand side panel.

Strainer is easily removed for cleaning

Dismantle the element for cleaning and lubrication

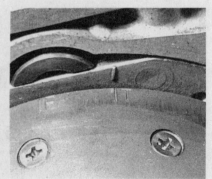

"T" mark should align as shown

Checking the condition of the contact breaker points

The contact breaker assembly can be viewed through one of the generator rotor slots; turn the rotor until the points open. Use a small screwdriver to push the moving point open against its spring. Examine the point contact faces. If they are burnt or pitted, remove the points for cleaning or renewal, see Chapter 3.4. Light surface deposits can be removed with crocus paper or a piece of stiff card.

If the contact faces are badly burnt or pitted, or if the moving contact fibre heel shows signs of wear or damage, renew the assembly. It is essential that the points are in good condition if the ignition timing is to be correct; use only genuine Honda parts when renewing. If the faces are only mildly marked, clean them using an oilstone or fine emery but be careful to keep them square. If it is necessary to separate the moving contact from the fixed one, carefully remove the circlip fitted to the pivot post and note carefully the arrangement of washers at both the pivot post and spring blade fixing. On reassembly, the moving contact must be able to move freely; apply a smear of grease to the pivot post. Note also that the low tension lead terminal and the moving contact spring blade must be connected to each other via the small bolt, but that both must be completely insulated from the fixed contact. *The engine will not run if a short-circuit occurs at this point.*

Refit the points to the stator plate and the rotor to the crankshaft. Tighten the rotor nut to a torque setting of 4.0 – 5.0 kgf m (29 – 36 lbf ft), then apply a few drops of oil to the cam lubricating wick.

Checking the ignition timing

Disconnect the generator wiring at the connector block joining it to the main wiring loom and identify the black or black/white wire leading to the points. The best way of establishing exactly when the points open is to use either a multimeter set to its most sensitive resistance scale, or a battery and bulb test circuit; refer to Chapter 3 for details. The meter needle will flicker to indicate increased resistance as the points open, or the bulb (which will be lit when the points are closed) will glow dimmer; note that a high-wattage bulb must be used to make this more obvious to the eye.

Turn the rotor anticlockwise until the meter needle deflects (or the bulb dims); at this point the rotor 'F' mark should align exactly with the raised index mark on the stator plate.

The setting is adjusted by opening or closing the points gap to advance or retard respectively the ignition timing. Repeat the procedure to check that the timing is now correct.

When the timing is correct, measure very carefully the points gap, to ensure that the dwell angle is correct for the maximum spark intensity. If the gap is found to be outside the permitted tolerance the contact breaker points are excessively worn and must be renewed.

Fit a new set of contact breaker points; note that it is essential that only genuine Honda points are used. Refit the rotor and set the points gap to exactly 0.35 mm (0.014 in), then repeat the procedure given above. The ignition timing should be correct.

Note: The above procedure is described in full as it is the most accurate means of setting the ignition timing. In practice there is no need to repeat the full procedure at every service interval. Instead it is sufficient to check that the points gap is within tolerances.

If a strobe timing light is available the ATU's performance can be checked. Connect the light following its manufacturer's instructions, then start the engine and allow it to idle. At idle speed the 'F' mark should align with the raised index mark; at just above idle speed the mark should appear to move as the advance begins until at 3000 rpm the two parallel lines of the full advance mark are aligned with the index mark. If the movement is stiff and jerky, or if the advance range is restricted, the rotor must be removed so that the ATU can be dismantled for cleaning and greasing.

5 General checks and lubrication

At regular intervals the control cables must be thoroughly lubricated, using light machine oil. This can be done by either disconnecting the cable upper end and fitting a proprietary cable oiler to pump oil through, or by removing the cable from the machine and hanging it up overnight so that oil can drain through the cable from a small funnel attached to its upper end. Ensure that the cables are correctly routed and adjusted on refitting. Grease the speedometer drive cable as described in Chapter 4.17.

Check all pivots and control levers, cleaning and lubricating them to prevent wear or corrosion. Where necessary, dismantle and clean any moving part which may have become stiff in operation. Similarly clean, check and grease the stand pivots and ensure that the return spring holds the stand securely.

Check around the machine, looking for loose nuts, bolts or screws, retightening them as necessary.

It is advisable to lubricate the handlebar switches and stop lamp switches with WD40 or a similar water dispersant lubricant.

6 Check the fuel system

Referring to the relevant Sections of Chapter 2 (or of Chapter 7 for (T)PFC carburettors) for full details check that the petrol tank, tap, and feed pipe are in good condition and securely fastened with no leaks. Check also that the choke operates correctly. If rough running of the engine has developed, some adjustment of the carburettor pilot setting and tickover speed may be required. Do not make these adjustments unless they are obviously required; there is little to be gained by unwarranted attention to the carburettor.

Switch on the petrol tap and unscrew the float bowl drain plug, allowing a small quantity of petrol to flush through. If large amounts of dirt or water are found in the petrol, the system components must be drained and cleaned out.

Once the carburettor has been checked and reset if necessary, the throttle cable free play can be checked. Open

Set clearance so that the feeler gauge is a sliding fit

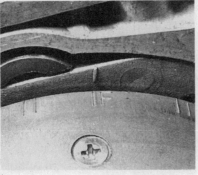

"F" mark should align just as points separate

Contact breaker gap is measured via aperture

and close the throttle several times, allowing it to snap shut under its own pressure. Ensure that it is able to shut off quickly and fully at all handlebar positions, then check that there is 2 – 6 mm (0.08 – 0.24 in) of cable free play, measured in terms of twistgrip rotation. If adjustment is necessary, use first the adjuster which is set below the twistgrip. If there is an insufficient range of adjustment the surplus free play can be eliminated by peeling back the rubber cover and by using the adjuster on the carburettor top.

7 Check the clutch adjustment

Fine adjustment is provided on the handlebar lever by way of a threaded adjuster and lockring. Should this prove insufficient, a second adjuster nut and locknut can be found at the cable lower end. These should be set to give 10 – 20 mm (0.4 – 0.8 in) movement at the lever end before the clutch begins to lift.

8 Check the brakes

The brakes are adjusted by a nut at the end of the brake cable or rod, as appropriate, with the front brake having an additional fine adjuster at the cable handlebar end. To adjust the brakes place the machine on its centre stand with the wheel to be adjusted clear of the ground. Spin the wheel and tighten the adjusting nut until a rubbing sound is heard as the shoes begin to contact the drum, then unscrew the nut by $\frac{1}{2}$ – 1 turn until the sound ceases. Spin the wheel hard and apply the brake firmly to settle all components, then re-check the setting. This procedure should give the specified setting of 20 – 30 mm (0.8 – 1.2 in) free play, measured at the lever or pedal tip. Check that the stop lamp rear switch is set so that the lamp lights just as pedal free play is taken up and the brake is beginning to engage.

At regular intervals the wheels should be removed so that each brake assembly can be cleaned and checked for wear. Renew any worn components and apply a smear of grease to the camshaft bearing surfaces on reassembly. See Chapter 5.4.

9 Check the wheels

Referring to Chapter 5.2 check the wheel rims for runout, the spokes for straightness, security and even tension, and the bearings for signs of free play. Any faults found must be rectified immediately.

10 Check the suspension and steering

Support the machine so that it is secure with the front wheel clear of the ground, then grasp the front fork legs near the wheel spindle and push and pull firmly in a fore and aft direction. If play is evident between the top and bottom fork yokes and the steering head, the steering head bearings are in need of adjustment. Imprecise handling or a tendency for the front forks to judder may be caused by this fault.

Bearing adjustment is correct when the lockring is tightened until resistance to movement is felt and then loosened by $\frac{1}{8}$ to $\frac{1}{4}$ of a turn. The lockring should be rotated by means of a C-spanner after slackening the steering stem nut.

Take great care not to overtighten the lockring. It is possible to place a pressure of several tons on the head bearings by over-tightening even though the handlebars may seem to turn quite freely. Overtight bearings will cause the machine to roll at low speeds and give imprecise steering. Adjustment is correct if there is no play in the bearings and the handlebars swing to full lock either side when the machine is supported with the front wheel clear of the ground. Only a light tap on each end should cause the handlebars to swing. Secure the lockring by tightening the steering stem nut to a torque setting of 6.0 – 9.0 kgf m (43 – 65 lbf ft) then check that the setting has not altered.

Examine closely the front and rear suspension. Ensure that the front forks work smoothly and progressively by pumping them up and down whilst the front brake is held on. Any faults revealed by this check should be investigated further. Check carefully for signs of leaks around the front fork oil seals. If any damage is found, it must be repaired immediately as described in the relevant Sections of Chapter 4.

To check the swinging arm place the machine on its centre stand then pull and push horizontally at the rear end of the swinging arm; there should be no discernible play at the pivot.

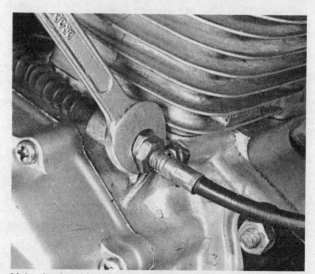

Main clutch cable adjuster is at lower end of cable

Annually, or every 7500 miles (12 000 km)

Repeat all service operations listed under previous headings, then carry out the following:

1 Renew the spark plug

The spark plug should be renewed at this interval, regardless of its apparent condition.

Front brake adjuster nut

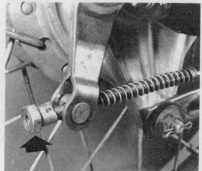

Rear brake adjuster nut

Clean out accumulated sediment from housing

2 Clean the centrifugal oil filter

Remove the crankcase right-hand cover, as described in Chapter 1.10, then remove its three retaining screws and withdraw the filter cover; note the gasket. Carefully clean out the deposits which will have accumulated around the inner edge of the unit, noting that these may have become quite compacted and may need scraping off. Wash each part out using a lint-free rag soaked in solvent, then dry them off before refitting the cover. Refit the crankcase cover and refill the engine to the correct level with the specified oil.

3 Change the front fork oil

Place the machine on the centre stand then remove the fork top bolts. Unscrew the drain plug from each fork lower leg and allow the oil to drain into a suitable container. This is accomplished most easily if the legs are attended to in turn. Take care not to spill any oil onto the brake or tyre. The forks may be pumped up and down to expel any remaining oil. Refit and tighten the drain plugs to a torque setting of 0.3 – 0.6 kgf m (2 – 4 lbf ft). Refill each fork leg with the specified oil. Refit and tighten the fork top bolts to a torque setting of 3.0 – 4.0 kgf m (22 – 29 lbf ft).

Quick glance maintenance data

Oil capacity	
Engine/gearbox unit approx	1.0 litre (1.76 Imp pint)
Front forks – at oil change	
CG125	120 – 130 cc (4.22 – 4.58 Imp fl oz)
CG125 K1, B, C, E	130 – 140 cc (4.58 – 4.93 Imp fl oz)
Valve clearances – inlet and exhaust, cold engine	0.08 mm (0.003 in)
Contact breaker gap	
Nominal	0.35 mm (0.014 in)
Tolerance – for ignition timing	0.30 – 0.40 mm (0.012 – 0.016 in)
Spark plug gap	0.6 – 0.7 mm (0.024 – 0.028 in)
Tyre pressures – solo, tyres cold	
Front	25 psi (1.75 kg/cm^2)
Rear	28 psi (2.00 kg/cm^2)

Recommended lubricants

Petrol	Either leaded three- or four-star (minimum octane rating of 91) or unleaded premium
Engine/gearbox unit	Good quality SAE10W/40 engine oil, API class SE, SF or SG
Front forks	Automatic transmission fluid (ATF) or equivalent fork oil
Air cleaner	SAE80 or 90 gear oil – SAE30 engine oil if gear oil not available
Final drive chain	Commercial chain lubricant
Brake camshafts, wheel bearings and speedometer drive	High melting-point grease
All other greasing points	General purpose grease
Control cables	Engine oil or light machine oil

Working conditions and tools

When a major overhaul is contemplated, it is important that a clean, well-lit working space is available, equipped with a workbench and vice, and with space for laying out or storing the dismantled assemblies in an orderly manner where they are unlikely to be disturbed. The use of a good workshop will give the satisfaction of work done in comfort and without haste, where there is little chance of the machine being dismantled and reassembled in anything other than clean surroundings. Unfortunately, these ideal working conditions are not always practicable and under these latter circumstances when improvisation is called for, extra care and time will be needed.

The other essential requirement is a comprehensive set of good quality tools. Quality is of prime importance since cheap tools will prove expensive in the long run if they slip or break when in use, causing personal injury or expensive damage to the component being worked on. A good quality tool will last a long time, and more than justify the cost.

For practically all tools, a tool factor is the best source since he will have a very comprehensive range compared with the average garage or accessory shop. Having said that, accessory shops often offer excellent quality tools at discount prices, so it pays to shop around. There are plenty of tools around at reasonable prices, but always aim to purchase items which meet the relevant national safety standards. If in doubt, seek the advice of the shop proprietor or manager before making a purchase.

The basis of any tool kit is a set of open-ended spanners, which can be used on almost any part of the machine to which there is reasonable access. A set of ring spanners makes a useful addition, since they can be used on nuts that are very tight or where access is restricted. Where the cost has to be kept within reasonable bounds, a compromise can be effected with a set of combination spanners – open-ended at one end and having a ring of the same size on the other end. Socket spanners may also be considered a good investment, a basic $3/8$ in or $1/2$ in drive kit comprising a ratchet handle and a small number of socket heads, if money is limited. Additional sockets can be purchased, as and when they are required. Provided they are slim in profile, sockets will reach nuts or bolts that are deeply recessed. When purchasing spanners of any kind, make sure the correct size standard is purchased. Almost all machines manufactured outside the UK and the USA have metric nuts and bolts, whilst those produced in Britain have BSF or BSW sizes. The standard used in USA is AF, which is also found on some of the later British machines. Others tools that should be included in the kit are a range of crosshead screwdrivers, a pair of pliers and a hammer.

When considering the purchase of tools, it should be remembered that by carrying out the work oneself, a large proportion of the normal repair cost, made up by labour charges, will be saved. The economy made on even a minor overhaul will go a long way towards the improvement of a toolkit.

In addition to the basic tool kit, certain additional tools can prove invaluable when they are close to hand, to help speed up a multitude of repetitive jobs. For example, an impact screwdriver will ease the removal of screws that have been tightened by a similar tool, during assembly, without a risk of damaging the screw heads. And, of course, it can be used again to retighten the screws, to ensure an oil or airtight seal results. Circlip pliers have their uses too, since gear pinions, shafts and similar components are frequently retained by circlips that are not too easily displaced by a screwdriver. There are two types of circlip pliers, one for internal and one for external circlips. They may also have straight or right-angled jaws.

One of the most useful of all tools is the torque wrench, a form of spanner that can be adjusted to slip when a measured amount of force is applied to any bolt or nut. Torque wrench settings are given in almost every modern workshop or service manual, where the extent to which a complex component, such as a cylinder head, can be tightened without fear of distortion or leakage. The tightening of bearing caps is yet another example. Overtightening will stretch or even break bolts, necessitating extra work to extract the broken portions.

As may be expected, the more sophisticated the machine, the greater is the number of tools likely to be required if it is to be kept in first class condition by the home mechanic. Unfortunately there are certain jobs which cannot be accomplished successfully without the correct equipment and although there is invariably a specialist who will undertake the work for a fee, the home mechanic will have to dig more deeply in his pocket for the purchase of similar equipment if he does not wish to employ the services of others. Here a word of caution is necessary, since some of these jobs are best left to the expert. Although an electrical multimeter of the AVO type will prove helpful in tracing electrical faults, in inexperienced hands it may irrevocably damage some of the electrical components if a test current is passed through them in the wrong direction. This can apply to the synchronisation of twin or multiple carburettors too, where a certain amount of expertise is needed when setting them up with vacuum gauges. These are, however, exceptions. Some instruments, such as a strobe lamp, are virtually essential when checking the timing of a machine powered by CDI ignition system. In short, do not purchase any of these special items unless you have the experience to use them correctly.

Although this manual shows how components can be removed and replaced without the use of special service tools (unless absolutely essential), it is worthwhile giving consideration to the purchase of the more commonly used tools if the machine is regarded as a long term purchase Whilst the alternative methods suggested will remove and replace parts without risk of damage, the use of the special tools recommended and sold by the manufacturer will invariably save time.

Chapter 1 Engine, clutch and gearbox

Refer to Chapter 7 for information relating to 1985-on models

Contents

Specifications

Engine (general)

Type	Air cooled, single cylinder, four stroke
Bore	56.5 mm (2.224 in)
Stroke	49.5 mm (1.949 in)
Capacity	124 cc (7.56 cu in)
Compression ratio	
CG125, CG125 K1, B	9.0:1
CG125-C, E	9.2:1

Piston

Type	Forged aluminium alloy
Skirt OD	56.45 – 56.48 mm (2.2224 – 2.2236 in)
Wear limit	56.35 mm (2.2185 in)
Gudgeon pin OD	14.99 – 15.00 mm (0.5902 – 0.5906 in)
Wear limit	14.96 mm (0.5890 in)
Gudgeon pin bore ID	15.00 – 15.01 mm (0.5906 – 0.5909 in)
Wear limit	15.04 mm (0.5921 in)

Piston rings : 2 compression, 1 oil scraper
  Ring to groove clearance
    Top ... ...   0.03 – 0.05 mm (0.0012 – 0.0020 in)
    2nd ... ...   0.02 – 0.05 mm (0.0008 – 0.0020 in)
  Wear limit (both) ... ...   0.10 mm (0.0039 in)
  End gap (Top and 2nd) – installed ... ...   0.15 – 0.35 mm (0.0059 – 0.0138 in)
  Wear limit ... ...   0.60 mm (0.0236 in)
  Thickness (Top and 2nd) ... ...   1.50 – 1.52 mm (0.0591 – 0.0598 in)
  Wear limit ... ...   1.45 mm (0.0571 in)

Cylinder bore diameter ... ...   56.50 – 56.51 mm (2.2244 – 2.2248 in) nominal
  Wear limit ... ...   56.60 mm (2.2283 in)
  Cylinder compression pressure – throttle open, engine fully warmed up
    CG125, CG125 K1, B ... ...   10.0 – 12.0 kg/cm^2 (142 – 171 psi)
    CG125-C, E ... ...   11.5 – 14.5 kg/cm^2 (164 – 206 psi)

Valves
  Valve timing
    Inlet valve opens at ... ...   TDC
    Inlet valve closes at ... ...   30° ABDC
    Exhaust valve opens at ... ...   30° BBDC
    Exhaust valve closes at ... ...   TDC
  Valve clearances – inlet and exhaust, cold engine ... ...   0.08 mm (0.003 in)

	Standard	Wear limit
Valve spring free length		
Inner	33.5 mm (1.3189 in)	30.0 mm (1.1811 in)
Outer	40.9 mm (1.6102 in)	39.8 mm (1.5669 in)
Valve seat width ...	1.2 – 1.5 mm (0.0472 – 0.0591 in)	2.0 mm (0.0787 in)
Valve stem diameter		
Inlet	5.45 – 5.46 mm (0.2146 – 0.2150 in)	5.42 mm (0.2134 in)
Exhaust ... ... ,.. ...	5.43 – 5.44 mm (0.2138 – 0.2142 in)	5.40 mm (0.2126 in)
Valve guide bore diameter	5.47 – 5.48 mm (0.2154 – 0.2157 in)	5.50 mm (0.2165 in)
Valve stem to guide clearance		
Inlet	0.01 – 0.03 mm (0.0004 – 0.0012 in)	0.12 mm (0.0047 in)
Exhaust	0.03 – 0.05 mm (0.0012 – 0.0020 in)	0.14 mm (0.0055 in)

Pushrods
  Length ... ...   141.15 – 141.45 mm (5.5571 – 5.5689 in)
  Wear limit ... ...   141.00 mm (5.5512 in)

Cam and followers
  Cam follower bore diameter ... ...   12.00 – 12.02 mm (0.4724 – 0.4732 in)
  Wear limit ... ...   12.05 mm (0.4744 in)
  Cam follower shaft diameter ... ...   11.976 – 11.994 mm (0.4715 – 0.4722 in)
  Wear limit ... ...   11.950 mm (0.4705 in)
  Cam lobe height ... ...   32.768 – 32.928 mm (1.2901 – 1.2964 in)
  Wear limit ... ...   32.628 mm (1.2846 in)

	Up to eng. no. 1486212	From eng. no. 1486212
Cam gear shaft diameter	11.970 – 11.980 mm (0.4713 – 0.4717 in)	13.996 – 13.984 mm (0.5498 – 0.5506 in)
Wear limit	N/Av	13.946 mm (0.5491 in)
Cam gear bore diameter	12.000 – 12.020 mm (0.4724 – 0.4732 in)	14.060 – 14.078 mm (0.5535 – 0.5543 in)
Wear limit	N/Av	14.098 mm (0.5550 in)
Gear to shaft clearance	0.020 – 0.050 mm (0.0008 – 0.0020 in)	0.076 – 0.112 mm (0.0030 – 0.0044 in)
Wear limit	0.060 mm (0.0024 in)	0.120 mm (0.0047 in)

Clutch
  Type ... ...   Wet, multiplate
  Number of plates
    Plain   4
    Friction   5
  Plate maximum warpage ... ...   0.20 mm (0.0079 in)
  Spring free length ... ...   35.50 mm (1.3976 in)
  Wear limit ... ...   34.20 mm (1.3465 in)
  Compressed length ... ...   23.00 mm (0.9055 in)
  Spring pressure (compressed) ...   23.8 kg (52.5 lbs)
  Wear limit ... ...   21.8 kg (48.1 lbs)
  Friction plate thickness ... ...   2.90 – 3.00 mm (0.1142 – 0.1181 in)
  Wear limit ... ...   2.60 mm (0.1024 in)

Gearbox

Reduction ratios...	
Primary drive	4.055:1 (18/73T)
1st	2.769:1 (13/36T)
2nd	1.882:1 (17/32T)
3rd	1.450:1 (20/29T)
4th	1.174:1 (23/27T)
5th	1.000:1 (25/25T)
Final drive	2.267:1 (15/34T)
Selector fork claw end thickness	4.93 – 5.00 mm (0.1941 – 0.1969 in)
Wear limit	4.70 mm (0.1850 in)
Selector fork bore diameter	12.00 – 12.02 mm (0.4724 – 0.4732 in)
Wear limit	12.05 mm (0.4744 in)
Selector fork shaft diameter	11.98 – 11.99 mm (0.4717 – 0.4721 in)
Wear limit	11.96 mm (0.4709 in)
Kickstart shaft diameter – at pinion	
Up to engine number 1020010	N/Av
Engine number 1020011 on	19.959 – 19.980 mm (0.7858 – 0.7866 in)
Wear limit	19.900 mm (0.7835 in)
Kickstart pinion bore diameter	
Up to engine number 1020010	24.900 – 24.920 mm (0.9803 – 0.9811 in)
Wear limit	24.940 mm (0.9819 in)
Engine number 1020011 on	20.000 – 20.021 mm (0.7874 – 0.7882 in)
Wear limit	20.050 mm (0.7894 in)

1 General description

The engine unit employed in the Honda CG125 models is of the single cylinder air cooled four stroke type. Unlike most other machines in the Honda range, the CG125 utilises a pushrod operated valve arrangement.

The unit is of all-alloy construction, employing vertically split crankcases which house both the crankshaft assembly and the gear clusters. The cylinder head and cylinder barrel are also of light alloy, the latter incorporating a steel liner in which the cylinder bore is machined.

Lubrication is provided by a small trochoidal oil pump feeding the major engine components. The lubricating oil is contained in the lower portion of the crankcase which forms a combined sump and an oil bath for the gearbox components.

2 Operations with the engine unit in the frame

It is not necessary to remove the engine unit from the frame unless the crankshaft assembly and/or the gearbox internals require attention. Most operations can be accomplished with the engine in place, such as:
1 Removal and replacement of the cylinder head.
2 Removal and replacement of the cylinder barrel and piston.
3 Removal and replacement of the camshaft.
4 Removal and replacement of the generator.
5 Removal and replacement of the contact breaker assembly.
6 Removal and replacement of the clutch assembly.
7 Removal and replacement of the centrifugal oil filter.
8 Removal and replacement of the oil pump.

When several operations need to be undertaken simultaneously, it will probably be advantageous to remove the complete engine unit from the frame, an operation that should take approximately one hour, working at a leisurely pace. This will give the advantage of better access and more working space.

3 Operations with engine removed

1 Removal and replacement of the crankshaft assembly.
2 Removal and replacement of the gear cluster, selectors and gearbox main bearings.

4 Method of engine/gearbox removal

As mentioned previously, the engine and gearbox are of unit construction, and it is necessary to remove the unit complete, in order to gain access to the internal components. Separation and reassembly are only possible with the engine unit removed from the frame. It is recommended that the procedure detailed below is adhered to, as in certain instances, components are much easier to remove whilst the unit is supported by the frame.

5 Removing the engine/gearbox unit

1 Place the machine securely on its centre stand, ensuring that there is no likelihood of it falling over during engine removal. Engine removal can be made much easier if the machine is raised about two feet by means of a stand. A stout table can be modified for this purpose, or alternatively, a few substantial planks and sorne concrete blocks will suffice. This procedure is by no means essential, but will greatly ease the discomfort of squatting or kneeling down to work.
2 Place a container of at least one litre beneath the engine unit, then remove the drain plug and leave the oil to drain while further dismantling is carried out. Turn the fuel tap to the off position and prise off the fuel pipe from the stub at the base of the tap. A small screwdriver can be used to ease the pipe off without straining it.
3 Release the seat mounting bolts, which are located immediately above the rear indicator lamps, and lift the seat away from the frame. Disengage the rear of the petrol tank from the rubber block which retains it. The tank can then be pulled upwards and back to release the front mounting blocks.
4 Slacken off the clutch cable adjuster nuts, and release the cable from the actuating arm on the top of the engine casing. Disengage the cable and lodge it clear of the engine. The spark plug lead should also be detached and placed out of the way on the top frame tube.
5 Unscrew the carburettor top and withdraw the throttle valve assembly. There is no need to disconnect the cable, but the assembly should be positioned where it will not get damaged during engine removal. Disconnect the rubber intake hose, then remove the two nuts which hold the carburettor flange to the cylinder head. The carburettor body should be lifted away, together with the heat shield and spacer or inlet stub. Pull off the crankcase breather pipe.
6 Remove the two nuts which retain the exhaust pipe to the cylinder head, sliding the flange clear and removing the two

packing pieces behind it. The exhaust is secured by two nuts to its mounting bracket, which is secured to the frame by a bolt and by the swinging arm pivot bolt retaining nut. These should be removed and the complete system withdrawn. The footrest assembly should be removed after unscrewing the four bolts which hold it to the underside of the crankcase.

7   Remove the gearchange pedal pinch bolt and slide the pedal off its splines. Remove the left-hand outer cover, and place it to one side to await reassembly. The gearbox sprocket is retained by a locking plate which in turn is held in position by two bolts. Remove the bolts, to allow the plate to be turned slightly and drawn off the splined shaft.

8   Remove the left-hand side panel which is a push fit in the frame lugs. It is also worth removing the right-hand panel to avoid any risk of damage to the paint finish. Remove the screw from the battery negative (–) terminal and release the two green leads to isolate the battery from the electrical system. Separate the white multiple connector block to disconnect the generator; this will be found adjacent to the battery.

9   The engine is now held only by the five mounting bolts. Remove the two front bolts and place them to one side. It is worthwhile removing the entire engine plate to gain the maximum amount of manoeuvring room. Remove the lower rear mounting bolt, noting that the nut may be difficult to reach if the exhaust mounting bracket has not been removed, followed by the upper bolt which passes through a lug in the cylinder head. Finally, release the remaining rear mounting bolt, disengaging the generator harness from its clip. As the bolt is withdrawn, the unit will drop free, and it is advisable to have an

assistant to hand to help with these final stages. Note that whilst not strictly necessary, it was found helpful to remove the left-hand head steady plate to provide better clearance. The unit is not heavy, and can easily be lifted clear of the frame by one person.

5.3 Seat is retained by two bolts at rear

5.4 Slacken off and remove the clutch cable

5.5a Remove the carburettor, heatshield and spacer (early models)

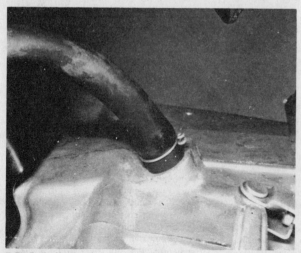
5.5b Pull off the crankcase breather pipe

5.6a Remove exhaust pipe flange followed by ...

5.6b ... rear mounting nuts to release complete exhaust system

5.7 Release the locking plate to permit sprocket removal

5.8a Disconnect the battery to isolate the electrical system ...

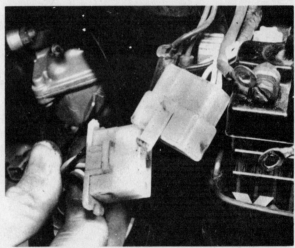

5.8b ... then separate the generator output lead connector

6 Dismantling the engine and gearbox unit: general

1   Before commencing work on the engine unit, the external surfaces should be cleaned thoroughly. A motor cycle engine has very little protection from road grit and other foreign matter, which will find its way into the dismantled engine if this simple precaution is not taken. One of the proprietary cleaning compounds, such as 'Gunk' or 'Jizer' can be used to good effect, particularly if the compound is permitted to work into the film of oil and grease before it is washed away. Special care is necessary, when washing down to prevent water from entering the now exposed parts of the engine unit.

2   Never use undue force to remove any stubborn part unless specific mention is made of this requirement. There is invariably good reason why a part is difficult to remove, often because the dismantling operation has been tackled in the wrong sequence.

3   Mention has already been made of the benefits of owning an impact driver. Most of these tools are equipped with a standard $\frac{1}{2}$ inch drive and an adaptor which can take a variety of screwdriver bits. It will be found that most engine casing screws will need jarring free due to both the effects of assembly by power tools and an inherent tendency for screws to become pinched in alloy castings.

4   A cursory glance over many machines of only a few years

use, will almost invariably reveal an array of well-chewed screw heads. Not only is this unsightly, it can also make emergency repairs impossible. It should also be borne in mind that there are a number of types of crosshead screwdrivers which differ in the angle and design of the driving tangs. To this end, it is always advisable to ensure that the correct tool is available to suit a particular screw.

5   In addition to the above points, it is worth noting before any dismantling work is undertaken that it is desirable to have two service tools available. The first, and most important, is a flywheel puller, Honda part number 07933-0010000 or a cheaper pattern version, and secondly, a special peg spanner for releasing the centrifugal oil filter housing, Honda part number 07916-6390001. The latter can be fabricated from a piece of tubing, if necessary, but it is much less easy to make do without the flywheel extractor as the flywheel proved to be a very tight fit.

7 Dismantling the engine and gearbox unit: removing the cylinder head, barrel and piston

1   If the cylinder head is to be removed with the engine unit in the frame, start by removing the carburettor and heat shield, the

spark plug lead, the exhaust pipe and the cylinder head steady bolt, as described in Section 5 of this Chapter.

2   Slacken and remove the three rocker cover mounting bolts, and lift the cover away, taking care not to damage the rubber sealing ring. The rocker arms may be removed as a unit together with their common support bracket. This is retained by a single bolt at each end, and a central bolt. Lift out the pushrods and push them through holes in a piece of card which has been marked to denote inlet and exhaust. Although the pushrods are identical, it is preferable to replace them in their original positions.

3   The cylinder head is retained by four large sleeve bolts, one of which is recessed into the large diameter oil passage. An additional special bolt passes down into the end of the cam follower shaft, and this should also be removed. Note that the pushrod guide bracket will be released as the two left-hand cylinder head sleeve bolts are removed. The cylinder head can now be lifted away and placed to one side to await further attention. Make a note of the position and sizes of the dowels fitted over three of the four studs. One of these is fitted with an

O ring and acts as an oil feed passage.

4   The cylinder barrel is retained by two bolts passing through a flange on the left-hand side. Once these have been removed, the barrel can be slid upwards off its mounting studs. As soon as the bottom of the barrel is clear of the crankcase mouth, the latter should be packed with clean rag to obviate any risk of pieces of broken piston ring or other foreign matter falling into the crankcase. Be careful not to twist the barrel as it is removed, or the cam follower feet may be scratched on the sharp cam gear teeth.

5   Use a pair of pointed nose pliers or a small screwdriver to dislodge the circlips, which should then be discarded. Note that new circlips should always be fitted in view of the risk of a displaced circlip causing engine damage. If the gudgeon pin should prove to be a particularly tight fit, the piston should be warmed first, to expand the alloy and release the grip on the steel pin. If it is necessary to tap the gudgeon pin out of position, make sure that the connecting rod is supported to prevent distortion. On no account use excess force.

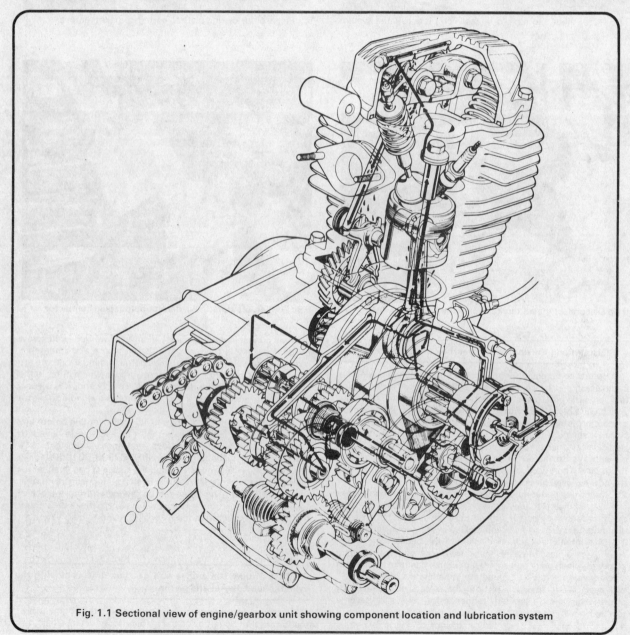

Fig. 1.1 Sectional view of engine/gearbox unit showing component location and lubrication system

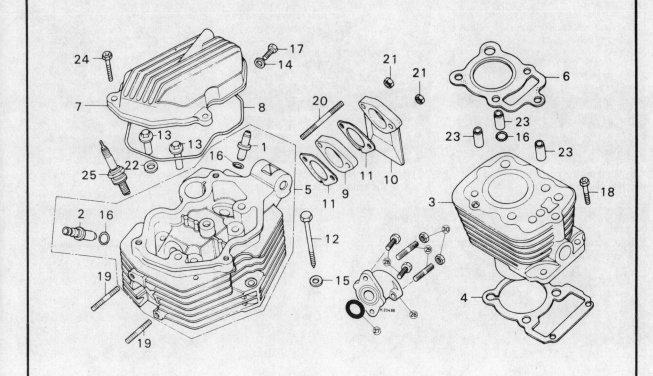

Fig. 1.2 Cylinder head and barrel – component parts

1 Inlet valve guide	11 Gasket – 2 off ◁	21 Nut – 2 off
2 Exhaust valve guide	12 Special bolt	22 Washer – 2 off
3 Cylinder barrel	13 Sleeve bolt – 4 off	23 Dowel – 3 off
4 Cylinder base gasket	14 Sealing washer	24 Bolt – 3 off
5 Cylinder head complete	15 Sealing washer	25 Sparking plug
6 Cylinder head gasket	16 O ring – 3 off	26 Inlet stub ◀
7 Cylinder head cover	17 Plug	27 O-ring ◀
8 Rubber seal	18 Bolt – 2 off	28 Bolt – 2 off ◀
9 Spacer ◁	19 Stud – 2 off	29 Stud – 2 off ◀
10 Heat shield ◁	20 Stud – 2 off	30 Nut – 2 off ◀

◁ early models   ◀ later models

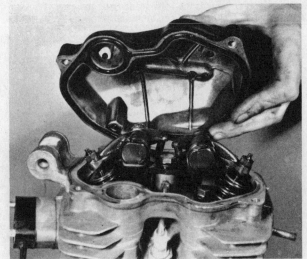

7.2a Remove the cylinder head cover to expose the valve gear

7.2b Release the three mounting bolts, and lift rocker assembly away as a unit

7.2 Withdraw the pushrods, noting which is inlet and exhaust

7.3 Note the additional, special bolt, which retains head and cam follower shaft

7.4a Slide barrel carefully off its studs

7.4b Pack the crankcase mouth with rag if the crankcase is not to be separated

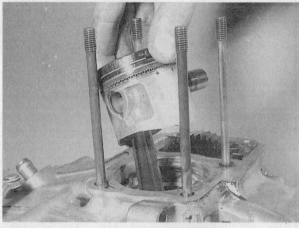

7.5 Remove piston, discarding the used circlips

8 Dismantling the engine and gearbox unit: removing the generator assembly

1　As mentioned earlier, it is recommended that the Honda flywheel puller, part number: 07933-0010000 or a chapter pattern version is used to draw the flywheel/rotor off its taper. Whilst it is possible to use a conventional legged puller, it should be noted that the flywheel can prove exceedingly stubborn. It is also necessary to lock the flywheel/rotor while the centre nut is removed. If the cylinder head and barrel have already been removed, a bar can be passed through the small end eye and rested on a wooden block placed at each side of the crankcase mouth (**never** directly on the jointing face) to prevent crankshaft rotation. If the cylinder head and barrel are in place, the rotor can be held by inserting a holding tool in its two slots. The tool shown in the accompanying photograph has been made from two strips of steel bolted together in the middle to form a pivot. The ends of the tool have been drilled to accept suitable sized bolts to engage the rotor slots – ensure that the bolts don't extend far enough into the rotor to damage the coils. With the rotor securely held, the nut can be unscrewed.

8.1 Using a holding tool in the rotor slots whilst the retaining nut is removed

8.2 The rotor puller threads into the rotor centre

2   To draw the rotor off the crankshaft, thread the puller boss (left-hand thread) into the rotor centre, then hold the hexagon of the boss and tighten the puller's centre bolt to draw the rotor off. If the rotor proves stubborn, tap the end of the puller's centre bolt to jar the rotor off its taper. On no account strike the rotor itself as this can damage the unit.

3   With the flywheel/rotor removed as described above, release the three countersunk screws which secure the generator stator. It will also be necessary to release the output leads from beneath the guide before lifting the assembly clear. There is no need to mark the stator position as this is not variable.

9   Dismantling the engine/gearbox unit: removing the cam gear and shaft

1   If this job is being tackled with the engine in the frame, it is first necessary to remove the cylinder head and pushrods, the cylinder barrel and cam followers and the generator assembly. Refer to the preceding Sections in this Chapter for details.

2   The cam gear takes the form of a skew-cut gear driven by the crankshaft and producing rotation at half engine speed. The cam lobe is retained on the gear by a circlip, and the assembly runs on a special shaft which is retained by the generator stator. When the latter is removed, the small thrust spring in the end of the shaft will probably fall away. A screwdriver can be used to lever the head of the shaft gently outwards against the resistance of the O ring seal. The gear and cam assembly will be freed as the shaft is withdrawn, and can be lifted out through the aperture adjacent to the crankcase mouth.

10 Dismantling the engine/gearbox unit: removing the centrifugal oil filter

1   If the engine is in the frame the oil must be drained, the clutch cable must be disconnected and the exhaust system and footrest assembly must be removed first. Remove its pinch bolt and pull the kickstart pedal off its shaft, then remove all the screws around the outer edge of the crankcase right-hand cover. Tap the cover smartly with a soft-faced mallet to break the seal and withdraw the cover, noting the two locating dowels in the mating surface, also the pushrod in the centre of the clutch. Peel off the cover gasket.

2   Slacken and remove the three screws which secure the oil filter cover. As the cover is lifted away, place some rag beneath the unit to catch the residual oil which will be caught inside the filter assembly.

3   The inner half of the filter housing is retained by a slotted nut which will require the use of a peg spanner to release it. This tool is available as a Honda service tool, part number: 07916–6390001. If this is not available, it is possible to fabricate a suitable tool from a length of thick-walled tubing. Refer to the accompanying photograph for details, cutting away the segments shown with a hacksaw to leave four tangs. If the machine is to be regarded as a long term purchase, it may be considered worthwhile spending some time with a file to obtain a good fit. The end can then be heated to a cherry red colour and quenched in oil to harden the tangs. An axial hole can be drilled to accept a tommy bar.

4   Lock the crankshaft either by selecting top gear and applying the rear brake (engine in frame) or by passing a bar through the small end eye and resting the ends on a wooden block placed each side of the crankcase mouth. The securing nut can then be removed, and the inner housing pulled off the crankshaft. Note that the special washer, fitted behind the nut, is marked 'outside' for reference during reassembly.

11 Dismantling the engine/gearbox unit: removing the oil pump

1   The oil pump is retained by two screws which pass through the inner pinion casing into the crankcase. It will be noted that the front half of the pinion casing has two holes in it. A screwdriver can be passed through these, and the corresponding holes in the pinion in order to release the retaining screw. The pump can then be lifted away as an assembly.

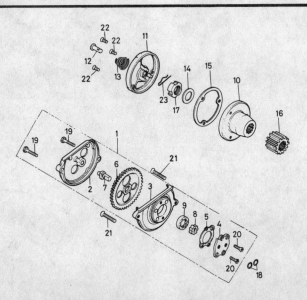

Fig. 1.3 Oil pump and centrifugal filter – component parts

1	Oil pump assembly	7	Pump spindle	13	Spring	19 Bolt – 2 off
2	Pinion casing	8	Inner rotor	14	Special washer	20 Screw – 2 off
3	Inner casing half	9	Outer rotor	15	Gasket	21 Screw – 2 off
4	Backplate	10	Inner housing	16	Primary gear	22 Screw – 3 off
5	Gasket	11	Cover	17	Nut	23 R pin
6	Drive pinion	12	Plunger	18	O ring – 2 off	

9.2a Note thrust washer when removing cam gear shaft

9.2b Lift out the cam gear/cam unit

10.3 Home-made peg spanner is crude but proved effective

10.4 With the nut removed, slide inner housing off its splines

11.1a Pass screwdriver through holes in pump to release mounting screws

11.1b Pump can be lifted away as a unit

12 Dismantling the engine/gearbox unit: removing the clutch assembly and crankshaft pinion

1   Lift out the clutch pushrod together with the cup in which it seats, then remove the four bolts which secure the clutch thrust plate, unscrewing them in a diagonal sequence until the clutch spring pressure is released. Lift off the thrust plate and the four clutch springs and place them to one side.

2   Remove the circlip which retains the outer half of the clutch centre, then remove it, followed by the clutch plain and friction plates. The inner half of the clutch centre can now be lifted out followed by the clutch drum, noting the special thrust washer interposed between the two. The crankshaft pinion can simply be slid off its splines once the filter has been removed.

13 Dismantling the engine/gearbox unit: removing the gearchange shaft and mechanism

1   The gearchange shaft runs in a bore through the crankcase, emerging on the left-hand side of the engine. The complete unit can be withdrawn from the right-hand side of the unit, the quadrant centring spring disengaging from its locating lug.

2   Unscrew the detent roller arm retaining bolt and carefully release the detent spring pressure before withdrawing the bolt, arm and spring. Note how the arm rotates against spring pressure on the shouldered portion of the bolt's shank. Remove the camplate retaining bolt from the end of the selector drum and withdraw the camplate, noting that it is located by a small pin which should be removed to prevent its loss.

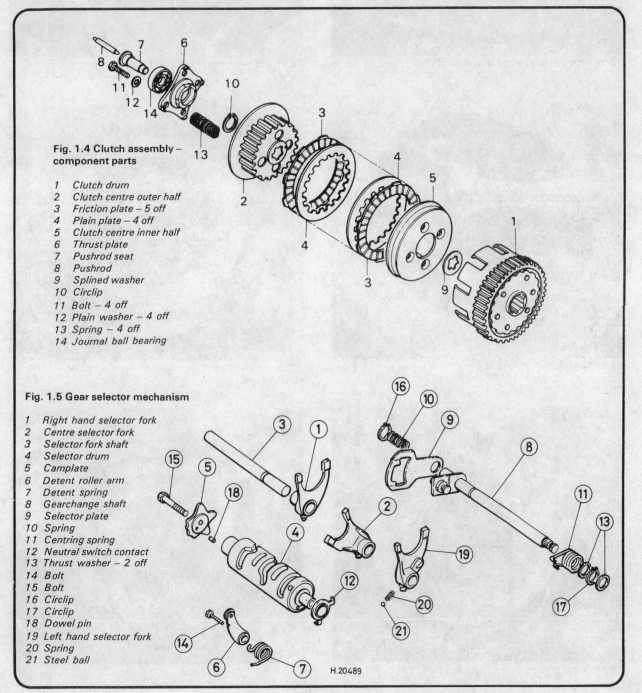

Fig. 1.4 Clutch assembly – component parts

1   Clutch drum
2   Clutch centre outer half
3   Friction plate – 5 off
4   Plain plate – 4 off
5   Clutch centre inner half
6   Thrust plate
7   Pushrod seat
8   Pushrod
9   Splined washer
10 Circlip
11 Bolt – 4 off
12 Plain washer – 4 off
13 Spring – 4 off
14 Journal ball bearing

Fig. 1.5 Gear selector mechanism

1   Right hand selector fork
2   Centre selector fork
3   Selector fork shaft
4   Selector drum
5   Camplate
6   Detent roller arm
7   Detent spring
8   Gearchange shaft
9   Selector plate
10 Spring
11 Centring spring
12 Neutral switch contact
13 Thrust washer – 2 off
14 Bolt
15 Bolt
16 Circlip
17 Circlip
18 Dowel pin
19 Left hand selector fork
20 Spring
21 Steel ball

H.20489

12.1a Remove the pushrod and pushrod seat

12.1b Lift away the thrust plate after releasing bolts

12.2a Remove the circlip to allow ...

12.2b ... outer half of clutch centre to be removed, followed by clutch plates . . .

12.2c ... and inner half of clutch centre

12.2d Clutch drum will slide off, complete with slotted washer

12.2e Crankshaft pinion can be slid off splined crankshaft end

13.1 Disengage gearchange shaft and withdraw from casing

14 Dismantling the engine/gearbox unit: removing the end-float plunger and neutral switch

1   Although the above mentioned components will not prevent crankcase separation, it is advisable to remove them as this will need to be done prior to reassembly. The plunger assembly is retained by a single fixing bolt, and can be withdrawn from the crankcase after this has been released.

2   The neutral indicator switch is normally retained by a rubber pad on the inside of the outer casing. After this has been removed, the switch body can be withdrawn from the crankcase.

15 Dismantling the engine/gearbox unit: separating the crankcase halves

1   Slacken and remove the crankcase retaining screws from each side of the unit. Note that the bolt which retains the clutch cable guide must be removed if this has not been done already. It is recommended that an impact driver is used to loosen and tighten these screws as it is likely that the heads will be damaged if an ordinary screwdriver is employed. The screws will probably prove to be very tight, as they are machine-assembled in the factory. It is worth noting that it is possible to obtain sets of Allen screws to replace all the crossheaded screws on the engine. These are usually far more durable and better looking then the original fitments and do not require the use of an impact driver.

2   Check that all the casing screws are removed, then lay the unit on its side, right-hand casing half uppermost, and support it on suitable wooden blocks. The right-hand casing half will probably lift away quite easily, but should it prove stubborn it can be tapped off using a **soft headed** mallet. Make sure that all the components remain in the left-hand casing half. Place the right-hand casing half to one side while the crankcase components are removed.

16 Dismantling the engine/gearbox unit: removing the kickstart mechanism, crankshaft assembly and gearbox components

1   With the left-hand casing half still in position on the blocks,

the kickstart mechanism may be lifted out of the casing, having first lifted the ratchet to release spring tension.

The crankshaft assembly can be lifted out of position. The use of steel inserts in each crankcase half means that the main bearings are a light sliding fit, and offer little resistance during removal. They will remain in position on the crankshaft.

2   Lift the selector fork shaft slightly, so that the selector drum can be pulled out of the casing. The selector fork assembly can be eased out of position, noting that it may be necessary to lift the gear cluster and then tip the fork assembly away from it. **Do not** withdraw the selector fork shaft from the forks, as the lower fork contains a spring loaded locating ball which is easily lost.

3   The gear clusters together with the shafts can now be lifted out of the case, noting the shim(s) fitted to the shaft end. If the gearbox assembly is not to be dismantled, it is advisable to assemble the gear clusters, selector forks and the selector drum in their correct relative positions, and to secure the assembled unit with elastic bands before placing it to one side to await reassembly.

17 Examination and renovation: general

1   Before examining the component parts of the dismantled engine/gear unit for wear, it is essential that they should be cleaned thoroughly. Use a paraffin/petrol mix to remove all traces of oil and sludge which may have accumulated within the engine.

2   Examine the crankcase castings for cracks or other signs of damage. If a crack is discovered, it will require professional attention, or in an extreme case, renewal of the casting. The machine dismantled for the photographic sequences proved to have sustained damage to one of the crankcase lugs due to the kickstart mechanism breaking away part of its stop. (See photograph). This necessitated the renewal of the damaged casing.

3   Examine carefully each part to determine the extent of wear. If in doubt, check with the tolerance figures whenever they are quoted in the text or specifications. The following sections will indicate what type of wear can be expected and in many cases, the acceptable limits.

4   Use clean, lint-free rags for cleaning and drying the various components, otherwise there is a risk of small particles obstructing the internal oilways.

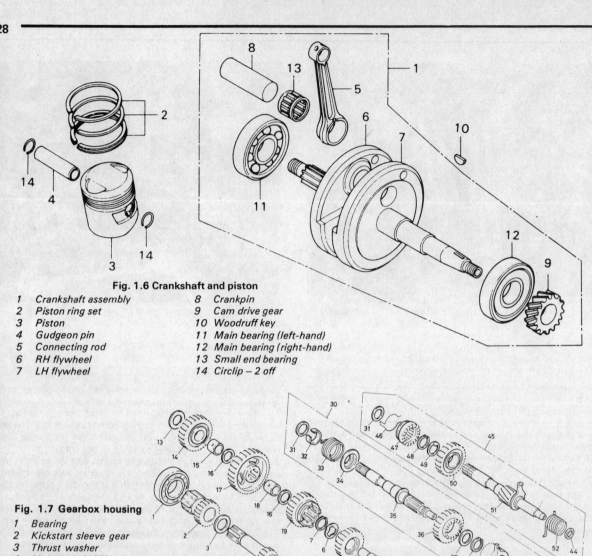

Fig. 1.6 Crankshaft and piston

1	Crankshaft assembly	8	Crankpin
2	Piston ring set	9	Cam drive gear
3	Piston	10	Woodruff key
4	Gudgeon pin	11	Main bearing (left-hand)
5	Connecting rod	12	Main bearing (right-hand)
6	RH flywheel	13	Small end bearing
7	LH flywheel	14	Circlip – 2 off

Fig. 1.7 Gearbox housing

1 Bearing
2 Kickstart sleeve gear
3 Thrust washer
4 Mainshaft (13T)
5 Mainshaft 3rd gear pinion
   (20T)
6 Splined thrust washer – 3 off
7 Circlip – 3 off
8 Mainshaft 4th gear pinion
   (23T)
9 Mainshaft 5th gear pinion
   (25T)
10 Mainshaft 2nd gear pinion
   (17T)
11 Thrust washer
12 Bearing
13 Thrust washer
14 Kickstart idler pinion
15 Bush – later models
16 Thrust washer – 2 off*
17 Layshaft 1st gear pinion
   (36T)
18 Bush – later models
19 Layshaft 3rd gear pinion
   (29T)
20 Layshaft 4th gear pinion
   (27T)
21 Layshaft
22 Layshaft 5th gear pinion
   (25T)
23 Layshaft 2nd gear pinion
   (32T)

24 Thrust washer
25 Bearing
26 Oil seal
27 Gearbox sprocket (15T)
28 Locking plate
29 Bolt – 2 off
30 Kickstart shaft assembly –
   later models
31 Thrust washer
32 Spring guide
33 Kickstart spring
34 Spring seat
35 Kickstart shaft
36 Kickstart pinion (29T)
37 Thrust washer
38 Circlip
39 Kickstart ratchet
40 Coil spring

41 Thrust washer
42 Ratchet guide plate
43 Circlip
44 Thrust washer
45 Kickstart shaft assembly –
   early models
46 Friction clip
47 Kickstart ratchet
48 Circlip
49 Thrust washer
50 Kickstart pinion (29T)
51 Kickstart shaft
52 Kickstart spring

*item 16 located between items 18 and 19 fitted to CG125 K1 on models. Note – items 2, 14 and 50 only available as a set for early CG125 models.

14.1 End-float plunger is retained by a single bolt

14.2 Neutral indicator switch is easily withdrawn

16.1a Disengage and remove the kickstart mechanism

16.1b Crankshaft assembly lifts easily out of case

16.2a Lift selector fork assembly slightly to allow selector drum to be withdrawn

16.2b Remove the selector forks and pin as an assembly - *Do not dismantle*

16.3a Lift out mainshaft and layshaft clusters complete

16.3b Do not lose these shims which may remain in case

17.1a Clean cases thoroughly and check bearings etc

17.1b Ensure that oilways are kept clear

17.2 This casing has been damaged by the kickstart mechanism; it required renewal

18 Crankshaft and gearbox main bearings: removal

1   The crankshaft bearings will remain on their shafts when the crankshaft assembly is withdrawn from the crankcase. A puller or an extractor will be necessary for their removal as they are a tight fit on the shafts.

2   The gearbox bearings are a light press fit in the crankcase castings. They can be drifted out of position, using a mandrel of the correct size and a hammer.

3   If necessary, warm the crankcases slightly, to aid the release of the bearings.

19 Examination and renovation: Big-end and main bearings

1   Failure of the big-end bearing is invariably accompanied by a knock from within the crankcase that progressively becomes worse. Some vibration will also be experienced. There should be no vertical play in the big-end bearing after the old oil has been washed out. If even a small amount of play is evident, the bearing is due for replacement. Do not run the machine with a worn big-end bearing, otherwise there is risk of breaking the connecting rod or crankshaft.

A certain amount of side play is intentional, and should be between 0·05 – 0·30 mm (0·002 – 0·012 in) on a new crankshaft. The maximum allowable side play is 0·80 mm (0·032 in) and can be checked with a feeler gauge between the flywheel face and the edge of the connecting rod.

2   It is not possible to separate the flywheel assembly in order to replace the bearing because the parallel sided crankpin is pressed into the flywheels. Big-end repair should be entrusted to a Honda agent, who will have the necessary repair or replacement facilities.

3   Failure of the main bearings is usually evident in the form of an audible rumble from the bottom end of the engine, accompanied by vibration. The vibration will be most noticeable through the footrests.

4   The crankshaft main bearings are of the journal ball type. If wear is evident in the form of play or if the bearings feel rough as they are rotated, replacement is necessary. To remove the main bearings if the appropriate service tool is not available, insert two thin steel wedges, one on each side of the bearing, and with these clamped in a vice hit the end of the crankshaft squarely with a rawhide mallet in an attempt to drive the crankshaft through the bearing. When the bearing has moved the initial amount, it should be possible to insert a conventional two or three legged sprocket puller, to complete the drawing-off action.

18.1a Use steel wedges and a puller to remove worn main bearings

18.1b Mark pinion relative to shaft before withdrawing pinion

18.2 Bearings can be tapped out of the cases using large drift

20 Examination and renovation: gudgeon pin, small end and piston bosses

1   The fit of the gudgeon pin in both the small end eye of the connecting rod, and in the piston bosses should be checked. In the case of the small end eye, slide the pin into position and check for wear by moving the pin up and down. The pin should be a light sliding fit with no discernible radial play. If play is detected, it will almost certainly be the small end eye which has worn rather than the gudgeon pin, although in extreme cases, the latter may also have become worn. The connecting rod is not fitted with a bush type of small end bearing, and consequently a new connecting rod will have to be fitted if worn. This is not a simple job, as the flywheels must be parted to fit the new component, and is a job for a Honda Service Agent. It should be borne in mind that if the small end has worn, it is likely that the big-end bearing will require attention.

2   Check the fit of the gudgeon pin in the piston. This is normally a fairly tight fit, and it is not unusual for the piston to have to be warmed slightly to allow the pin to be inserted and removed. After considerable mileages have been covered, it is possible that the bosses will have become enlarged. If this proves to be the case, it will be necessary to renew the piston to effect a cure. It is worth noting, as an aid to diagnosis, that wear

in the above areas is characterised by a metallic rattle when the engine is running.

21 Examination and renovation: piston and piston rings

1   If a rebore is necessary, the existing piston and rings can be disregarded because they will be replaced with their oversize equivalents as a matter of course.

2   Remove all traces of carbon from the piston crown, using a soft scraper to ensure the surface is not marked. Finish off by polishing the crown, with metal polish, so that carbon does not adhere so easily in the future. Never use emery cloth.

3   Piston wear usually occurs at the skirt or lower end of the piston and takes the form of vertical streaks or score marks on the thrust side. There may also be some variation in the thickness of the skirt. Measure the piston skirt outside diameter at right angles to the gudgeon pin axis and at a point 10 mm (0.4 in) above the base of the skirt; renew the piston if it is found to be scored, damaged or worn to the specified wear limit or beyond.

4   The piston ring grooves may also become enlarged in use, allowing the piston rings to have greater side float. If the clearance exceeds 0·10 mm (0·004 in) for the two compression rings, the piston is due for renewal. It is unusual for this amount of wear to occur on its own.

5   Piston ring wear is measured by removing the rings from the piston and inserting them in the cylinder bore using the crown of the piston to locate them approximately 25 mm (1 in) from the top of the bore. Make sure they rest square with the bore. Measure the end gap with a feeler gauge; if it exceeds 0·6 mm (0·024 in) the rings require renewal.

22 Examination and renovation: cylinder barrel

1   The usual indications of a badly worn cylinder barrel and piston are excessive oil consumption and piston slap, a metallic rattle that occurs when there is little or no load on the engine. If the top of the bore of the cylinder barrel is examined carefully, it will be found that there is a ridge on the thrust side, the depth of which will vary according to the amount of wear that has taken place. This marks the limit of travel of the uppermost piston ring.

2   Measure the bore diameter just below the ridge, using an internal micrometer. Compare this reading with the diameter at the bottom of the cylinder bore, which has not been subject to wear. If the difference in readings exceeds 0·09 mm (0·0035 in) it is necessary to have the cylinder rebored and to fit an over-size piston and rings.

3   If an internal micrometer is not available, the amount of cylinder bore wear can be measured by inserting the piston without rings so that it is approximately 20 mm ($\frac{3}{4}$ in) from the top of the bore. If it is possible to insert a 0·10 mm (0·004 in) feeler gauge between the piston and the cylinder wall on the thrust side of the piston, remedial action must be taken.

4   Check the surface of the cylinder bore for score marks or any other damage that may have resulted from an earlier engine seizure or displacement of the gudgeon pin. A rebore will be necessary to remove any deep indentations, irrespective of the amount of bore wear, otherwise a compression leak will occur.

5   Check the external cooling fins are not clogged with oil or road dirt; otherwise the engine will overheat.

23 Cylinder head: valve removal, examination and renovation

1   Remove each valve in turn, using a valve spring compressor, and place the valves, springs, seats and collet halves in a suitable box or bag marked to denote inlet or exhaust as appropriate. Assemble the valve spring compressor in position on the cylinder head, and gradually tighten the threaded portion to place pressure on the upper spring seat. Do not exert undue force to compress the springs, the tool should be placed under slight load, and then tapped on the end to jar the collet halves free. Continue to compress the springs until the collet halves can be dislodged using a small screwdriver. Note that the valve springs exert considerable force, and care should be taken to avoid the compressed assembly flying apart. To this end, a small magnet is invaluable for retrieving the collet halves, being more delicate than fingers.

2   After cleaning the valves to remove all traces of carbon, examine the heads for signs of pitting and burning. Examine also the valve seats in the cylinder head. The exhaust valve and its seat will probably require the most attention because these are the hotter running of the two. If the pitting is slight, the marks can be removed by grinding the seats and valves together, using fine valve grinding compound.

3   Valve grinding is a simple task, carried out as follows: Smear a trace of fine valve grinding compound (carborundum paste) on the seat face and apply a suction grinding tool to the head of the valve. With a semi-rotary motion, grind in the valve head to its seat. It is advisable to lift the valve occasionally, to distribute the grinding compound evenly. Repeat this operation until an unbroken ring of light grey matt finish is obtained on both valve and seat. This denotes the grinding operation is complete. Before passing to the next operation, make quite sure that all traces of the grinding compound have been removed from both the valve and its seat and that none has entered the valve guide. If this precaution is not observed, rapid wear will take place, due to the abrasive nature of the carborundum base.

4   When deeper pit marks are encountered, it will be necessary to use a valve refacing machine and also a valve seat cutter, set to an angle of 45°. Never resort to excessive grinding because this will only pocket the valve and lead to reduced engine efficiency. If there is any doubt about the condition of a valve, fit a new replacement.

5   Examine the condition of the valve collets and the groove on the valve in which they seat. If there is any sign of damage, new replacements should be fitted. If the collets work loose whilst the engine is running, a valve will drop in and cause extensive damage.

6   Measure the valve stems for wear, making reference to the tolerance values given in the Specifications Section of this Chapter.

7   Check the free length of the valve springs against the list of tolerances in the Specifications. If the springs are reduced in length or if there is any doubt about their condition, they should be renewed.

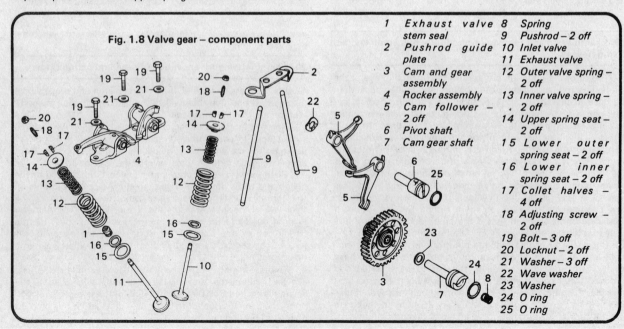

Fig. 1.8 Valve gear – component parts

1	Exhaust valve stem seal	8	Spring
2	Pushrod guide plate	9	Pushrod – 2 off
3	Cam and gear assembly	10	Inlet valve
4	Rocker assembly	11	Exhaust valve
5	Cam follower – 2 off	12	Outer valve spring – 2 off
6	Pivot shaft	13	Inner valve spring – 2 off
7	Cam gear shaft	14	Upper spring seat – 2 off
		15	Lower outer spring seat – 2 off
		16	Lower inner spring seat – 2 off
		17	Collet halves – 4 off
		18	Adjusting screw – 2 off
		19	Bolt – 3 off
		20	Locknut – 2 off
		21	Washer – 3 off
		22	Wave washer
		23	Washer
		24	O ring
		25	O ring

23.1a Compress springs and prise out collet halves, to release …

23.1b … the top spring seat …

23.1c … and valve springs

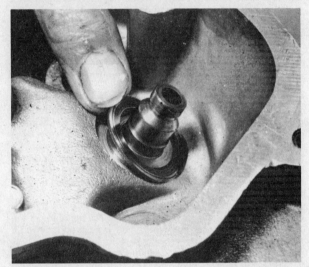

23.1d Note lower outer spring seat around valve guide

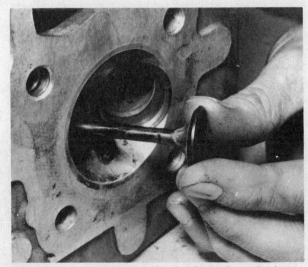

23.1e Valve can be withdrawn for cleaning and examination

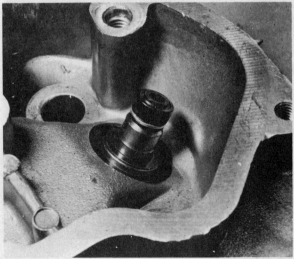

23.1f Seal (on exhaust valve only) should be renewed

24 Examination and decarbonisation: cylinder head

1   Remove all traces of carbon from the cylinder head and valve ports, using a soft scraper. Extreme care should be taken to ensure the combustion chamber and valve seats are not marked in any way, otherwise hot spots and leakages may occur. Finish by polishing the combustion chamber so that carbon does not adhere so easily in the future. Use metal polish and NOT emery cloth.
2   Check to make sure the valve guide bores are free from carbon or any other foreign matter that may cause the valves to stick.
3   Make sure the cylinder head fins are not clogged with oil or road dirt, otherwise the engine will overheat. If necessary, use a wire brush.
4   Reassemble the valves, using a valve spring compressor to compress the springs. Make sure the valve stems have a coating of oil before they are replaced in the valve guides. Also check that the split collets are located positively before the spring compressor is released. A misplaced collet can cause a valve to drop in whilst the engine is running and cause serious damage. To ensure that the collets are firmly located, tap the top of each valve stem sharply with a hammer, taking care to strike squarely on the stem and not on the seat. Note that the outer springs must be positioned with the closely wound coils nearest the head.

25 Examination and renovation: rocker arms, adjusters and pushrods

1   It is unlikely that excessive wear will occur on the valve gear components unless the engine has been run without changing the oil or the machine has covered a very large mileage.
2   Examine the condition of the rocker assembly, which should operate smoothly, but without discernible radial play. If worn, it will be necessary to renew the complete rocker assembly, as the unit cannot be dismantled.
3   Check the condition of the adjuster and lock nut threads, and renew these if stretched or damaged. The ball-ends of the pushrods should also be examined, and the pushrod renewed if they are worn or cracked.
4   Check the pushrods for straightness by rolling them on a flat surface. If they are bent, this is often a sign that the engine has been over-revved on some previous occasion. It is better to fit replacements than attempt to straighten the originals.

26 Examination and renovation: cam gear and lobe, and cam followers

1   Examine the condition of the cam gear teeth, looking for signs of chipping and wear. At the same time, examine the corresponding teeth of the driving gear on the crankshaft. The camshaft gear can be separated from the cam lobe, if desired, by removing the circlip which retains it.
2   The cam lobe itself is unlikely to exhibit any great degree of wear due to its wide profile, but after extended mileage a flat may begin to appear at the top of the lobe. This can be checked by measuring the lobe across its widest point. The nominal size is 32.768 – 32.928 mm (1.2901 – 1.2964 in). The cam will require renewal if worn to less than 32.628 mm (1.2846 in).
3   The clearance between the cam gear and the shaft on which it is carried should not exceed the specified amount. The condition of the cam followers should also be checked, especially if the cam lobe is worn. The clearance between the cam follower bores and the pivot shaft must not exceed 0.1 mm (0.004 in). The rubbing face of each cam follower should be examined for signs of scuffing or scores, indicating wear due to poor lubrication.

27 Examination and renovation: trochoidal oil pump

The trochoidal oil pump is removed as a sub assembly as described earlier in this Chapter. Dismantling and renovation are covered in Chapter 2. The condition of the pump should be checked as a matter of course if the engine is being overhauled, especially if signs of scuffing are evident on the various shafts and bushes.

28 Examination and renovation: clutch and primary drive

1   After a considerable mileage has been covered, the bonded linings of the clutch friction plates will wear down to or beyond the specified wear limit, allowing the clutch to slip.
2   The degree of wear is measured across the faces of the friction material, the nominal or new size being 2·9 – 3·00 mm (0·114 – 0·118 in). If the plates have worn to 2·6 mm (0·102 in) they should be renewed, even if slipping is not yet apparent.
3   The plain plates should be free from scoring and signs of overheating, which will be apparent in the form of blueing. The plates should also be flat. If more than 0.20 mm (0.0079 in) out of true, judder or snatch may result.

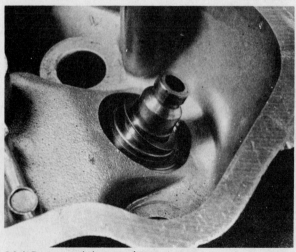

24.4 Do not omit inner spring seat

26.3 Check fit of followers on pivot shaft – note thrust washer

4   Measure the uncompressed length of the clutch springs which should be 35.5 mm (1.398 in) when new. Should any spring have settled to the specified service limit or shorter, all four springs should be renewed as a set.

5   Check the condition of the thrust bearing assembly and pushrod, which are located in the clutch centre. Excessive play or wear will cause noise and erratic operation.

6   Check the condition of the slots in the outer surface of the clutch centre and the inner surfaces of the outer drum. In an extreme case, clutch chatter may have caused the tongues of the inserted plates to make indentations in the slots of the outer drum, or the tongues of the plain plates to indent the slots of the clutch centre. These indentations will trap the clutch plates as they are freed, and impair clutch action. If the damage is only slight the indentations can be removed by careful work with a file and the burrs removed from the tongues of the clutch plates in a similar fashion. More extensive damage will necessitate renewal of the parts concerned.

7   The clutch release mechanism attached to the inside of the crankcase right-hand cover takes the form of a vertical spindle with a cam on the lower end. A light return spring ensures that pressure is taken off the end of the pushrod once the handlebar lever has been released. No attention is normally required, other than greasing prior to reassembly.

8   The primary drive is by means of a crankshaft-mounted gear driving the clutch by way of teeth on the outer drum. The two gears should be examined for signs of wear or chipped teeth, and replaced as necessary, preferably as a pair.

29 Examination and renovation: gearbox components

1   Examine each of the gear pinions to ensure that there are no chipped or broken teeth and that the dogs on the end of the pinions are not rounded. Gear pinions with these defects must be renewed; there is no satisfactory method of reclaiming them.

2   Examine the selector forks carefully, ensuring that there is no scoring or wear where they engage in the gears, and that they are not bent. Damage and wear rarely occur in a gearbox which has been properly used and correctly lubricated, unless very high mileages have been covered.

3   The tracks in the selector drum, which co-ordinate the movement of the selector forks, should not show signs of undue wear. Check also that the detent arm spring has not weakened, and that no play has developed in the gear selector linkages.

4   Unless the unit has shown signs of wear or malfunctioning, it is unnecessary to dismantle the kickstart assembly. It is however, a very simple unit to deal with.

5   Check the movement of the gear on the spiral which brings it into engagement with the coupling gear. Look for chipped or broken teeth and excessive wear, replacing the gear if necessary.

30 Engine casings and covers: examination and repair

1   The aluminium alloy casings and covers are unlikely to suffer damage through ordinary use. However, damage can occur if the machine is dropped, or if sudden mechanical breakages occur, such as the rear chain breaking.

2   Small cracks or holes may be repaired with an epoxy resin adhesive, such as Araldite, as a temporary expedient. Permanent repairs can only be effected by argon-arc welding, and a specialist in this process is in a position to advise on the viability of proposed repair. Often it may be cheaper to buy a new replacement.

3   Damaged threads can be economically reclaimed by using a diamond section wire insert, of the Helicoil type, which is easily fitted after drilling and re-tapping the affected thread. The process is quick and inexpensive, and does not require as much preparation and work as the older method of fitting brass, or similar inserts. Most motorcycle dealers and small engineering firms offer a service of this kind.

4   Sheared studs or screws can usually be removed with screw extractors, which consist of tapered, left-hand thread screws, of very hard steel. These are inserted by screwing anti-clockwise, into a pre-drilled hole in the stud, and usually succeed in dislodging the most stubborn stud or screw. The only alternative to this is spark erosion, but as this is a very limited, specialised facility, it will probably be unavailable to most owners. It is wise, however, to consult a professional engineering firm before condemning an otherwise sound casing. Many of these firms advertise regularly in the motorcycle papers.

31 Engine reassembly: general

1   Before reassembly of the engine/gear unit is commenced, the various component parts should be cleaned thoroughly and placed on a sheet of clean paper, close to the working area.

2   Make sure all traces of old gaskets have been removed and that the mating surfaces are clean and undamaged. One of the best ways to remove old gasket cement is to apply a rag soaked in methylated spirit. This acts as a solvent and will ensure that the cement is removed without resort to scraping and the consequent risk of damage.

3   Gather together all the necessary tools and have available an oil can filled with clean engine oil. Make sure all the new gaskets and oil seals are to hand, also all replacement parts required. Nothing is more frustrating than having to stop in the middle of a reassembly sequence because a vital gasket or replacement has been overlooked.

4   Make sure that the reassembly area is clean and that there is adequate working space. Many of the smaller bolts are easily sheared if over-tightened. Always use the correct size screwdriver bit for the crosshead screws and never an ordinary screwdriver or punch. If the existing screws show evidence of maltreatment in the past, it is advisable to renew them as a complete set.

5   If the purchase of a replacement set of screws is being contemplated, it is worthwhile considering a set of socket or Allen screws. These are invariably much more robust than the originals, and can be obtained in sets for most machines, in either black or nickel plated finishes. The manufacturers of these screw sets advertise regularly in the motorcycle press.

32 Engine reassembly: gear clusters and selector mechanism reassembly and replacement

1   Having examined and renewed the gearbox components as necessary, the clusters can be built up and assembled as a complete unit for installation in the engine/gearbox casings.

2   Study the line drawing carefully (Fig. 1.7) and assemble the layshaft components in the exact order shown, ensuring that the thrust washers and circlips are correctly positioned. The gearbox mainshaft (input shaft) should be tackled in a similar manner. See also the accompanying photographic sequence.

33 Engine reassembly: replacing the crankcase components

1   Place the larger, left-hand, crankcase half on blocks on the workbench, checking that a reasonable amount of room is allowed for the shafts to protrude when fitted. The gearbox mainshaft and layshaft clusters should be placed into position first, ensuring that the shim fitted on the mainshaft end is not omitted. The selector forks, having previously been fitted to their pivot shaft, can now be placed in position. This operation calls for a certain amount of patience, as the three forks must be eased into their respective grooves before the pivot shaft will locate correctly.

2   Fit the neutral switch contact to the end of the selector drum, and then lower it, contact downwards, into the crankcase half, so that the contact aligns with the neutral switch. It will be necessary to lift the selector fork assembly slightly, so that the selector fork pins can be engaged in their tracks in the selector drum. When the assembly has been installed correctly, lubricate it with engine oil, and check gearbox operation by turning the selector drum.

3   Lubricate the crankshaft big end and main bearings with clean engine oil, then lower the assembly into position in the crankcase. The main bearing bosses will not require heating in order that the bearings may be fitted, as they are fitted with steel inserts which mean that a simple, sliding, fit is possible.

4   The assembled kickstart mechanism should now be installed in the right-hand crankcase half; slide the assembly into position, ensuring that the return spring engages in its hole in the casing. The upper half of the ratchet should be pulled upwards, the assembly twisted clockwise, and then pushed inwards to engage the stop. The assembly will now be retained by the pressure of the return spring.

32.2a Slide 3rd gear pinion (20T) onto mainshaft, fit washer and circlip, then ...

32.2b ... fit 4th gear pinion (23T), washer and circlip

32.2c Fit circlip, followed by ...

32.2d ... slotted washer and ...

32.2e ... 5th gear pinion (25T), dogs inwards

32.2f Slide 2nd gear pinion (17T) into position

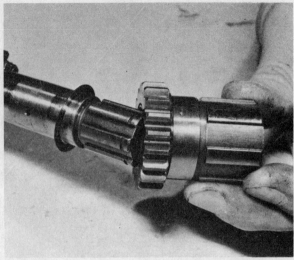

32.2g Slide shim and sleeve gear onto other end of shaft

32.2h Place 4th gear pinion (27T) in position on layshaft and fit washer and clip

32.2i Fit 3rd gear pinion (29T)

32.2j Bottom gear pinion (36T) has renewable bush ...

32.2k ... and fits as shown

32.2l Fit kickstart pinion (also bushed)

32.2m *Note:* If layshaft has this circlip groove, it must be ignored. Do not fit circlip

32.2n Slide 5th gear pinion (25T) into position – no circlip

32.2o Fit 2nd gear pinion (32T), and thrustwasher

32.2p The assembled clusters should look like this:

32.2q View of gearbox components with selector forks in position

33.1 Lower fork is retained by spring-loaded ball

33.2a Do not omit the neutral switch contact during reassembly

33.2b Place gearbox components into left-hand casing

33.3 The crankshaft will drop into position

33.4a Fit the kickstart mechanism ...

33.4b ... ensuring that it engages correctly

34 Preparation of crankcase jointing surfaces: joining the crankcase

1   Coat the jointing surfaces of both crankcases with a thin layer of gasket cement, and fit the crankcase gasket to the left-hand casing half.
2   With the left-hand crankcase lying on its left side on the workbench, lower the right-hand crankcase on to it, taking care to locate the right-hand main bearing in its housing and the gearshafts in their respective bearings. It may be necessary to give the right-hand crankcase a few light taps with a soft faced mallet before the jointing surfaces will mate up correctly. **Do not use force.** If the crankcases will not align, one of the main bearings is not seating correctly.
3   Refit and tighten the various retaining screws. The operation and free-running of the crankshaft and gearbox assembly should be ascertained at this stage. Any tight spots or resistance must be investigated and rectified before further reassembly takes place.

35 Replacing the crankshaft pinion, oil pump and gearchange mechanism

1   Slide the crankshaft pinion into position on the splined mainshaft end. Fit two new O rings in their recesses in the oil pump seating face, then place the pump unit in position, aligning the holes in the top cover and pinion so that the two countersunk retaining screws can be fitted and tightened.
2   Fit the detent roller arm in position in the casing, and tighten the single retaining bolt. Check that the arm is free to move against spring pressure. Place the camplate locating pin in the end of the selector drum, followed by the camplate and its retaining bolt. The gearchange pedal shaft can now be slid into place in its bore in the crankcase, and the operating claw engaged with the camplate.

34.2 Check that all is well, then fit right-hand casing half

35.1a Slide the crankshaft pinion into position

35.1b Fit two new O rings to the oil pump jointing face ...

35.1c ... then position pump and tighten the retaining screw

35.2a Detent roller arm is retained by a shouldered bolt

35.2b Note locating pin which engages in camplate

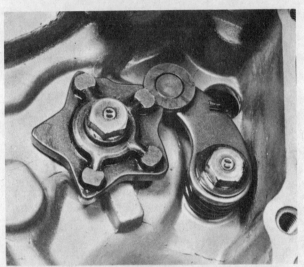

35.2c Fit camplate and tighten bolt

35.2d If the gearchange pedal shaft has been dismantled, reassemble . . .

35.2e . . . ensuring that springs are aligned properly

35.2f Fit assembly as shown

36 Replacing the clutch assembly and centrifugal oil filter

1   Place the clutch outer drum in position on the gearbox mainshaft end, followed by the splined thrust washer and inner clutch centre half. Fit the clutch plates, starting with a friction plate, then a plain plate. Build up the layers of plates, finishing with a friction plate, and ensuring that the internal splines of the plain plates are in line. If this is not done, it will be impossible to fit the clutch centre.

2   Lower the clutch centre into position and secure with the circlip, then fit the clutch springs over the projecting threaded pillars. The thrust plate can now be placed in position, and the four retaining bolts fitted and tightened. Install the cup and pushrod in the centre of the thrust bearing.

3   Place the inner half of the centrifugal oil filter over the crankshaft end, followed by the special washer, noting the markings denoting the outside face. Fit and tighten the slotted securing nut to a torque setting of 4.0 – 5.0 kgf m (29 – 36 lbf ft), using the Honda service tool or improvised peg spanner. Install a new gasket, followed by the outer half of the filter unit, tightening the three retaining screws evenly to avoid any risk of warpage.

4   Fit the two locating dowels into the crankcase mating surface and place a new gasket over them, using a smear of grease to stick it in place. Check that the clutch pushrod is in place and the release mechanism is correctly refitted and greased, then apply a smear of grease to the lips of the kickstart

shaft oil seal. Press the crankcase right-hand cover into place, using a few taps from a soft-faced mallet to seat it. Refit and tighten securely and evenly the cover retaining screws. Check that the clutch release mechanism is working properly.

36.1a Place clutch drum in position ...

36.1c ... and inner centre half

36.1b ... and fit thrust washer ...

36.1d Fit friction and plain plates as shown

36.2a Upper clutch centre half can now be fitted and retained by circlip

36.2b Position springs over threaded pillars

36.2c Fit pressure plate and pushrod and cup

36.3a Slide on the inner half of centrifugal filter

36.3b Note markings on special washer ...

36.3c ... which should be fitted thus

36.3d Use home-made tool to tighten lockring

36.3e Fit new gasket and replace the cover

37 Replacing the camshaft, generator and left-hand casing fittings

1   Turn the unit over and support it on wooden blocks with the left-hand side uppermost. Fit the gauze crankcase strainer, its spring and the large hexagon-headed cover. Push the neutral indicator switch into position in the crankcase bore. It is worthwhile ensuring that the rubber plug, which retains the switch, is fitted to the outer casing, as this is easily overlooked.

2   The crankshaft pinion which drives the cam gear is marked with a centre-punched timing dot. The crankshaft should be rotated so that this mark is at the top, nearest to the cam gear. The cam gear has a corresponding mark, and should be placed in position so that these two marks correspond exactly. As long as this precaution is observed, the valve timing will be set correctly, but on no account overlook this setting as it is critical to the operation of the engine.

3   Place the shim under the head of the cam gear shaft, then fit the gear shaft in the crankcase bore, taking care that the O ring is not nipped as the head of the shaft enters its recess. The head of the shaft should be positioned so that the small projecting segment is uppermost; do not forget the small spring.

Fit the endfloat plunger in its bore, and depress it against spring pressure while the retaining bolt is tightened.

4   Place the generator stator in position, noting the flat at the top which engages with the head of the cam gear shaft. Ensure that the rubber fillet through which the generator cables pass is located correctly. The generator rotor can now be placed over the mainshaft, and its securing nut tightened to a torque setting of 4.0 – 5.0 kgf m (29 – 36 lbf ft), having locked the crankshaft in the same way as described during the removal sequence. Route the neutral switch lead between the casting webs, noting the rubber packing piece, and reconnect the end at the switch. Make sure that the main output leads pass beneath the small guide plate at the top of the casing.

38 Replacing the gearbox sprocket

1   Place the gearbox sprocket in position on the splined shaft end, followed by the locking plate, which is similarly splined. When the plate is aligned with the groove in the shaft, it can be rotated sufficiently to allow the securing bolts to be fitted. Note that if the rear chain was removed together with the sprocket, this stage should be left until the engine has been installed in the frame.

37.1a Refit gauze crankcase filter assembly

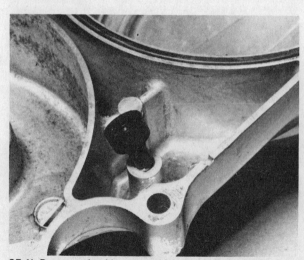

37.1b Do not omit rubber stop which retains neutral switch

37.2a Lower cam assembly into position ...

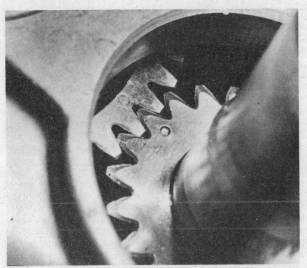

37.2b ... aligning the timing marks as shown

37.3a Do not omit thrust washer or small spring when refitting cam gear shaft

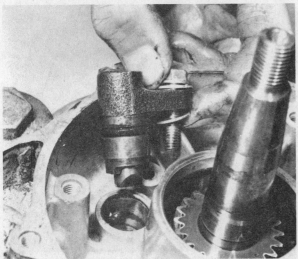

37.3b Depress end float plunger while single bolt is tightened

37.4a Reconnect lead to neutral switch

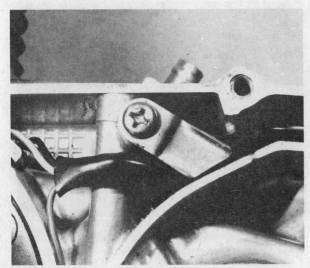

37.4b Ensure that generator leads pass behind guide plate

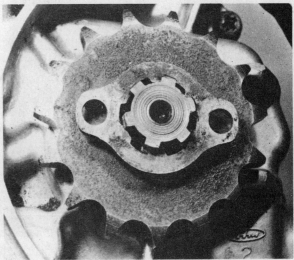

38.1 Fit sprocket and retain with the locking plate and bolts

39 Refitting the piston, cylinder barrel, cylinder head and rocker arms

1   Raise the connecting rod to its highest point and pad the mouth of the crankcase with clean rag as a precaution against displaced parts falling in.

2   The piston is marked 'IN' denoting the inlet valve cutaway, and must be fitted in the correct relative position ie, towards the rear.

3   Lightly oil and fit the piston onto the connecting rod by inserting the gudgeon pin. Replace the circlips that retain the gudgeon pin, making doubly sure that they are correctly seated in their grooves and that the circlip gap does not coincide with the slot in the piston. Always renew the circlips as it is false economy to re-use the originals.

4   Trim off any excess crankcase gasket from the cylinder mounting face with a sharp knife. Refit the locating dowel to each of the left-hand studs and install a new cylinder base gasket, using a smear of grease to stick it in place. Ensure that the cam followers have been correctly refitted on their shaft.

5   When fitting the piston rings first fit the oil scraper ring centre section, ensuring that its ends butt together, then fit the side rails on each side of it; these are fitted with their top surfaces (identified by etched markings) upwards and with their end gaps spaced 20 – 30 mm on each side of the centre section gap. Of the two compression rings, the second is identified by its tapered outer edge (the top ring being rectangular in section) and the top surface of both is identified by the letter T, R or N etched near the gap. Fit the compression rings with their top surfaces upwards, each in its correct groove and with their end gaps at 120° to that of the oil scraper ring. Lightly oil the piston and the cylinder bore, place the barrel over the studs and lower it onto the piston, compressing each ring in turn by hand to feed them into the bore.

6   When all three piston rings are in the bore, the padding in the crankcase can be removed and the cylinder barrel located on the two dowels and secured with two bolts at the left-hand side. Check that the cam followers are correctly located either side of the cam lobe as the cylinder barrel is lowered into position and be careful not to scratch their feet on the cam gear teeth.

7   Note the position of the three dowels, (see photograph) which should be positioned over three of the four studs. The front right-hand stud does not have a dowel. A new cylinder head gasket can now be placed in position, plus a new O ring around the right-hand rear dowel. The cylinder head can now be lowered over the holding down studs, and the pointed bolt fitted and screwed lightly into the head of the cam follower pivot shaft. Fit the two pushrods, ensuring that they seat in the cam follower cups. The pushrod guide plate can now be fitted and retained by two of the four cylinder head sleeve bolts.

8   Fit the remaining two sleeve bolts to the cylinder head, then tighten all four bolts evenly and diagonally, finally tightening them to 2.3 – 2.8 kgf m (16.5 – 20 lbf ft). Tighten the special bolt which screws into the cam follower pivot to 1.8 – 2.3 kgf m (13 – 16.5 lbf ft). Slacken off the valve rocker adjusters, and fit the rocker assembly to the cylinder head, tightening the retaining bolts. Ensure that the pushrods engage in the rocker cups.

9   Turn the engine over to align the T mark on the generator rotor with the index mark on the crankcase, and set the valve clearances to 0·08 mm (0·003 in) using a feeler gauge. Tighten the locknuts, then recheck the clearances. Examine the rubber seal in the cylinder head cover for signs of cracking or scuffing, and renew if it at all suspect. Before fitting the cover, liberally lubricate the rocker assembly with engine oil, and prime the circular oil feed passage. Place the cover in position, and fit the retaining screws, tightening them evenly.

39.2 Cutout for inlet valve is marked appropriately

39.3 Refit the piston using new circlips

39.5 Feed piston into bore, then lower barrel into position

39.7a Fit new head gasket. Note position of dowels

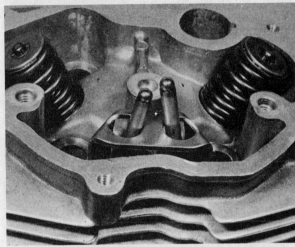
39.7b Ensure that pushrods engage in cam followers correctly

39.8a Refit pushrod guide and rocker assembly ...

39.8b ... oiling them liberally

39.9 Adjust valve clearances, then refit cylinder head cover

40 Refitting the engine/gearbox unit in the frame

1 It is worth checking at this stage that nothing has been omitted during the rebuilding sequences. It is better to discover any left-over components at this stage rather than just before the rebuilt engine is to be started.

2 Installation is, generally speaking, a reversal of the removal sequence. The unit should be lifted into its approximate position in the frame, where it can be lodged between the frame members. Loosely assemble the front engine plate, fitting, but not tightening, the mounting bolts. Place the rear bolts in position, noting that all bolts should be fitted from the left-hand side. Assemble the head steady plates, if these have been removed. When all the bolts are in position, tighten them evenly to 2.0 – 3.0 kgf m (14.5 – 22 lbf ft). Note that the generator output leads should be routed through the pressed steel guide which fits beneath the upper mounting bolt head.

3 Reconnect the generator output leads at the connector block adjacent to the battery. Refit the clutch operating cable and adjust it as described in Routine maintenance. Push the crankcase breather pipe onto its stub. Refit the carburettor,

ensuring that all gaskets and/or O-rings are renewed if necessary, that all components are refitted the correct way round and in the correct order and that the fasteners are securely tightened. Refit the throttle valve assembly which will have been left attached to the throttle cable, and screw down the mixing chamber top. The air hose from the air filter box can now be reconnected to the carburettor.

4   Thread the footrest assembly into position beneath the crankcase, and fit the four retaining bolts, tightening them to a torque setting of 2.0 – 3.0 kgf m (14.5 – 22 lbf ft). Note that it will fit in one position only, and if turned round, the mounting bolt holes will not align. Place a new exhaust port sealing ring in position, and fit the exhaust system, first placing the pipe in the exhaust port and then loosely assembling the rear mounting. Fit the two packing pieces as shown in the accompanying photograph, place the flange over then so that they are located inside the flange recess, and tighten the two retaining nuts securely, followed by the rear mounting fasteners.

5   Refit the rear chain, together with the gearbox sprocket if it was removed in this manner. Replace the left-hand cover, having first checked the contact breaker gap and ignition timing as described in Chapter 3. Refit the gearchange and kickstart pedals and tighten their pinch bolts to a torque setting of 0.8 – 1.2 kgf m (6 – 9 lfb ft).

6   Reconnect the fuel pipe to the carburettor, and install the air filter element if this has been removed for cleaning. Fit the battery leads, observing the polarity markings, and check that the electrical system functions correctly. Refit the petrol tank, the seat and the side panels. Check that the drain plug is tightened to a torque setting of 2.0 – 3.5 kgf m (14.5 – 25 lbf ft), then refill the engine to the correct level with oil, as described in Routine maintenance.

40.2a Assemble engine front plate loosely – do not tighten

40.2b Refit both rear mounting bolts . . .

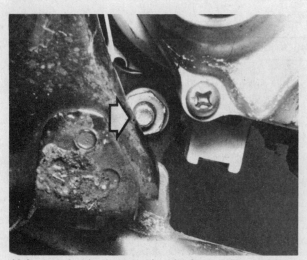

40.2c . . . noting that lower nut is rather inaccessible

40.2d Replace head steady plate, if this was removed

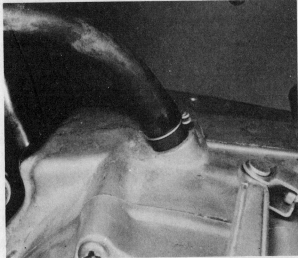

40.3a Push breather pipe over crankcase stub

40.3b Reconnect clutch cable, and check adjustment

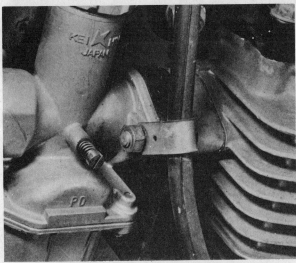

40.3c Refit the carburettor, noting guide for HT cable

40.4a Footrest assembly bolts onto underside of crankcase

40.4b Fit new sealing ring in the exhaust port ...

40.4c ... then fit exhaust system. Note packing pieces

41 Starting and running the rebuilt engine

1   Make a final check around the engine to ensure that everything has been refitted correctly and tightened down securely. Before starting the engine, unscrew the plug at the top of the cylinder head cover, and watch this carefully during the first few seconds of running to ensure that the oil is circulating properly. If all is well, oil will be expelled with considerable force, so have a rag to hand to wipe off the inevitable deluge.

Bear in mind that the engine parts should be liberally coated with oil during assembly, so the engine will tend to smoke heavily for a few minutes until the excess oil is burnt away. Do not despair if the engine will not fire up at first, as it is quite likely that the excess oil will foul the spark plug, necessitating its removal and cleaning. When the engine does start, listen carefully for any unusual noises, and if present, establish, and if necessary rectify, the cause. Check around the engine for any signs of leaking gaskets.

Before using the machine on the road, check the operation of the clutch and brakes. Remember that if a number of new parts have been fitted or if the engine has been rebored, it will be necessary to follow the original running-in instructions so that the new parts have ample opportunity to bed-down in a satisfactory manner.

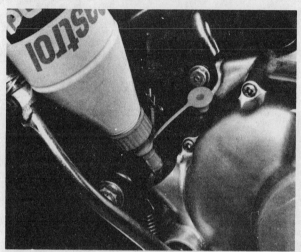

40.6 Refill crankcase to correct level with engine oil

41.1 Prime oil system before starting the engine

42 Fault diagnosis: engine

Symptom	Cause	Remedy
Engine does not start	Lack of compression:	
	Valve stuck open	Adjust tappet clearance.
	Worn valve guides	Renew.
	Valve timing incorrect	Check and adjust.
	Worn piston rings	Renew.
	Worn cylinder	Rebore.
	No spark at plug:	
	Fouled or wet spark plug	Clean.
	Fouled contact breaker points	Clean.
	Incorrect ignition timing	Check and adjust.
	Open or short circuit in ignition	Check wiring.
	No fuel flowing to carburettor:	
	Blocked fuel tank cap vent hole	Clean.
	Blocked fuel tap	Clean.
	Faulty carburettor float valve	Renew.
	Blocked fuel pipe	Clean.
Engine stalls whilst running	Fouled sparking plug or contact breaker points	Clean.
	Ignition timing incorrect	Check.
	Blocked fuel line or carburettor jets	Clean.

Symptom	Cause	Remedy
Noisy engine	Tappet noise:	
	Excessive tappet clearance	Check and reset.
	Weakened or broken valve spring	Renew springs.
	Knocking noise from cylinder:	
	Worn piston and cylinder bore	Rebore cylinder and fit oversize piston.
	Carbon in combustion chamber	Decoke engine.
	Worn gudgeon pin or connecting rod small end	Renew.
Engine noise	Excessive run-out of crankshaft	Renew.
	Worn crankshaft bearings	Renew.
	Worn connecting rod	Renew flywheel assembly.
	Worn transmission splines	Renew.
	Worn or binding transmission gear teeth	Renew gear pinions.
Smoking exhaust	Too much engine oil	Check oil level and adjust as necessary.
	Worn cylinder and piston rings	Rebore and fit oversize piston and rings.
	Worn valve guides	Renew.
	Damaged cylinder	Renew cylinder barrel and piston.
Insufficient power	Valve stuck open or incorrect tappet adjustment	Re-adjust.
	Weak valve springs	Renew.
	Valve timing incorrect	Check and reset.
	Worn cylinder and piston rings	Rebore and fit oversize piston and rings.
	Poor valve seatings	Grind in valves.
	Ignition timing incorrect	Check and adjust.
	Defective plug cap	Fit replacement.
	Dirty contact breaker points	Clean or renew.
Overheating	Accumulation of carbon on cylinder head	Decoke engine.
	Insufficient oil	Refill to specified level.
	Faulty oil pump and/or blocked oil passage	Strip and clean.
	Ignition timing too far retarded	Check

43 Fault diagnosis: clutch

Symptom	Cause	Remedy
Clutch slip	Worn clutch plates	Renew.
Clutch drag	Engine idle speed too high	Re-adjust.
	Broken springs	Renew.
	Clutch drum or centre damage	Rectify or renew as required.

44 Fault diagnosis: gearbox

Symptom	Cause	Remedy
Excessive mechanical noise	Lack of oil	Refill.
	Broken pinions or chain	Renew.
Difficulty in engaging gears	Selector forks or rods bent	Renew.
	Broken springs in gear selector mechanism	Check and renew.
	Clutch drag	See Preceding Section.
Machine jumps out of gear	Worn dogs on ends of gear pinions	Strip gearbox and renew worn parts.
	Worn selector forks	
Kickstarter does not return	Broken return spring	Renew spring
Kickstarter slips or jams	Worn ratchet assembly	Dismantle kickstarter assembly and renew worn parts.
Gear change lever does not return	Broken return spring	Remove right-hand crankcase cover and renew spring.

Chapter 2 Fuel system and lubrication

Refer to Chapter 7 for information relating to 1985-on models

Contents

Specifications

Fuel tank capacity

Overall	10 litres (2.2 Imp gal)
Including reserve of	2 litres (0.4 Imp gal)
Fuel grade and type	Either leaded three- or four-star (minimum octane rating of 91) or unleaded premium

Carburettor

ID number – by machine serial (engine) number:

CG125 up to 1020010	077A-A
CG125 1020011 to 1104204	PD88E-A/B
CG125 1104205 on, CG125 K1, CG125-B up to 1422468	PD88E-C
CG125-B 1422469 on	PD88E-E
CG125-C up to 1608462	PD45C-A*
CG125-C 1608463 on, CG125-E...	PD45C-C*

*Indicates (T)PFC type carburettor – see Chapter 7 for details

	077A-A	PD88E-A/B/C/E	PD45C-A/C
Main jet	92	100	95(-A), 85(-C)
Pilot (slow) jet	38	40(-E only)*	38(-A), 40(-C)
Needle clip position – grooves from top	3rd	3rd	N/Av
Pilot screw – turns out from fully closed	$1\frac{3}{8}$	$1\frac{3}{4}$	N/Av
Float height	24.0 mm (0.95 in)	18.5 mm (0.73 in)	N/Av
Idle speed	1100 – 1300 rpm	1200 rpm	1200 rpm

* Pilot jet not removable on PD88E-A/B/C carburettors

Engine/gearbox lubrication

Capacity – approx	1.0 litre (1.76 Imp pint)
Recommended oil	Good quality SAE10W/40 engine oil, API class SE, SF or SG

1 General description

The fuel system comprises a petrol tank from which petrol is fed by gravity to the float chamber. It is controlled by a petrol tap with a built-in filter. The tap has three positions: 'Off', 'On', 'Reserve', the latter providing a reserve supply of petrol when the main supply has run out. For cold starting the carburettor has a manually operated choke. The machine should run on 'Choke' for the least amount of time.

The lubrication system is of the pressure fed type, supplying oil to almost every part of the engine. There is a centrifugal filter mounted directly on the end of the crankshaft. Centrifugal force caused by the rotation of the engine throws the heavier impurities outwards where they stick to the walls, allowing only the clean, lighter oil through. Oil is picked up by the oil pump and pressure fed through the right-hand crankcase where it is diverted into two routes. In one direction it goes through a passage in the right-hand crankcase cover and then through the oil filter to the crankshaft. The other direction takes the oil through a passage via a cylinder head stud to the rocker arms. The transmission also receives oil under pressure, relying upon this simple yet very efficient system.

2 Petrol tank: removal and replacement

1 The fuel tank is not bolted to the machine in any way. It is held in place by three rubbers; two at the inner front and one at the rear under the seat, which it is necessary to remove.

2 Unfasten the bolt on each side of the rear of the seat. Lift up the back a little and pull back until the seat disengages with its location bracket and lifts clear.

3 Turn the fuel to 'Off' position and ease off the rubber fuel feed pipe clip and pipe. Lift the rear of the tank, pull to the rear, then lift away.

4 If difficulty is found in replacing the tank, apply a small amount of lubricant to the tank front rubbers before reassembly.

3 Petrol feed pipe: examination

The petrol feed pipe is made from thin walled synthetic rubber and is of the push-on type. It is only necessary to replace the pipe if it becomes hard or splits. It is unlikely that the retaining clips should need replacing due to fatigue as the main seal between the pipe and union is effected by an 'interference' fit.

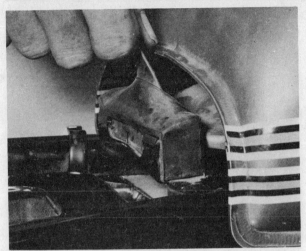

2.2 Rubber strap retains rear of petrol tank

4 Petrol tap: removal, repair and replacement

1   Before the petrol tap can be removed, it is first necessary to drain the tank. This is easily accomplished by removing the feed pipe from the carburettor and allowing the contents of the tank to drain into a clean receptacle, with the tap turned to the 'reserve' position. Alternatively, the tank can be removed and placed on one side, so that the fuel level is below the tap outlet. (Take care not to damage the paintwork.)
2   The tap unit is retained by a gland nut to the threaded stub on the underside of the tank. It can be removed after the fuel pipe has been pulled off the tap.
3   If the tap lever leaks, it will be necessary to renew it as a complete unit. It is not possible to dismantle the tap for repair.

5 Carburettor: removal – pre (T)PFC type

1   Before the carburettor is removed from the inlet stub, it is necessary to detach the petrol pipe, air cleaner hose, and carburettor top and throttle valve assembly. It is easier to remove the petrol tank to lessen the risk of damage to the paintwork, and to improve access. (Make sure the fuel tap is turned off first!). Prise off the air hose from the carburettor intake.
2   Unscrew the carburettor top, and withdraw the valve assembly. If the valve or needle require attention, they can be detached by compressing the return spring against the

underside of the top, and disengaging the cable end from its recess in the valve. The needle is held by a spring clip, which is itself positioned by a second clip inside the valve. It is normally advisable to leave this assembly undisturbed unless obviously worn.
3   Slacken and remove the two flange mounting nuts, and pull the carburettor body clear of the mounting studs. Do not remove the heat shield or spacing block unless necessary. The carburettor components can now be dismantled for examination.

6 Carburettor: overhaul – pre (T)PFC type

1   On early models, prise back the spring clip retaining the float bowl, tap the bowl gently to break the seal and withdraw it. On later models remove the three retaining screws and withdraw the float bowl. Note the seal set in the gasket surface, which must be renewed if damaged or worn, and check that the drain plug passage is clean, that the plug seal is in good condition and that the plug is securely fastened.
2   Displace the float pivot pin to release the float assembly, then withdraw the float needle. Check the float for leakage and renew the assembly if damaged or worn; repairs are not possible. Check the float needle tip for wear. After lengthy service a ridge or groove will appear; even if this is so small that it can be seen only with the aid of a magnifying glass, the needle must be renewed to restore the valve's seal and the

4.2 Petrol tap is secured by a gland nut

4.3 Tap is riveted together, and must be renewed if worn

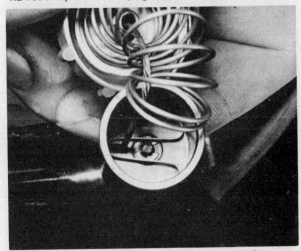

5.2 Throttle valve may be detached for access to needle

5.3a Remove carburettor body from inlet port

5.3b It is not normally necessary to remove heat shield

carburettor fuel level. If the needle seat is worn or damaged it must be renewed also; on later models note that this means renewing the complete carburettor assembly.

3   The main jet is screwed into the jet holder which is itself screwed into the central column projecting from the carburettor underside. On certain models (see Specifications) the pilot jet can be unscrewed from its location next to the central column; on all others it is fixed and can only be cleaned in place, using compressed air. When removing jets use only a close-fitting screwdriver or spanner to minimise the risk of damage, and do not exert excessive force. Before removing the needle jet, note carefully exactly how it is positioned above the jet holder, before pressing it out using a slim wooden rod.

4   The throttle stop screw is located in the right-hand side of the carburettor body, at the base of the throttle valve bore; the pilot screw is located either adjacent to the throttle stop screw (early models) or projecting downwards from the carburettor body, at the front of the float bowl. To remove these, first screw each in until it seats lightly and note the **exact** number of turns required to do this, then unscrew it and note the presence of the small spring under each. On refitting, screw it in until it seats lightly then unscrew it by the previously noted number of turns to restore it to its original position.

5   Check the throttle valve components for wear or damage and renew any defective item. If the valve is slack in the carburettor body, then either the valve or the complete carburettor assembly must be renewed. Similarly, check the choke mechanism for wear or damage, noting that the complete carburettor assembly must be renewed to rectify any problems. On early models check particularly that the spring-loaded flap is in one piece and free from cracks; on later models check that the butterfly retaining screws are securely fastened.

6   Before the carburettor is reassembled, using the reverse of the dismantling procedure, it should be cleaned out thoroughly using compressed air. Avoid using a piece of rag since there is always risk of particles of lint obstructing the internal passageways or the jet orifices.

7   Never use a piece of wire or any pointed metal object to clear a blocked jet. It is only too easy to enlarge the jet under these circumstances, and increase the rate of petrol consumption. If compressed air is not available, a blast of air from a tyre pump will usually suffice. As a last resort, a fine **nylon** bristle may be used.

8   Do not use excessive force when reassembling a carburettor because it is easy to shear a jet or some of the smaller screws. Furthermore, the carburettor is cast in a zinc-based alloy which itself does not have a high tensile strength. If any of the castings are damaged during reassembly, they will almost certainly have to be renewed.

7   Carburettor adjustment – pre (T)PFC type

1   Commence operations by checking the float height, which will involve detaching the carburettor, if not already removed, inverting it and removing the float bowl. If the float height is correct, the bottom of each float should be the specified distance away from the carburettor body mating surface when the valve has just closed. To adjust the setting bend the float arm.

2   Replace the carburettor, check that free play is present in the throttle cable, and with the engine at normal operating temperature turn the pilot screw inwards until the engine misfires or decreases in speed. Note the position of the screw, then turn it outwards until similar symptoms are observed. The screw should then be set exactly between these two positions, which should approximate the specified setting.

3   When the mixture setting is correct, use the throttle stop screw to set the idle speed. If a suitable tachometer is not available the correct speed can be approximated by finding the lowest speed at which the engine will tick over smoothly and reliably. Adjust the throttle cable, using the adjuster at either end of the cable, to give 2 – 6 mm (0.08 – 0.24 in) free play measured at the twistgrip flange, ie 10 – 15° of twistgrip rotation. Ensure the idle speed remains steady at all handlebar positions.

4   Note that these adjustments should always be made with the engine at normal operating temperature and with the air cleaner connected, otherwise a false setting will be obtained.

8   Carburettor settings

1   Some of the carburettor settings, such as the sizes of the needle jet, main jet, and needle position etc are pre-determined by the manufacturer. Under normal circumstances, it is unlikely that these settings will require modification, even though there is provision made. If a change appears necessary, it can often be attributed to a developing engine fault.

2   As an approximate guide the pilot jet setting controls engine speed up to $\frac{1}{8}$ throttle. The throttle slide cutaway controls engine speed from $\frac{1}{8}$ to $\frac{3}{4}$ throttle. The size of the main jet is responsible for engine speed at the final $\frac{3}{4}$ to full throttle. It should be added however that these are only guide lines. There is no clearly defined demarcation line due to a certain amount of overlap that occurs between the carburettor components involved.

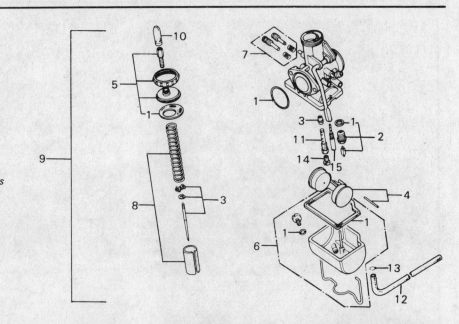

Fig. 2.1 Carburettor –
077A type

1 *Gasket set*
2 *Needle valve assembly*
3 *Needle jet*
4 *Float assembly*
5 *Mixing chamber top*
6 *Float bowl assembly*
7 *Pilot and throttle stop screws*
8 *Throttle valve assembly*
9 *Carburettor complete*
10 *Rubber cap*
11 *Needle jet holder*
12 *Drain pipe*
13 *Clip*
14 *Main jet*
15 *Pilot jet*

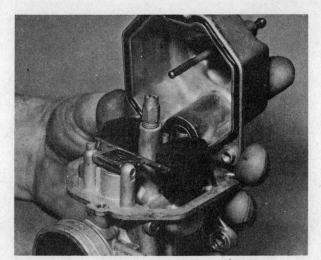

6.1 Float bowl is retained by three screws – later type

6.2a Displace the float pivot pin to free the float assembly

3   Always err slightly on the side of a rich mixture, since a weak mixture will cause the engine to overheat. Reference to Chapter 3 will show how the condition of the spark plug can be interpreted with some experience as a reliable guide to carburettor mixture strength.

9   Carburettor: (T)PFC type

1   CG125-C and E models are fitted with Honda's (Transient) Power Fuel Control carburettor. This is an economy carburettor designed to run on a weaker mixture, so reducing fuel consumption. The (T)PFC system consists of an accelerator pump mounted on the underside of the carburettor. It provides a richer mixture during acceleration. A linkage depresses the pump rod causing a metered quantity of fuel to be injected as the throttle is opened.

2   Refer to Chapter 7 for details of overhaul and adjustment.

6.2b Take care not to lose the float needle!

6.3a Main jet can be unscrewed for cleaning ...

6.3b . . . as can the jet holder

6.4 Pilot screw is located here – later type

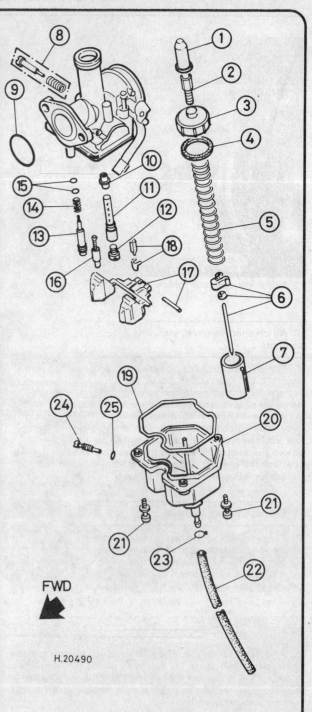

FWD

H.20490

Fig. 2.2 Carburettor – PD88E type

1	Rubber cap	14	Spring
2	Cable adjuster	15	O-ring
3	Mixing chamber top	16	Pilot jet
4	Gasket	17	Float and pivot pin
5	Return spring	18	Float needle valve
6	Jet needle assembly	19	Gasket
7	Throttle valve	20	Float bowl
8	Throttle stop screw	21	Screw and washer – 3 off
9	O-ring	22	Drain pipe
10	Needle jet	23	Clip
11	Needle jet holder	24	Drain screw
12	Main jet	25	O-ring
13	Pilot screw		

7.2 Adjust idle speed by means of this screw

10 Air cleaner: removal, cleaning and replacement of elements

1   Pull off the right-hand side panel to gain access to the air cleaner case. Release the lid of the air cleaner case, then displace the leaf spring to enable removal of the element. The foam filter sleeves can be slid off the central core, and the whole unit washer thoroughly in a high flash-point solvent such as white spirit (Stoddard solvent). Dry each part carefully, then soak each sleeve in the specified oil and squeeze it gently to remove the surplus oil. Rebuild the assembly and refit it. Make sure that the element and cover are both correctly seated to prevent air leakage.

11 Exhaust system: general

1   The exhaust system on a four-stroke motor-cycle will require very little attention, as, unlike two-stroke machines, it is not prone to the accumulation of carbon. The only points requiring attention are the general condition of the system, including mountings and the chromium plating, and ensuring that the

system is kept airtight, particularly at the exhaust port. Air leaks here will cause mysterious backfiring when the machine is on overrun, as air will be drawn in causing residual gases to be ignited in the exhaust pipe. To this end, make sure that the composite sealing ring is renewed each time the system is removed.

12 Oil pump: removal, examination and renovation

1   Access to the oil pump is gained after removing the right-hand outer casing. The driving gear housing will be seen to have two holes in its outer face. Turn the engine over until the holes in the driving gear are in line, then pass a screwdriver through to release the two countersunk retaining screws. The pump can now be lifted away.

2   Remove the end plate from the back of the unit, noting the locating pip and corresponding recess which must align during reassembly. Shake out the inner and outer rotor. The driving gear housing can be separated, if desired, and the gear and spindle removed.

3   Examine each component for signs of scuffing and wear. Note especially the condition of the rotors and pump body. If these are at all worn, the pump must be renewed. Temporarily fit the rotors to the pump body and use feeler gauges to measure the clearance between the rotors and a straightedge placed acoss the pump body mating surface (ie rotor endfloat). This clearance should be in the range 0.15 – 0.20 mm (0.0059 – 0.0079 in) if the pump is in good condition; if the clearance is 0.25 mm (0.0098 in) or more the worn components must be renewed. Similarly measure the clearance between any two tips of the inner and outer rotors. The correct clearance is 0.15 mm (0.0059 in); if it is 0.20 mm (0.0079 in) or more the rotors must be renewed as a matched set.

4   When reassembling the pump, lubricate each component with clean engine oil, and make sure that a new gasket is fitted. Note that the end plate pip and the depression in the pump body must align. Fit new O rings when fitting the pump unit to the engine.

13 Oil filters: location and cleaning

1   The engine is equipped with two types of oil filter; a gauze element located in the lower part of the left-hand crankcase, behind a large hexagon-headed plug, and a crankshaft mounted centrifugal oil filter. Removal and cleaning of these components is covered in Routine Maintenance.

10.1a Air filter element is retained by spring clip . . .

10.1b . . . and can be dismantled for cleaning

12.2a Note alignment marks on oil pump components

12.2b Casing is secured by two bolts, and can be removed ...

12.2c ... to allow pinion ...

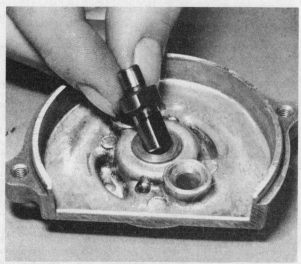

12.2d ... and spindle to be withdrawn

12.3 Check pump components as described

13.1 Centrifugal filter can be dismantled for cleaning

14 Fault diagnosis: fuel system and lubrication

Symptom	Cause	Remedy
Excessive fuel consumption	Air cleaner choked or restricted	Clean or renew.
	Fuel leaking from carburettor. Float sticking	Check all unions and gaskets. Float needle seat needs cleaning.
	Badly worn or distorted carburettor	Replace.
	Jet needle setting too high	Adjust to figure given in Specifications.
	Main jet too large or loose	Fit correct jet or tighten if necessary.
	Carburettor flooding	Check float valve and replace if worn.
Idling speed too high	Throttle stop screw in too far. Carburettor top loose	Adjust screw. Tighten top.
	Pilot jet incorrectly adjusted	Refer to relevant paragraph in this Chapter.
	Throttle cable sticking	Disconnect and lubricate or replace.
Engine dies after running for a short while	Blocked air hole in filler cap	Clean.
	Dirt or water in carburettor	Remove and clean out.
General lack of performance	Weak mixture; float needle stuck in seat	Remove float chamber or float and clean.
	Air leak at carburettor joint	Check joint to eliminate leakage, and fit new O ring.
Engine does not respond to throttle	Throttle cable sticking	See above.
	Petrol octane rating too low	Use higher grade (star rating) petrol.
Engine runs hot and is noisy	Lubrication failure	Stop engine immediately and investigate cause. Do not restart until cause is found and rectified.

Chapter 3 Ignition system

Refer to Chapter 7 for information relating to 1985-on models

Contents

Specifications

Ignition timing

Initial – 'F' mark aligned	20° BTDC static or at idle speed
Advance starts at	1800 rpm
Full advance at	35° BTDC @ 3000 rpm

Ignition system

Ignition HT coil spark gap	8 mm (0.32 in) minimum
Condenser capacity	0.22 – 0.26 microfarad
Contact breaker gap:	
Nominal	0.35 mm (0.014 in)
Tolerance for ignition timing	0.30 – 0.40 mm (0.012 – 0.016 in)
Contact breaker spring pressure	750 g (1.65 lb)

Spark plug

	NGK	ND
Make		
Type:		
CG125 model – original/current recommendation	D8ES-L/D8EA	X24ES/X24ES-U
CG125 K1, B, C, E	DR8ES-L	X24ESR-U
Electrode gap	0.6 – 0.7 mm (0.024 – 0.028 in)	

1 General description

The spark which is necessary to ignite the petrol/air mixture in the combustion chamber is derived from an ignition coil mounted on the frame and a flywheel generator attached to the left-hand crankshaft of the engine. A contact breaker assembly within the generator determines the exact moment at which the spark will occur; as the points separate the electrical circuit is interrupted and a high tension voltage is developed across the points of the spark plug which jumps the gap and ignites the mixture.

2 Generator: checking the output

1   The generator coil is instrumental in creating the power in the ignition system, and any failure or malfunction will affect the operation of the ignition system. Should a generator fault be indicated, reference should be made to Chapter 6.

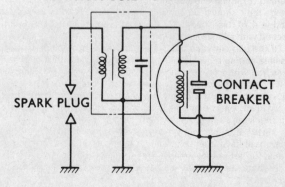

IGNITION COIL / CONDENSER

Fig. 3.1 Ignition system: schematic diagram

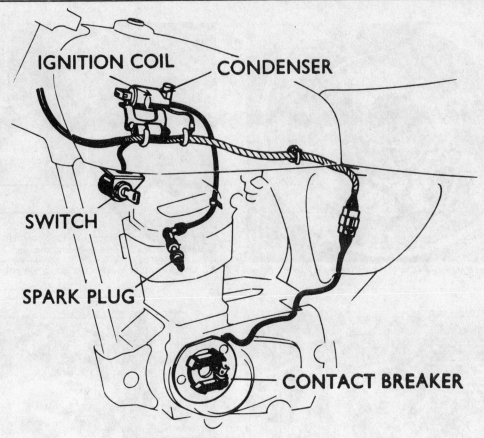

IGNITION COIL **CONDENSER**

SWITCH

SPARK PLUG

CONTACT BREAKER

Fig. 3.2 Ignition system: component location

3 Contact breaker: adjustment

1 To gain access to the contact breaker assembly, the left-hand outer casing should be removed. It is retained by four screws. The contact breaker is mounted on the stator or back-plate, and operated by a cam which is fitted to the centre boss inside the flywheel/rotor. A centrifugally-operated automatic timing unit (ATU) is fitted to advance the ignition timing as engine speed increases.

2 Rotate the engine until the contact breaker fibre heel is at the highest point of the cam and the points are at their widest opening. Examine the contact faces. If they are dirty, burnt or pitted, they should be removed for renewal as described in Section 4 of this Chapter. If the points are in sound condition, proceed with adjustment as follows:

3 If the gap between the breaker points is not within the permissible setting range of 0.3 - 0.4 mm (0.012 - 0.016 in) when measured with a feeler gauge, they should be adjusted. Slacken very slightly the cross point screw which locks the fixed contact adjustment. It should barely nip the contact support. Using a screwdriver, open or close the contact, tighten the lockscrew and check the setting. Repeat until correct.

4 **Note:** if adjustment has proved necessary, the ignition timing will have been affected, and this should be checked. It should be noted that wear in the contact breaker will normally necessitate its renewal, as no ignition timing adjustment is provided.

4 Contact breaker: removal and renewal

1 If examination has shown the contact breaker points to be worn, or if a timing check has shown them to have worn outside the limits given, it will be necessary to renew the assembly. Do not attempt to reface the contact breaker points, as this will make it impossible to obtain the required gap and timing settings. Use only genuine Honda replacement parts when obtaining new points.

2 It is necessary to remove the flywheel/rotor from the crankshaft in order to gain access to the contact breaker assembly. This can be expected to be a tight fit on the mainshaft taper, and although it may be possible to remove it with a conventional legged puller, this course of action must be regarded as a last resort, and wherever possible, the proper Honda puller or a cheaper pattern version of it must be used. The genuine tool is available from Honda agents under part number 07933 – 0010000.

3 Unscrew the centre nut, having locked the crankshaft by selecting top gear and applying the rear brake, or by applying a holding tool. Fit the extractor in place, and gradually tighten the T handle to draw the rotor off. Check the ATU for wear or damage; if it is stiff in operation it should be dismantled for cleaning and greasing.

4 Prise off the E clip from the contact breaker pivot post, and place it in a safe place. Disconnect the leads from the terminal, and at the same time release the moving contact spring. Note the order in which the various terminal components are assembled. Remove the fixed contact securing screw and lift the fixed contact away.

5 Reassemble the new contact breaker assembly in the reverse order of that described for dismantling, taking care to assemble the terminal components in the correct order. Replace the rotor and tighten the securing nut to a torque setting of 4.0 – 5.0 kgf m (29 – 36 lbf ft). Set the contact breaker gap to exactly 0.35 mm (0.014 in) as described in Section 3, then check the ignition timing as described in Section 5.

3.1 Automatic timing unit in flywheel rotor may be lubricated lightly

3.3 Check contact breaker gap using feeler gauge

4.3 Flywheel rotor centre has thread to accept extractor

4.4 A : E clip. B : Fixed contact securing screw C : Terminal

5 Checking the ignition timing

1   The ignition timing can be checked using a battery and bulb arrangement connected as shown in the accompanying diagram. Owners of multimeter test instruments may prefer to use these, set to the most sensitive resistance scale, as continuity testers. Note that the easiest way to connect the probe to the contact breaker assembly is to disconnect the generator output lead connector and locate the black or black/white lead to the points.

2   Set the rotor so that the F mark registers with its datum mark, then adjust the fixed contact so that the points **just** start to separate. This will be indicated by the test lamp flickering (or the meter needle deflecting). Check that the contact breaker gap is within the tolerance given.

6 Ignition coil: checking

1   The ignition coil is a sealed unit and designed to give long service without need for attention., The coil is located under the petrol tank, which must be removed to gain access.

2   A number of tests can be performed using a basic test lamp

6.1 Coil and condenser are located beneath the fuel tank

and battery arrangement connected as shown in the accompanying diagrams. Should any of these checks not produce the expected result, the coil should be removed and taken to a Honda Service Agent or Auto-Electrical specialist for a more thorough check.

7 Condenser: location, removal and replacement

1 A condenser is included in the contact breaker circuitry to prevent arcing across the contact breaker points as they separate. The condenser is connected in parallel with the points and if a fault develops, ignition failure is liable to occur.

2 If the engine proves difficult to start, or misfiring occurs, it is possible that the condenser is at fault. To check, watch the points via the rotor apertures when the engine is running. If a spark occurs across the points and they have a blackened and burnt appearance, the condenser can be regarded as un-serviceable.

3 It is not possible to fully check the condenser without the appropriate equipment. In view of the low cost involved, it is preferable to fit a new replacement and observe the effect on engine performance although an approximate test can be carried out as shown in the accompanying diagram.

4 The condenser is mounted on the ignition coil assembly by means of a metal clamp. Since this fitting provides the earth connection of the condenser, it follows that the clip should make good contact and be tightened fully.

8 Spark plug: checking and re-setting the gap

1 The spark plug specified as original equipment will prove satisfactory in most operating conditions; alternatives are available to allow for varying altitudes, climatic conditions and the use to which the machine is put. It a spark plug is suspected of being faulty it can be tested only by the substitution of a brand new (not second-hand) plug of the correct make, type, and heat range; always carry a spare on the machine.

2 Note that the advice of a competent Honda Service Agent or similar expert should be sought before the plug heat range is altered from standard. The use of too cold, or hard, a grade of plug will result in fouling and the use of too hot, or soft, a grade of plug will result in engine damage due to excess heat being generated. If the correct grade of plug is fitted, however, it will be possible to use the condition of the spark plug electrodes to diagnose a fault in the engine or to decide whether the engine is operating efficiently or not.

3 Also, always ensure that the plug is of the resistor type (indicated by the letter 'R'), where applicable, so that its resistance value is correct for the ignition system. The same applies to the suppressor cap; if a cap or plug of the wrong type is fitted, thus producing a much greater or lesser resistance value than that for which the ignition system was designed, one or more components of the system may break down.

4 The electrode gap can be assessed using feeler gauges. If necessary, alter the gap by bending the outer electrode, preferably using a proper electrode tool. **Never** bend the centre electrode, otherwise the ceramic insulator will crack, and may cause damage to the engine if particles break away whilst the engine is running. If the outer electrode is seriously eroded as shown in the photographs, or if the spark plug is heavily fouled, it should be renewed. Clean the electrodes using a wire brush or a sharp-pointed knife, followed by rubbing a strip of fine emery across the electrodes. If a sand-blaster is used, check carefully that there are no particles of sand trapped inside the plug body to fall into the engine at a later date. For this reason such cleaning methods are no longer recommended; if the plug is so heavily fouled it should be renewed.

5 Before replacing a spark plug into the cylinder head coat the threads sparingly with a graphited grease to aid future removal. Use the correct sized spanner when tightening the plug otherwise the spanner may slip and damage the ceramic insulator. The plug should be tightened sufficiently to seat firmly on the sealing washer, and no more.

6 Never overtighten a spark plug otherwise there is risk of stripping the threads from the cylinder head, especially as it is cast in light alloy. A stripped thread can be repaired without having to scrap the cylinder head by using a 'Helicoil' thread insert. This is a low-cost service, operated by a number of dealers.

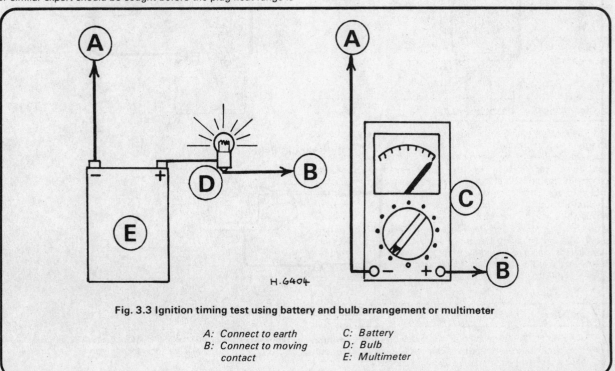

H.6404

Fig. 3.3 Ignition timing test using battery and bulb arrangement or multimeter

A: Connect to earth
B: Connect to moving
   contact

C: Battery
D: Bulb
E: Multimeter

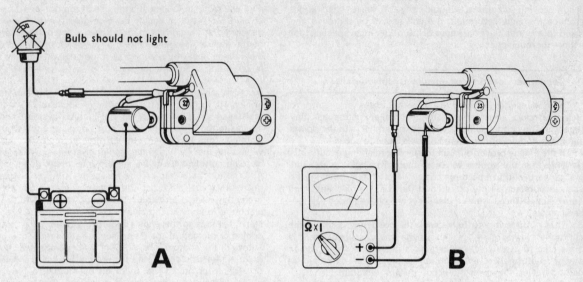

Bulb should not light

Fig. 3.4 Condenser: test sequence

A: *Using a battery/bulb arrangement*
B: *Using a multimeter*

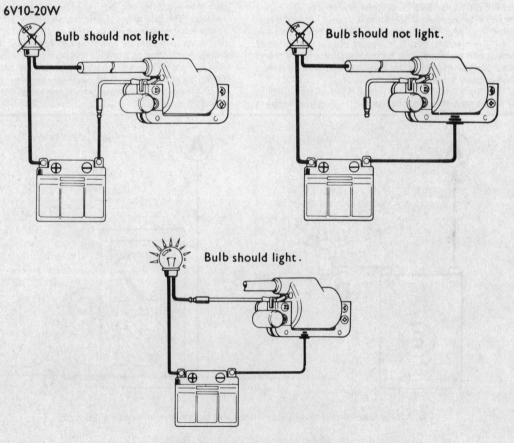

6V10-20W

Bulb should not light .

Bulb should not light .

Bulb should light .

Fig. 3.5 Ignition coil: test procedure

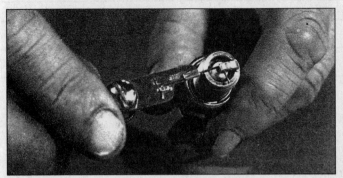

Electrode gap check - use a wire type gauge for best results

Electrode gap adjustment - bend the side electrode using the correct tool

Normal condition - A brown, tan or grey firing end indicates that the engine is in good condition and that the plug type is correct

Ash deposits - Light brown deposits encrusted on the electrodes and insulator, leading to misfire and hesitation. Caused by excessive amounts of oil in the combustion chamber or poor quality fuel/oil

Carbon fouling - Dry, black sooty deposits leading to misfire and weak spark. Caused by an over-rich fuel/air mixture, faulty choke operation or blocked air filter

Oil fouling - Wet oily deposits leading to misfire and weak spark. Caused by oil leakage past piston rings or valve guides (4-stroke engine), or excess lubricant (2-stroke engine)

Overheating - A blistered white insulator and glazed electrodes. Caused by ignition system fault, incorrect fuel, or cooling system fault

Worn plug - Worn electrodes will cause poor starting in damp or cold weather and will also waste fuel

9 Fault diagnosis : ignition system

Symptom	Cause	Remedy
Engine will not start	Plug faulty	Check plug and adjust gap or renew.
	Defective ignition coil	Renew.
	Dirty points	Clean or renew and check gap.
	Poor points contact	Check for arcing. Renew condenser.
Engine starts but runs erratically	Plug gap incorrect or has whiskered	Adjust and clean or renew.
	Incorrect ignition timing	Check timing and points gap.
	Weak points arm return spring	Renew.
	Defective ignition coil	Renew after expert testing.
	Low output from flywheel generator	Have tested and renew.
	Plug lead insulation breaking down	Check and renew.

Chapter 4 Frame and forks

Refer to Chapter 7 for information relating to 1985-on models

Contents

Specifications

Front forks

	Standard	Wear limit
Travel	108 mm (4.25 in)	
Lower leg bore diameter	31.000 – 31.039 mm (1.2205 – 1.2220 in)	31.100 mm (1.2244 in)
Bottom bush/damper piston diameter	30.936 – 30.975 mm (1.2180 – 1.2195 in)	30.900 mm (1.2165 in)
Fork spring free length		
CG125	185.90 mm (7.3189 in)	170.00 mm (6.6929 in)
CG125 K1, B, C, E	411.60 mm (16.2047 in)	391.00 mm (15.3937 in)
Fork oil capacity – per leg		
CG125 – at oil change	120 – 130 cc (4.22 – 4.58 Imp fl oz)	
CG125 – at rebuild, CG125 K1, B, C, E	130 – 140 cc (4.58 – 4.93 Imp fl oz)	
Recommended fork oil	Automatic transmission fluid (ATF) or equivalent fork oil	

Rear suspension

	Standard	Wear limit
Travel	70 mm (2.76 in)	
Suspension unit spring free length	179.80 mm (7.0787 in)	171.00 mm (6.7323 in)
Swinging arm pivot bolt to bush clearance	0.10 – 0.30 mm (0.0039 – 0.0118 in)	0.50 mm (0.0197 in)

1 General description

The Honda CG 125 utilises a frame of open diamond type, being a composite structure of tubular construction with a monocoque spine. The engine unit is bolted between the spine and the downtube to form a structural part of the frame. The front forks are of traditional telescopic design, being controlled by hydraulic dampers. Rear suspension is provided by a swinging arm fork, pivoting on replaceable bushes, and controlled by adjustable, hydraulically damped, suspension units.

2 Front forks: removal – general

1   It is unlikely that the forks will require removal from the frame unless the fork seals are leaking or accident damage has been sustained. In the event that the latter has occurred, it should be noted that the frame may also have become bent, and whilst this may not be obvious when checked visually, could prove to be potentially dangerous.

2   If attention to the fork legs only is required, it is unnecessary to detach the complete assembly, the legs being easily removed individually.

3   If, on the other hand, the headstock bearings are in need of attention, the forks complete with bottom yoke must be removed.

4   Before any dismantling work can be undertaken, the machine should be placed on the centre stand and blocked securely so that the front wheel is held off the ground. Detach the speedometer drive cable at the wheel, by unscrewing the knurled gland nut which retains it. Remove the front brake cable.

5   Remove the wheel spindle nut and split pin, and withdraw the spindle with the aid of a tommy bar. The wheel can now be lowered clear of the forks and put to one side.

6   To avoid damage to the paintwork, it is a good idea to remove the front mudguard at this stage, irrespective of whether removal will later be necessary, as in the case of individual fork leg removal.

3 Front forks: removing the fork assembly from the frame

1   Before the forks can be detached, it will be necessary to remove the handlebars, complete with controls, the mudguard, (if this has not already been removed), and the headlamp unit. Start by covering the petrol tank with an old blanket, or similar, to protect the paintwork from damage. Slacken and remove the handlebar clamp retaining bolts, noting that the right-hand clamp incorporates a helmet lock. The clamp halves can now be lifted off, and the handlebar assembly rested across the top of the petrol tank.

2   Disconnect the speedometer drive cable, and then release its retaining bolts and lift the instrument head away, detaching the bulbholders from the base as this is done.

3   Remove the headlamp unit from its shell, by releasing the single screw which secures the rim. The headlamp can be removed completely by disconnecting the colour coded leads inside the shell. Alternatively, the unit can be left in place, the

two mounting bolts released, and the leads threaded around the stanchions as the forks are removed. Note that whilst this will save disconnecting and then reconnecting the headlamp wiring, care must be taken to avoid damage to the unit during the fork dismantling sequence.

4   Slacken the two fork top bolts which pass through the top yoke, and the large chromium plated nut which retains the top yoke to the top of the steering stem. With these removed, the top yoke can be lifted away. If it proves stubborn, it may be tapped free using a soft-faced mallet. If the headlamp has been left in place, this should be positioned clear of the forks, as should any trailing cables. Note that it will be necessary to release the front indicator lamp leads from the inside of the headlamp shell.

5   Using a 46mm C spanner (available as a Honda service tool, part number: 07902 - 2400000), slacken off the lockring which retains the steering column. Have to hand two small tins or jars in which the head race balls can be kept safely. The balls from the lower race will drop free as the cup and cone part, and should be caught. Make sure none are left clinging to the race. Support the fork assembly while the lockring and cone are removed, and the balls from the upper race are removed and placed in the second container. The lower yoke can now be removed complete with the fork legs.

2.4 Release brake and speedometer cable, then remove wheel

2.5 Mudguard is secured by four bolts

3.1 Right-hand handlebar clamp incorporates helmet lock

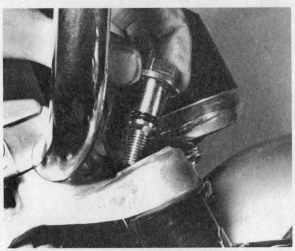

3.2 Remove fork top bolt to release yoke

4   Front forks: removing the fork legs from the yokes

1   It is not necessary to remove the complete headstock assembly if attention to the fork legs alone is required. The instructions in Section 2 of this Chapter should be followed, then proceed as described below:

2   Remove the fork top bolts and slacken the pinch bolts which clamp the stanchions in the lower yoke. The fork legs can now be removed individually. If necessary, the fork top bolts can be screwed partly home, and tapped with a soft faced mallet to jar the leg out of position. On CG125 models the shrouds will remain in position.

5   Steering head bearings: examination and renovation

1   Before reassembly of the forks is commenced, examine the steering head races. The ball bearing tracks of the respective cup and cone bearings should be polished and free from indentations or cracks. If wear or damage is evident, the cups and cones must be renewed as a complete set. They are a tight press fit and should be drifted out of position.

2   Ball bearings are cheap. If the originals are marked or discoloured, they should be renewed. To hold the steel balls in position during reassembly, pack the bearings with grease.

6   Fork yokes: examination

1   To check the top yoke for accident damage, push the fork stanchions through the bottom yoke and fit the top yoke. If it lines up, it can be assumed the yokes are not bent. Both must also be checked for cracks. If they are damaged or cracked, fit new replacements.

7   Fork legs: dismantling, examination and renovation – CG125 model

1   This type of fork is fully shrouded, and has an external variable rate spring. After the leg concerned has been removed from the yokes, the spring and headed spring guide may be slid off the stanchion. The guide serves to hold the top of the spring concentric to the stanchion, and thereby removes any tendency for the spring to chatter. It is unlikely to suffer any noticeable degree of wear. It will be noted that the forks are fitted with variable rate springs which mean that the forks are deflected easily at the start of their movement, and that subsequent compression produces progressively greater tension. It is important that the tighter coils are fitted at the top of the fork. Check the free length of the springs and compare it with the dimensions given in the specification. Always renew the springs as a pair.

2   Remove the lower shroud half and lower spring guide/seat to expose the bare stanchion and lower leg. Remove the circlip which retains the seal in the top of the lower leg. The lower leg should be clamped lightly in a vice, using soft aluminium jaws or some rag to prevent the surface of the leg from becoming scarred. If the restrictor is to be removed, press the stanchion fully into the lower leg to prevent the restrictor from rotating while its retaining screw is released.

3   The stanchion can now be pulled out of the lower leg, the oil seal being displaced by the headed upper fork bush. The seal should be renewed as a matter of course, each time the forks are dismantled.

4   Examine the inner surface of the headed top bush for signs of scuffing, and check that it is not slack when fitted on the stanchion. Any discernible axial play will necessitate renewal. The outer surface of the plain lower bush (which acts as the damper piston), should also be examined, and if possible, the

4.2a Stanchion is held by pinch bolt in lower yoke

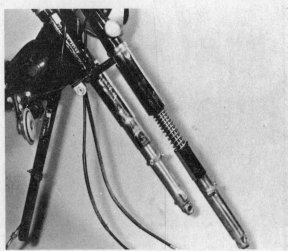

4.2b Fork leg can be pulled free from yokes.

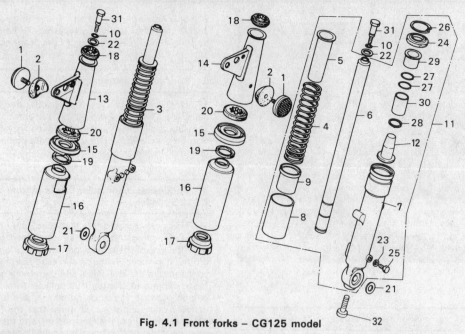

Fig. 4.1 Front forks – CG125 model

1	Reflector – 2 off	11	Left-hand fork assembly	22	Washer – 2 of
2	Seat – 2 off	12	Restrictor – 2 off	23	Fibre washer – 2 off
3	Right-hand fork assembly	13	Upper shroud	24	Oil seal – 2 off
4	Fork spring – 2 off	14	Upper shroud	25	Drain plug – 2 off
5	Spring guide – 2 off	15	Shroud seat – 2 off	26	Circlip – 2 off
6	Stanchion	16	Lower shroud – 2 off	27	Spring ring – 4 off
7	Lower leg	17	Spacer – 2 off	28	Spring ring – 2 off
8	Sleeve – 2 off	18	Sleeve – 2 off	29	Top bush – 2 off
9	Lower spring seat – 2 off	19	Sealing ring – 2 off	30	Bottom bush/piston – 2 off
10	O ring – 2 off	20	Sleeve – 2 off	31	Top bolt
		21	Washer – 2 off	32	Screw – 2 off

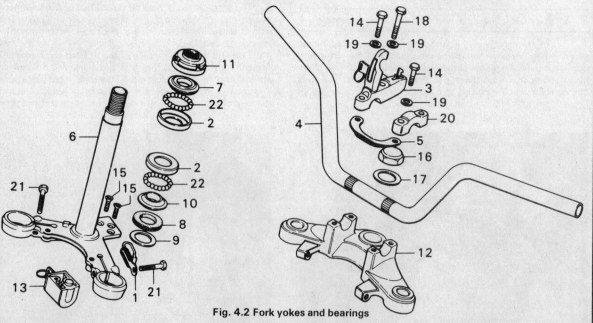

Fig. 4.2 Fork yokes and bearings

1	Cable clip	9	Washer	16	Steering stem nut
2	Bearing cup – 2 off	10	Lower cone	17	Washer
3	Right-hand clamp/helmet lock	11	Lockring	18	Bolt
4	Handlebars	12	Upper yoke	19	Washer – 2 off
5	Guide	13	Steering lock	20	Left-hand clamp
6	Lower yoke and stem	14	Bolt – 3 off	21	Bolt – 2 off
7	Upper cone	15	Screw – 2 off	22	Steel ball No. 6 ($\frac{3}{16}$ in) – 42 off
8	Dust seal				

diameter measured and compared with the figures given in the Specifications section of this Chapter. Play between the lower bush/piston and the inside of the lower leg, must not exceed 0.2 mm (0.008 in).

5   The lower leg bore and the fork stanchions must also be examined for signs of scoring, which is usually caused by grit particles becoming embedded in the seal lip. The stanchions should be checked for straightness, especially if accident damage is suspected. This can be done by mounting the stanchion between V blocks and measuring any eccentricity with a dial test indicator (DTI) or by rolling the stanchion on a surface plate or sheet of plate glass. It is possible to straighten a slightly bent stanchion in a hydraulic press or flypress. This is, however, a task for an expert, and his advice on the practicability of straightening a stanchion should be heeded.

6   When reassembling the forks, make sure the spring rings on the stanchion are seated correctly. When fitting the new seal, lubricate the sealing lip and stanchion, and tap it squarely into position in the top of the lower leg. Do not omit the retaining screw in the base of the lower leg if the restrictor was removed.

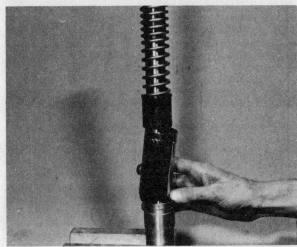
7.1 Note spring has tighter coils at top

7.2a Remove seal retaining circlip

7.2b Remove screw in base of lower leg if restrictor is to be withdrawn

7.3 New seals should be fitted as a precaution

7.4a Examine the headed top bush ...

7.4b ... and lower, plain bush, for wear

7.6a Note the position of spring rings ...

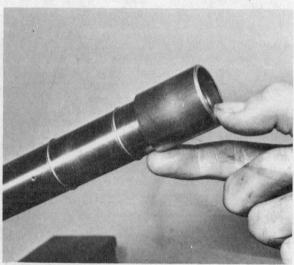

7.6b ... which locate the bushes on the stanchion

7.6c Do not omit restrictor, if removed

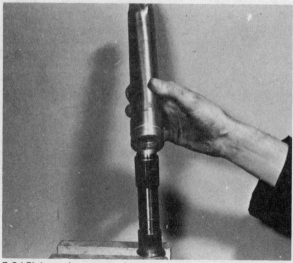

7.6d Fit lower leg over bushes

7.6e Renew seal and replace the circlip

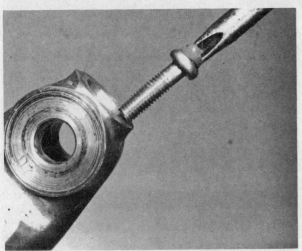

7.6f Do not omit the screw in base of lower leg, where necessary

8 Fork legs: dismantling, examination and renovation – CG125 K1, B, C and E models

1 The forks fitted to all later models differ in having longer fork springs that are much smaller in diameter so that they fit inside the fork stanchions. The metal shrouds of the early forks are replaced by a small rubber dust seal leaving the surface of the stanchion exposed.

2 The more exposed and thus unprotected design of these forks means that far greater attention must be paid to the condition of the stanchion surfaces. At regular intervals lift the dust seal from each lower leg and wipe away any accumulated dirt from its sealing lips and from above the oil seal; if the oil seal is leaking it must be renewed. Check the surface of the stanchion, looking for scratches or chips in the plating. These should be repaired by cleaning and degreasing so that they can be filled with Araldite or similar. Be careful to smooth down the filler, once it has set hard, to restore the original contour. If this sort of damage occurs repeatedly, fit a pair of gaiters to cover the stanchions.

3 To dismantle the legs remove the top bolt and drain plug from each and allow the oil to drain, then slide the dust seal off the lower leg and remove the circlip and backing ring from above the oil seal.

4 Clamp each lower leg by the spindle lug in a vice with padded jaws and sharply pull the stanchion out of the lower leg, using the headed top bush to displace the oil seal. Withdraw the spring from inside the stanchion, noting that it is fitted with its close-pitched coils at the top.

5 Be very careful to wash all traces of dirt and oil from the inside of the fork lower leg. Apart from the fact that the spring seat cannot be removed from inside the lower leg, the remainder of the overhaul procedure is exactly the same as that given in Section 7.

6 On reassembly, note that the oil seal retaining circlip should be renewed as a matter of course whenever it is disturbed, and that it should be fitted with its sharp-edged surface upwards. Pack grease above the oil seal as additional protection before pressing the dust seal firmly into place.

9 Refitting the forks in the frame

1 If it has been necessary to remove the fork assembly completely from the frame, refitting is accomplished by following the dismantling procedure in reverse. Check that none of the balls are misplaced whilst the steering head stem is passed through the head set. It has been known for a ball to be displaced, drop down and wear a groove or even jam the steering, so be extremely careful in this respect.

2 Take particular care when adjusting the steering head bearings; the lockring should be locked in place with the steering stem nut sufficiently to remove all the slack, but not tight otherwise damage to the cups or ball bearings will occur. When adjusted, lightly flick the handlebars with the finger. They should drop easily from side to side, but if the fork legs are held and pulled forwards and backwards no play should be felt. Tighten the steering stem nut to a torque setting of 6.0 – 9.0 kgf m (43 – 65 lbf ft) and re-check the bearing adjustment.

3 Difficulty may be experienced in raising the fork stanchions so that the end locates in the top yoke. If a stanchion puller is not available use a piece of wooden dowel with a tapered end, force it in the thread and use it to pull the stanchion into place.

4 Before refitting the top fork bolts do not forget to replace the oil, the quantity required is shown in the Specifications Section of this Chapter. **Do not** forget to tighten the drain plug first to a torque setting of 0.3 – 0.6 kgf m (2 – 4 lbf ft). Note that the fork leg with the brake plate location fits on the left-hand side of the machine. Where necessary attach the lower shroud and the headlamp bracket whilst sliding the stanchion into place.

5 Refit the front mudguard, headlamp, speedometer and handlebars; note that the handlebar punch marks should be aligned with the edge of the top yoke mounting, that the clamps should be installed with their punch-marked ends to the rear and that the clamp bolts should be tightened to a torque setting of 0.9 – 1.1 kgf m (6.5 – 8 lbf ft). Reconnect the cables and wiring.

6 When replacing the front wheel, first make sure that the speedometer drive pegs inside the front hub have not ridden up out of their location. After checking this, insert the wheel spindle (not forgetting the spacer on the opposite side to the brake; do not fail to check the brake location). The peg aligns with the slot on the outside of the brake plate. Push through the spindle and place on the washer and the nut. Tighten the nut to a torque setting of 3.5 – 5.0 kgf m (25 – 36 lbf ft) and fit a new split pin. Fit and adjust the brake cable, also the speedometer drive cable.

7 When everything is in place, bounce the forks a few times so that they settle into their natural position. Tighten the lower yoke pinch bolts to a torque setting of 2.0 – 3.0 kgf m (14.5 – 22 lbf ft) and the fork top bolts to a torque setting of 3.0 – 4.0 kgf m (22 – 29 lbf ft).

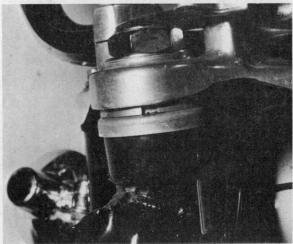

9.2 Adjust steering head races carefully

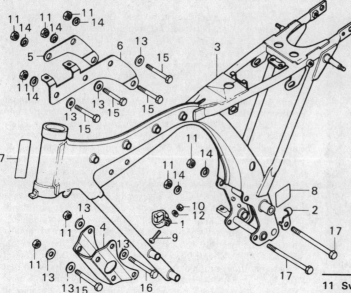

Fig. 4.3 Frame – component parts

1   Clamp
2   Wiring clip
3   Frame
4   Front engine plate
5   Right-hand head steady plate
6   Left-hand head steady plate
7   Frame identification plate
8   Decal
9   Screw
10 Nut
11 Nut – 10 off
12 Washer
13 Washer – 11 off
14 Spring washer – 6 off
15 Bolt – 2 off
16 Bolt – 2 off
17 Bolt – 2 off

10 Frame assembly: examination and renovation

1   If the machine is stripped for a complete overhaul, this affords a good opportunity to inspect the frame for cracks or other damage which may have occurred in service. Check the front downtube immediately below the steering head and the top tube immediately behind the steering head, the two points where fractures are most likely to occur. The straightness of the tubes concerned will show whether the machine has been involved in a previous accident.

2   If the frame is broken or bent, professional attention is required. Repairs of this nature should be entrusted to a competent repair specialist, who will have available all the necessary jigs and mandrels to achieve correct alignment.

Repair work of this nature can prove expensive and it is always worthwhile checking whether a good replacement frame of identical type can be obtained from a breaker or through any form of Service Exchange Scheme. The latter course of action is preferable because there is no safe means of assessing on the spot whether a secondhand frame is accident damaged too.

11 Swinging arm: examination and renovation

1   To check for wear in the swinging arm bushes, hold the frame firmly in one hand and with the other, shake the rear wheel. There should not be any side play at all; if there is, replacement of the swinging arm pivot bearings may be necessary.

2   Remove the rear wheel assembly as described in Chapter 5 and disconnect the chain, but do not pull it right off. Leave it on the gearbox sprocket.

3   Remove the two rear suspension units from their lower locating points and then remove the chainguard.

4   Undo the large nut on the end of the swinging arm pivot shaft and pull out the shaft whilst supporting the swinging arm in the other hand.

5   To replace the bushes a press is necessary with a few good fitting pieces of short tube. A vice clamped rigidly to a workbench will often suffice, if a fly-press is not available.

6   Position one piece of tube to support the swinging arm and line up another against the bush that has the same outside diameter in a vice fitted with soft jaws. Close the vice, using the tube to press the old bush out of position. Use the same method to press the new bush into position and when both have been renewed, reassemble in the reverse order of dismantling. Do not forget to replace and retighten the rear brake torque arm. Grease the pivot shaft, refit it from left to right and tighten the securing nut to a torque setting of 3.5 – 4.5 kgf m (25 – 32.5 lbf ft).

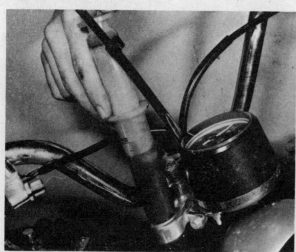

9.4 Refill fork legs with oil

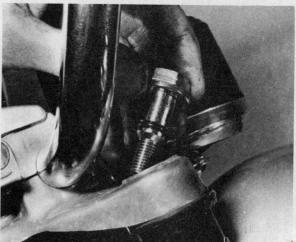

9.7 Bounce forks before final tightening of securing bolts

11.4a Slacken and remove pivot shaft nut ...

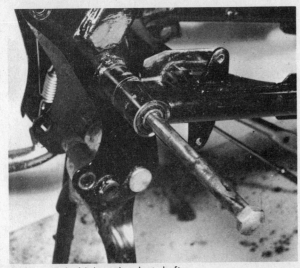

11.4b ... and withdraw the pivot shaft

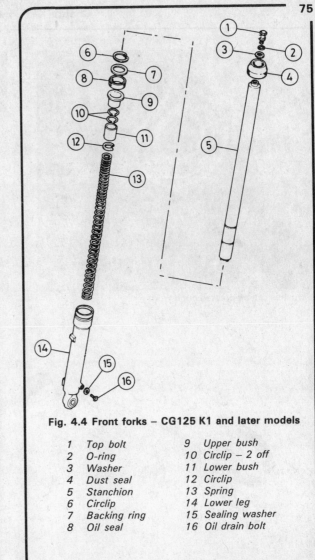

Fig. 4.4 Front forks — CG125 K1 and later models

1	Top bolt	9	Upper bush
2	O-ring	10	Circlip – 2 off
3	Washer	11	Lower bush
4	Dust seal	12	Circlip
5	Stanchion	13	Spring
6	Circlip	14	Lower leg
7	Backing ring	15	Sealing washer
8	Oil seal	16	Oil drain bolt

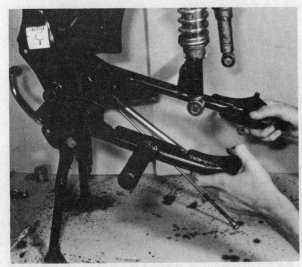

11.4c Remove swinging arm from frame ...

11.4d ... noting washers each side of exhaust mounting bracket

11.5 Bushes can be pressed out if worn

11.6 Check that torque arm mounting is secure

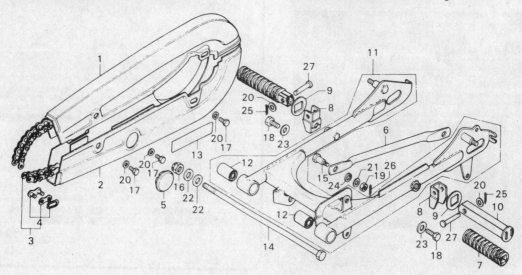

Fig. 4.5 Swinging arm and chain enclosure

1	Upper chain enclosure half	6	Torque arm
2	Lower chain enclosure half	7	Footrest rubber – 2 off
3	Final drive chain	8	Footrest bracket – 2 off
4	Joining link	9	Washer – 2 off
5	Inspection plug	10	Footrest – 2 off
		11	Swinging arm assembly
		12	Silentbloc bush – 2 off

13	Tyre pressure decal	20	Washer – 6 off
14	Swinging arm pivot shaft	21	Washer
15	Stepped bolt	22	Washer – 2 off
16	Locking nut	23	Washer – 2 off
17	Bolt – 4 off	24	Spring washer
18	Bolt – 2 off	25	Split pin – 2 off
19	Nut	26	Split pin
		27	Clevis pin – 2 off

12 Rear suspension units: removal, examination and renovation

1   The swinging arm rear fork assembly is supported by two suspension units, of the hydraulically damped spring type. Each unit consists of a hydraulic damper, effective primarily on rebound, and a concentric, chromed spring. It is mounted by way of rubber-bushed lugs at top and bottom.

2   The suspension units are provided with an adjustment of the spring tension, giving five settings. The settings can be easily altered without removing the units from the machine by using a 'C' spanner; both units should be positioned on the same setting.

3   Remove the suspension units by removing the chromed dome mounting nuts, then pull the unit sideways off its mounting lugs. Note carefully the position and number of the plain metal washers fitted next to the unit mounting eyes.

4   Refitting is the reversal of the above procedure. Refit the washers in their original positions and tighten the retaining nuts securely.

5   There is no means of draining the units or topping up, because the dampers are built as a sealed unit. If the damping fails or the units begin to leak, the complete damper assembly

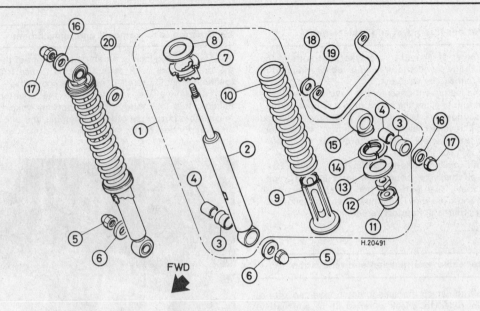

Fig. 4.6 Rear suspension units

1 Suspension unit – 2 off	6 Washer – 2 off	11 Bump stop	16 Washer – 2 off
2 Damper – 2 off	7 Adjustment cam	12 Locknut	17 Domed nut – 2 off
3 Rubber bush	8 Spacer	13 Spring seat	18 Washer
4 Metal sleeve	9 Spring guide	14 Spring retainer	19 Grab rail
5 Domed nut – 2 off	10 Spring	15 Top mounting eye	20 Washer

12.2 Use 'C' spanner to adjust rear suspension units

must be renewed. This applies equally if the damper rod has become bent. It is, however, possible to renew the springs independently of the sealed damper units. Removal of the spring however, does entail the use of some means of safely compressing the spring so that the suspension unit top mounting eye can be released.

6 To compress the spring, clamp the suspension unit at its bottom mounting in a vice and enlist the aid of an assistant to pull down the spring while the unit top mounting eye is unscrewed. Note that a slim spanner can be passed between the coils of the spring to slacken the locknut, while a bar is passed through the mounting eye to provide the necessary leverage for unscrewing it.

7 Examine the mounting bushes; if these are damaged or worn they must be renewed. They can be removed and refitted easily by pushing out both metal sleeves and rubber bushes as separate items.

13 Centre stand: examination

1 The centre stand shares a common pivot pin with the rear brake pedal, the right-hand end of the pin being fitted with a split pin. A strong return spring, attached to a small lug on the right-hand side of the stand, retracts and holds the stand in position when not in use.

2 Periodically the pivot pin should be lubricated with grease. This is fairly important as its exposed position renders it susceptible to corrosion if left unattended.

3 Be especially careful to check the condition and correct location of the return spring. If this fails, the stand will fall onto the road in use, and may unseat the rider if it catches in a drain cover or similar obstacle.

14 Footrests: examination

1 The footrests form an assembly mounted below the engine and can be detached as a complete unit. They are retained by four bolts. The assembly is easily removed after the bolts have been released. The complete unit must be manoeuvred to clear the silencer. On refitting, tighten the bolts to a torque setting of 2.0 – 3.0 kgf m (14.5 – 22 lbf ft).

2 Damage is likely only in the event of the machine being dropped. Slight bending can be rectified by stripping the assembly to the bare footrest bar, and straightening the bends by clamping the bar in a vice. A blowlamp should be applied to the affected area to avoid setting up stresses in the material, which may lead to subsequent fracturing.

15 Rear brake pedal: examination and renovation

1 The rear brake pedal is mounted on a spindle, which is also the pivot for the centre stand. It is retained, together with its return spring, by a circlip on the right-hand side of the machine.

2 Should the pedal become bent in an accident, it can be straightened in a similar manner to that given for footrests in the preceding Section. If severely distorted, it should be renewed.

16 Speedometer head: removal and replacement

1   The speedometer is secured to a bracket that bolts to the top yoke, on which the speedometer head is rubber mounted to prevent internal damage by vibration.

2   To remove the instrument unscrew the drive cable and take off the headlamp unit to allow the indicator and internal lighting lamps to be disconnected. Unscrew the mounting nuts and remove. Replace in reverse order of dismantling. Wire reconnection is easy due to the colour-coded system used.

3   Apart from defects in either the drive or the cable, a speedometer that malfunctions is difficult to repair. Fit a replacement or alternatively, obtain one from a crash repair specialist who may have perfectly good instruments with scratched cases and glass etc. Remember that a speedometer in good working order is a statutory requirement.

17 Speedometer cable: examination and renovation

1   It is advisable to detach the speedometer drive cable from time to time in order to check whether it is adequately lubricated and whether the outer cover is compressed or damaged at any point along its run. A jerky or sluggish movement at the instrument head can often be attributed to a cable fault.

2   To grease the cable, uncouple both ends and withdraw the inner cable. After removing the old grease, clean with a petrol-soaked rag and examine the cable for broken strands or other damage.

3   Regrease the cable with high melting point grease, taking care not to grease the last six inches closest to the instrument head. If this precaution is not observed, grease will work into the instrument and immobilise the sensitive movement.

4   If the cable breaks, it is usually possible to renew the inner cable alone, provided the outer cable is not damaged or compressed at any point along its run. Before inserting the new inner cable, it should be greased in accordance with the instructions given in the preceding paragraph. Try to avoid tight bends in the run of the cable because this will accelerate wear and make the instrument movement sluggish.

18 Dualseat: removal

1   The dualseat is fixed to the rear of the machine by two brackets bolted to the rear part of the frame assembly. At the front there is a bracket under the seat which engages with a location bracket on the frame just to the rear of the petrol tank.

2   To remove the seat, remove the two fixing bolts. Hold the seat firmly at the rear, pull gently and the seat will then become detached. Replace by reversing this procedure.

19 Steering lock: removal and replacement

1   The steering lock is situated at the front of the machine, by the bottom fork yoke. It is advisable to use it whenever the machine is left unattended, even for a short time.

2   To remove the lock, remove the countersunk screws holding the lock body to the bottom yoke. Replace and reassemble in reverse order. Remember you will have to carry an additional key for the new lock.

19.1 Steering lock is attached to lower yoke

20 Cleaning the machine: general

1   After removing all surface dirt with a rag or sponge washed frequently in clean water, the application of car polish or wax will give a good finish to the machine. The plated parts should require only a wipe over with a damp rag, followed by polishing with a dry rag. If, however, corrosion has taken place, which may occur when the roads are salted during the winter, a proprietary chrome cleaner can be used.

2   The polished alloy parts will lose their sheen and oxidise slowly if they are not polished regularly. The sparing use of metal polish or special polish such as Solvol Autosol will restore the original finish with only a few minutes labour.

3   The machine should be wiped over immediately after it has been used in the wet so that it is not garaged under damp conditions which will cause rusting and corrosion. Remember there is little chance of water entering the control cables if they are lubricated regularly, as recommended in the Routine Maintenance Section.

21 Fault diagnosis: frame and forks

Symptom	Cause	Remedy
Machine veers either to the left or the right with hands off handlebars	Bent frame Twisted forks Wheels out of alignment	Check, and renew. Check, and renew. Check and realign.
Machine rolls at low speed	Overtight steering head bearings	Slacken until adjustment is correct.
Machine judders when front brake is applied	Slack steering head bearings Worn fork bushes	Tighten, until adjustment is correct. Dismantle forks and renew bushes.
Machine pitches on uneven surfaces	Ineffective fork dampers Ineffective rear suspension units Suspension too soft	Check oil content of front forks. Check whether units still have damping action. Raise suspension unit adjustment one notch.
Fork action stiff	Fork legs out of alignment (twisted in yokes)	Slacken yoke clamps, and fork top bolts. Pump fork several times then retighten from bottom upwards.
Machine wanders. Steering imprecise. Rear wheel tends to hop.	Worn swinging arm pivot	Dismantle and renew bushes and pivot shaft.

Chapter 5 Wheels, brakes and tyres

Refer to Chapter 7 for information relating to 1985-on models

Contents

Specifications

Wheels

Rim size		
Front	1.40 x 18	
Rear	1.60 x 17	
Rim maximum runout – radial and axial	2.0 mm (0.0787 in)	
Spindle maximum warpage	0.2 mm (0.0079 in)	

Brakes

	Standard	Wear limit
Drum inside diameter	110 mm (4.3307 in)	111 mm (4.3701 in)
Brake shoe friction material thickness	3.9 – 4.1 mm (0.1535 – 0.1614 in)	2.0 mm (0.0787 in)

Tyres

	Front	Rear
Size	2.50 – 18 4PR	3.00 – 17 6PR
Pressures – tyres cold		
Solo	25 psi (1.75 kg/cm^2)	28 psi (2.00 kg/cm^2)
Pillion	25 psi (1.75 kg/cm^2)	40 psi (2.80 kg/cm^2)
Manufacturer's recommended minimum tread depth...	1.5 mm (0.06 in)	2.0 mm (0.08 in)

1 General description

All machines are equipped with two identical single leading shoe (sls) brake units, the drums being integral with the wheel hub.

On all models, chromium plated steel wheel rims are laced to the hub by spokes, the front and rear rims being of 18 in and 17 in diameter respectively. The front rim carries a 2·50 in section tyre, while the rear fitment is of 3·00 in section.

2 Front wheel: examination and renovation

1 Place the machine on the centre stand so that the front wheel is raised clear of the ground. Spin the wheel and check the rim alignment. Small irregularities can be corrected by tightening the spokes in the affected area, although a certain amount of practice is necessary to prevent over-correction. Any flats in the wheel rim should be evident at the same time. These are more difficult to remove and in most cases it will be necessary to have the wheel rebuilt on a new rim. Apart from the effect on stability, a flat will expose the tyre bead and walls to greater risk of damage.

2 Check for loose or broken spokes. Tapping the spokes is the best guide to tension. A loose spoke will produce a quite different sound and should be tightened by turning the nipple in an anti-clockwise direction. Always re-check for run-out by spinning the wheel again. If the spokes have to be tightened an excessive amount, it is advisable to remove the tyre and tube by the procedure detailed in Section 16 of this Chapter; this is so that the protruding ends of the spokes can be ground off, to prevent them from chafing the inner tube and causing punctures.

3 Front wheel: removal

1 With the machine supported on the centre stand, block the stand and crankcase to raise the wheel clear of the ground.

2 Detach the speedometer drive cable at the wheel, by unscrewing the knurled gland nut which retains it. Remove the front brake cable.

3 Remove the wheel spindle nut and split pin, and withdraw the spindle with the aid of a tommy bar. The wheel can now be lowered clear of the forks and put to one side.

4 Front brake: examination and renovation

1 With the wheel removed from the forks, as described in the preceding Section, the brake plate assembly can be removed from the drum.

2 Examine the drum surface for signs of scoring or oil contamination. Both of these conditions will impair braking efficiency. Remove all traces of dust, preferably using a brass wire brush, taking care not to inhale any of it, as it is of an asbestos nature, and consequently harmful. Remove oil or grease deposits, using a petrol soaked rag.

3 If deep scoring is evident, due to the linings having worn through to the shoe at some time, the drum must be skimmed on a lathe, or renewed. Whilst there are firms who will undertake to skim a drum whilst fitted to the wheel, it should be borne in mind that excessive skimming will change the radius of the drum in relation to the brake shoes, therefore reducing the friction area until extensive bedding in has taken place. Also full adjustment of the shoes may not be possible. If in doubt about this point, the advice of one of the specialist engineering firms who undertake this work should be sought.

4 If fork oil or grease from the wheel bearings has badly contaminated the linings, they should be renewed. There is no satisfactory way of degreasing the lining material, which in any case is relatively cheap to replace. Measure the thickness of the friction material; if it is worn at any point to or beyond the specified wear limit, both shoes must be renewed immediately. It is a false economy to try to cut corners with brake components; the whole safety of both machine and rider being dependent on their good condition.

5 The linings are bonded to the shoes, and the shoe must be renewed complete with the new linings. This is accomplished by folding the shoes together until the spring tension is relaxed, and then lifting the shoes and springs off the brake plate. Fitting new shoes is a direct reversal of the above procedure.

6 Before refitting existing shoes, roughen the lining surface sufficiently to break the glaze which will have formed in use.

7 The camshaft can be displaced for greasing prior to reassembly, after removing the actuating lever. No further attention is normally required. Note the alignment marks on the camshaft splined end, and on the lever. These must align on reassembly.

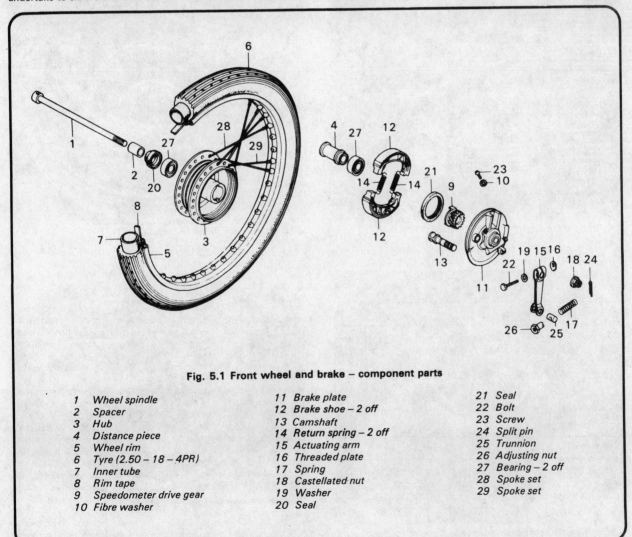

Fig. 5.1 Front wheel and brake – component parts

1 Wheel spindle	11 Brake plate	21 Seal
2 Spacer	12 Brake shoe – 2 off	22 Bolt
3 Hub	13 Camshaft	23 Screw
4 Distance piece	14 Return spring – 2 off	24 Split pin
5 Wheel rim	15 Actuating arm	25 Trunnion
6 Tyre (2.50 – 18 – 4PR)	16 Threaded plate	26 Adjusting nut
7 Inner tube	17 Spring	27 Bearing – 2 off
8 Rim tape	18 Castellated nut	28 Spoke set
9 Speedometer drive gear	19 Washer	29 Spoke set
10 Fibre washer	20 Seal	

3.2 Detach the speedometer and brake cables

3.3 Withdraw the wheel spindle, and lower the wheel clear

4.1a Brake plate assembly can be lifted out of drum ...

4.1b ... for examination and renovation

4.2 Examine the brake drum surface for signs of scoring

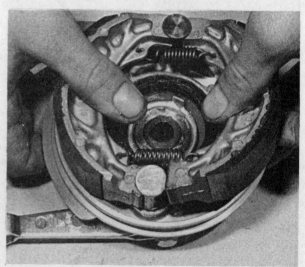

4.5 Method of removing brake shoes for inspection or renewal

4.7 Align punch marks to ensure operating arm is refitted correctly on brake camshaft

5 Adjusting the front brake

1   Adjusting the front brake is best accomplished with the front wheel free to rotate. Spin the wheel and carefully screw the adjusting nut down until you hear a rubbing sound which indicates that the brake shoes are lightly in contact with the drum surface. Turn the adjuster nut back by $\frac{1}{2} - 1$ turn until the noise stops. Spin the wheel and apply the brake hard once or twice to settle the brake. Check that the wheel is still free to rotate and that the adjustment has remained the same. This setting should give you 20 – 30 mm ($\frac{3}{4} - 1\frac{1}{4}$ inch) free play measured at the extreme tip of the handlebar brake lever.
2   Check the condition of the brake cable ensuring that all components are in good condition, properly lubricated and securely fastened. Note that the operating mechanism is at its most efficient when, with the brake correctly adjusted and applied fully, the angle between the cable and the operating arm on the brake backplate does not exceed 90°. This can be

adjusted by removing the operating arm from the brake camshaft and rotating it by one or two splines until the angle is correct. Ensure that all components are correctly secured on reassembly.

6 Front wheel bearings: removal and replacement

1   There are two bearings in the front wheel. If the wheel has any side play when fitted to the machine or any roughness, the wheel bearings need to be renewed.
2   Using a small flat ended drift, place it inside the hub against one of the wheel bearings and tap the bearing out of position. Remove the central spacer and then tap out the other bearing from the other side. Drive the bearings outwards in each case.
3   Use a good quality grease and grease the new bearings. Tap in one bearing, turn the wheel over, insert the central spacer and then tap in the other bearing. Fit each bearing with the dust seal facing outwards and do not cut or damage it when tapping it home.
4   Replace the outer left-hand oil seal which will have become dislodged. Renew it if necessary.

7 Front wheel: replacement

1   Locate the speedometer drive tabs with the slots in the hub.
2   Place the spacer on the left-hand side of the wheel and then, roll the wheel into the forks. The brake anchor slot and peg must locate correctly.
3   Hold the wheel in place and push the spindle through until it is right home. The spindle goes through the side opposite to the brake plate.
4   Reconnect the front brake cable and adjust the brake. Applying the front brake firmly with one hand, spin on the nut and tighten to a torque setting of 3.5 – 5.0 kgf m (25 – 36 lbf ft); when tight insert a new correct-sized split pin and bend it over.
5   Locate the speedometer cable and tighten the locking nut.

6.3a Do not omit central spacer

6.3b Bearing sealed surface must face outwards

6.3c Tap bearings into place using a socket as a drift

8 Rear wheel: examination

1   Place the machine on the centre stand and before removing the rear wheel, follow the procedure described for checking the front wheel for alignment of the rim, loose or broken spokes or any other defects.

9 Rear wheel: removal

1   Start by removing the two halves of the rear chain enclosure, and place these to one side. There is no need to remove the left-hand engine casing. Slacken the rear brake adjuster nut, and remove it to release the brake rod. Reassemble the rear brake rod components to avoid loss.
2   Turn the rear wheel until the joining link in the drive chain is accessible, then, using pointed-nosed pliers, prise off the spring link, and separate the chain. Reassemble the joining link parts on one end of the chain.

6.4 Renew seals together with bearings

7.2 Ensure that lug engages in backplate when refitting wheel

7.4 Tighten the wheel spindle nut and fit new split pin

9.2 Remove chain guard and separate the chain

3   Remove the spring pin which retains the torque arm nut, then remove the nut and disengage the torque arm from the brake plate. Slacken off the two wheel spindle drawbolt adjusters, having made a note of their position against the graduations on the fork ends. Pull out the split pin from the castellated wheel spindle nut, and remove the nut. It should be noted that if the spindle nut is on the left-hand side the exhaust system must be removed to allow the wheel spindle to be withdrawn. Alternatively, remove the lower suspension mounting bolts to allow the swinging arm to be moved to clear the end of the silencer. The spindle can now be withdrawn, and the wheel lowered clear of the frame.

10 Rear brake: examination and renovation

1   With the rear wheel removed from the frame, the brake plate assembly can be pulled clear of the drum for examination. The rear brake is identical to the front drum brake described in Section 4, and the remarks in that Section can be applied.

9.3a Exhaust must be removed if spindle is to be withdrawn from right-hand side

9.3b Torque arm secured by nut and spring pin

9.3c Wheel can be removed from frame

10.1a Lift out the brake plate assembly

10.1b Examine the shoes for signs of wear or contamination

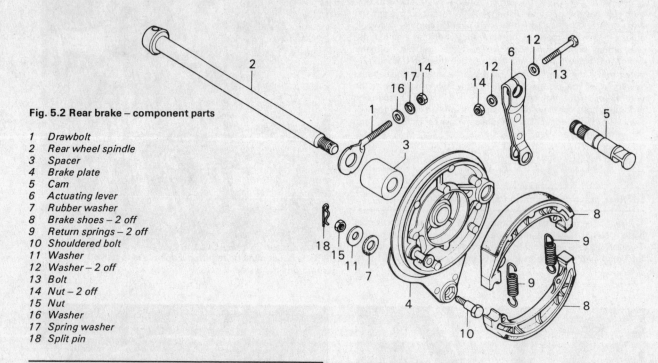

Fig. 5.2 Rear brake – component parts

1   Drawbolt
2   Rear wheel spindle
3   Spacer
4   Brake plate
5   Cam
6   Actuating lever
7   Rubber washer
8   Brake shoes – 2 off
9   Return springs – 2 off
10 Shouldered bolt
11 Washer
12 Washer – 2 off
13 Bolt
14 Nut – 2 off
15 Nut
16 Washer
17 Spring washer
18 Split pin

11 Rear wheel bearings: removal and replacement

1   Remove the oil seal and remember it has to be replaced by a new one. If the bearings are worn or rough, both should be renewed.
2   Tap out the old bearings and fit new ones, using the method recommended for the front wheel bearings. Do not forget to pack with new, clean grease.

12 Rear sprocket and shock absorber rubbers: examination and renovation

1   The rear sprocket is mounted on four pins which engage in bonded rubber bushes pressed into the hub casting. It is retained by a large circlip, which, when removed, allows the sprocket to be pulled free complete with the four driving pins. On older machines, it is possible that the pins may become jammed in place in the bonded bush centres, in which case, the four nuts may be removed to allow the sprocket to be detached. On refitting, tighten the nuts to a torque setting of 5.5 – 6.5 kgf m (40 – 47 lbf ft).
2   Should the above condition arise, or if the bushes are worn, the wheel should be taken to a Honda Service Agent who will have the equipment necessary to extract the old bushes, and fit the new ones. It is extremely unlikely that this operation can be performed at home due to the tight fit of the bushes. In all probability, any attempt to dislodge them will result in the inner metal sleeve tearing out of the rubber, making subsequent removal difficult.
3   Check the condition of the sprocket teeth, if they are hooked, chipped or badly worn, the sprocket must be renewed.
    It is considered bad practice to renew one sprocket on its own. The final drive sprockets should always be renewed as a pair and a new chain fitted, otherwise rapid wear will necessitate even earlier renewal on the next occasion.

13 Adjusting the rear brake

1   If the adjustment of the rear brake is correct, the rear brake pedal will have about 25 mm (1 inch) free play before the brake commences to operate.
2   The length of travel is controlled by the adjuster at the end of the brake operating rod, close to the brake operating arm. If the nut is turned clockwise, the amount of travel is reduced and vice-versa. Always check that the brake is not binding after adjustments have been made.
3   Note that it may be necessary to re-adjust the height of the stop lamp switch if the pedal height has been changed to any marked extent. The switch is located immediately below the right-hand side cover. The body of the switch is threaded, so that it can be raised or lowered, after the locknuts have been slackened. If the stop lamp lights too soon, the switch should be lowered, and vice-versa.

11.2a Spacer is fitted between wheel bearings

Tyre changing sequence - tubed tyres

A Deflate tyre. After pushing tyre beads away from rim flanges push tyre bead into well of rim at point opposite valve. Insert tyre lever adjacent to valve and work bead over edge of rim.

B Use two levers to work bead over edge of rim. Note use of rim protectors

C Remove inner tube from tyre

D When first bead is clear, remove tyre as shown

E When fitting, partially inflate inner tube and insert in tyre

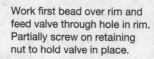

F Work first bead over rim and feed valve through hole in rim. Partially screw on retaining nut to hold valve in place.

G Check that inner tube is positioned correctly and work second bead over rim using tyre levers. Start at a point opposite valve.

H Work final area of bead over rim whilst pushing valve inwards to ensure that inner tube is not trapped

11.2b New bearings must be fitted if worn

11.2c A large socket makes a useful drift

11.2d New seals should be fitted together with bearings

12.1a Sprocket is retained by large diameter circlip

12.1b The pins engage in bonded rubber bushes

12.3 Number of teeth is stamped on the rear wheel sprocket

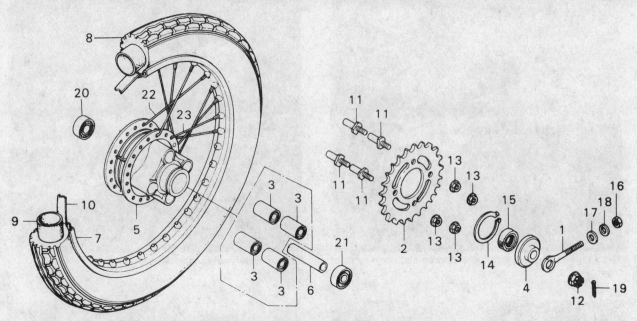

Fig. 5.3. Rear wheel and hub – component parts

1	Drawbolt	9	Inner tube	17	Washer – 2 off
2	Rear wheel sprocket	10	Rim tape	18	Spring washer – 2 off
3	Bonded rubber bush – 4 off	11	Sprocket mounting pin – 4 off	19	Split pin
4	Dust cover	12	Castellated nut	20	Bearing
5	Rear hub	13	Nut – 4 off	21	Bearing
6	Spacer	14	Circlip	22	Spoke set
7	Wheel rim	15	Seal	23	Spoke set
8	Tyre (3.00 x17 – 6PR)	16	Nut – 2 off		

14 Final drive chain: examination, adjustment and lubrication

1   The rear chain on CG125 models derives considerable benefit from its complete enclosure. The chain of any motorcycle is subjected to considerable loading in normal use, in addition to which the unfortunate dictates of fashion have resulted in the almost universal adoption of a small and inadequate guard covering the top run of the chain only. The full enclosure of the CG125 means that the chain is operating in almost ideal conditions, and this should be reflected in remarkably long chain life.

2   A small inspection plug is provided through which chain tension can be checked, and intermediate lubrication can take place. It is important that the drain holes in the bottom of the case are kept clear of obstruction, otherwise any water which finds its way into the enclosure will accumulate at the bottom of the case, giving rise to running conditions worse than complete non-enclosure.

3   Periodically the tension will need to be adjusted, to compensate for wear. This is accomplished by placing the machine on the centre stand and slackening the rear wheel spindle nut so that the wheel can be drawn backward by means of the drawbolt adjusters in the fork ends. The rear brake torque arm bolt must also be slackened during this operation. The chain is in correct tension if there is approximately 20 mm ($\frac{3}{4}$ in) slack in the middle of the lower run. Always check when the chain is at its tightest point as a chain rarely wears evenly during service.

4   Always adjust the drawbolts an equal amount in order to preserve wheel alignment. The fork ends are clearly marked with a series of horizontal lines above the adjusters, to provide a simple, visual check. If desired, wheel alignment can be checked by running a plank of wood parallel to the machine, so that it touches the side of the rear tyre. If wheel alignment is correct, the plank will be equidistant from each side of the front wheel tyre, when tested on both sides of the rear wheel. It will not touch the front wheel tyre because this tyre is of smaller cross section. See accompanying diagram.

5   Do not run the chain overtight to compensate for uneven wear. A tight chain will place undue stress on the gearbox and rear wheel bearings, leading to their early failure. It will also absorb a surprising amount of power.

6   After a period of running, the chain will require lubrication. Lack of oil will greatly accelerate the rate of wear of both the chain and sprockets and will lead to harsh transmission. The application of engine oil will act as a temporary expedient, but it is preferable to remove the chain and clean it in a paraffin bath before it is immersed in a molten lubricant such as 'Linklife' or 'Chainguard'. These lubricants achieve better penetration of the chain links and rollers and are less likely to be thrown off when the chain is in motion.

7   To check whether the chain is due for replacement, lay it lengthwise in a straight line and compress it endwise so that all the play is taken up. Anchor one end and measure the length. Now, pull the chain with one end anchored firmly, so that the chain is fully extended by the amount of play in the opposite direction. If there is a difference of more than $\frac{1}{4}$ inch per foot in the two measurements, the chain should be replaced in conjunction with the sprockets. Note that this check should be made **after** the chain has been washed out, but **before** any lubricant is applied, otherwise the lubricant may take up some of the play.

8   When replacing the chain, make sure that the spring link is seated correctly, with the closed end facing the direction of travel.

9   An equivalent British-made chain of the correct size is available from Renold Limited. When ordering a new chain always quote the size (length and width of each pitch), the number of links and the machine to which it is fitted.

14.2a Plug can be removed for lubrication and chain tension check

14.2b Ensure that drain holes remain clear – unblock if necessary

14.4 Marks ensure correct wheel alignment

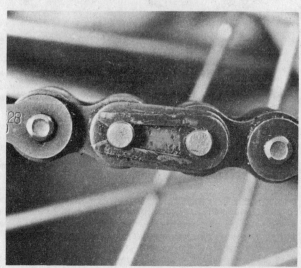

14.8 Closed end of link should face direction of travel

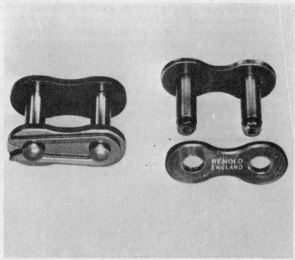

14.9 An equivalent British-made chain is available

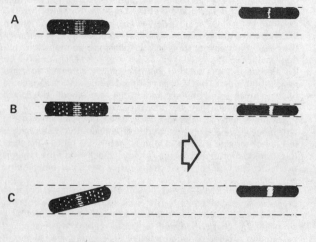

Fig. 5.4 Checking wheel alignment

A and C Incorrect   *B Correct*

15 Rear wheel: replacement

1   Clean and grease the rear wheel spindle, check that the sprocket and dust cover have been refitted to the hub left-hand side, and refit the brake plate assembly to the drum. Fit one of the chain adjusting drawbolts under the spindle head.

2   Note that while the spindle can physically be fitted either way round it is usually shown in the manufacturer's literature as being fitted from right to left and is generally found to be fitted this way on new machines. However, if it is fitted from left to right, so that the nut is on the right-hand side, the task of wheel removal is greatly eased by the fact that it is no longer necessary to remove the exhaust system.

3   Fit the wheel to the swinging arm fork ends and refit the spindle, ensuring that both spacers and drawbolts are correctly positioned. Refit and lightly tighten the spindle nut. Connect the brake torque arm to the brake plate, and the brake rod to the actuating lever, then adjust the chain as described in Section 14.

4   Applying the rear brake firmly, tighten the spindle nut to a torque setting of 4.0 – 5.0 kgf m (29 – 36 lbf ft) and secure it by fitting a new split pin with its ends bent over correctly. Tighten securely the torque arm retaining nut and refit its spring pin, then adjust the rear brake and stoplamp switch as described in Section 13.

5   Lubricate the chain and refit the enclosure, ensuring that all mating surfaces are correctly engaged before the mounting bolts are secured.

16 Tyres: removal and replacement

1   At some time or other the need will arise to remove and replace the tyres, either as the result of a puncture or because a replacement is required to offset wear. To the inexperienced, tyre changing represents a formidable task yet if a few simple rules are observed and the technique learned, the whole operation is surprisingly simple.

2   To remove the tyre from either wheel, first detach the wheel from the machine by following the procedure in Chapter 5.3 or 5.9, depending on whether the front or the rear wheel is involved. Deflate the tyre by removing the valve insert and when it is fully deflated, push the bead of the tyre away from the wheel rim on both sides so that the bead enters the centre well of the rim. Remove the locking cap and push the tyre valve into the tyre itself.

3   Insert a tyre lever close to the valve and lever the edge of the tyre over the outside of the wheel rim. Very little force should be necessary; if resistance is encountered it is probably due to the fact that the tyre beads have not entered the well of the wheel rim all the way round the tyre.

4   Once the tyre has been edged over the wheel rim, it is easy to work around the wheel rim so that the tyre is completely free on one side. At this stage, the inner tube can be removed.

5   Working from the other side of the wheel, ease the other edge of the tyre over the outside of the wheel rim that is furthest away. Continue to work around the rim until the tyre is free completely from the rim.

6   If a puncture has necessitated tyre removal, reinflate the inner tube and immerse it in a bowl of water to trace the source of the leak. Mark its position and deflate the tube. Dry the tube and clean the area around the puncture with a petrol soaked rag. When the surface has dried, apply the rubber solution and allow this to dry before removing the backing from the patch and applying the patch to the surface.

7   It is best to use a patch of self vulcanising type, which will form a very permanent repair. Note that it may be necessary to remove a protective covering from the top surface of the patch, after it has sealed in position. Inner tubes made from synthetic rubber may require a special type of patch and adhesive, if a satisfactory bond is to be achieved.

8   Before replacing the tyre, check the inside to make sure the agent that caused the puncture is not trapped. Check also the outside of the tyre – particularly the tread area, to make sure nothing is trapped that may cause a further puncture.

9   If the inner tube has been patched on a number of past occasions, or if there is a tear or large hole. it is preferable to discard it and fit a replacement. Sudden deflation may cause an accident, particularly if it occurs with the front wheel.

10   To replace the tyre, inflate the inner tube sufficiently for it to assume a circular shape but only just. Then put it into the tyre so that it is enclosed completely. Lay the tyre on the wheel at an angle and insert the valve through the rim tape and the hole in the wheel rim. Attach the locking cap on the first few threads, sufficient to hold the valve captive in its correct location.

11   Starting at the point furthest from the valve, push the tyre bead over the edge of the wheel rim until it is located in the central well. Continue to work around the tyre in this fashion until the whole of one side of the tyre is on the rim. It may be necessary to use a tyre lever during the final stages.

12   Make sure there is no pull on the tyre valve and again commencing with the area furthest from the valve, ease the other bead of the tyre over the edge of the rim. Finish with the area close to the valve, pushing the valve up into the tyre until the locking cap touches the rim. This will ensure the inner tube is not trapped when the last section of the bead is edged over the rim with a tyre lever.

13   Check that the inner tube is not trapped at any point. Reinflate the inner tube and check that the tyre is seating correctly around the wheel rim. There should be a thin rib moulded around the wall of the tyre on both sides, which should be equidistant from the wheel rim at all points. If the tyre is unevenly located on the rim, try bouncing the wheel when the tyre is at the recommended pressure. It is probable that one of the beads has not pulled clear of the centre well.

14   Always run the tyres at the recommended pressures and never under or over-inflate. The correct pressures for solo use are given in the Specifications Section of this Chapter.

15   Tyre replacement is aided by dusting the side walls, particularly in the vicinity of the beads, with a liberal coating of French chalk. Washing up liquid can also be used to good effect, but this has the disadvantage of causing the inner surfaces of the wheel rim to rust.

16   Never replace the inner tube and tyre without the rim tape in position. If this precaution is overlooked there is good chance of the ends of the spoke nipples chafing the inner tube and causing a crop of punctures.

17   Never fit a tyre that has a damaged tread or side walls. Apart from the legal aspects, there is a very great risk of a blow-out, which can have serious consequences on any two-wheel vehicles.

18   Tyre valves rarely give trouble, but it is always advisable to check whether the valve itself is leaking before removing the tyre. Do not forget to fit the dust cap, which forms an effective second seal.

17 Fault diagnosis: wheels, brakes and tyres

Symptom	Cause	Remedy
Ineffective brakes	Worn brake lining or pads	Renew.
	Foreign bodies on brake linings surface	Clean.
	Incorrect engagement of brake arm serration	Reset correctly.
	Worn brake cam	Renew.
Handlebars oscillate at low speeds	Buckle or flat in wheel rim, most likely front wheel	Check rim alignment by spinning wheel. Correct by retensioning spokes or building on new rim.
	Tyre not straight on rim	Check tyre alignment.
Machine lacks power and poor acceleration	Brakes binding	Warm brake drum provides best evidence. Re-adjust brakes.
Brakes grab when applied gently	Ends of brake shoes not chamfered	Chamfer with file.
	Elliptical brake drum	Lightly skim on lathe.
	Badly worn pads	Renew.
Brake pull-off spongy	Brake cam binding in housing	Free and grease.
	Weak brake shoe springs	Renew if springs have not become displaced
Harsh transmission	Worn or badly adjusted final drive chain	Adjust or renew.
	Hooked or badly worn sprockets	Renew as a pair.
	Loose rear sprocket	Check bolts.
	Worn damper rubbers	Renew rubber inserts.

Chapter 6 Electrical system

Refer to Chapter 7 for information relating to 1985-on models

Contents

Specifications

Electrical system

Voltage	6
Earth connection	Negative (−)
Generator output	81W @ 6000 rpm
Fuse rating	10A

Battery

Make and type	Yuasa 6N6-3B
Capacity	6Ah

Bulbs

Headlamp...	6V, 25/25W
Pilot lamp	
Early CG125 models	N/App
Later CG125 models, CG125 K1, B	6V, 4W
CG125-C, E	6V, 3W
Speedometer illumination	
CG125, CG125 K1, B	6V, 1.7W
CG125-C, E	6V, 3.4W
Flashing indicator warning	6V, 1.7W
Neutral indicator	
CG125, CG125 K1, B	6V, 3W
CG125-C, E	6V, 3.4W
Flashing indicator lamps	6V, 18W
Stop/tail lamp	6V, 21/5W

Note: *Some CG125-C and E models may use 6V, 17/5.3W stop/tail lamp bulbs – check bulbholder marking for correct bulb rating*

1 General description

The electrical system is powered by a generator mounted on the left-hand end of the crankshaft. It is normally of ND (Nippon Denso) manufacture, though occasionally a Hitachi unit is used. The latter can be identified by its having three generating coils, as opposed to the ND unit which has two. Care must be taken to obtain parts which are designed for each type of generator, but apart from this, they can be regarded as identical in function.

Alternating current produced by the generator is passed through a silicon rectifier which converts it to direct current, which in turn is fed to the battery. Output from the generator is matched to differing loadings on the system in accordance with the various switch positions.

2 Checking the electrical system: general

Many of the test procedures applicable to motorcycle electrical systems require the use of test equipment of the multimeter type. Although the tests themselves are quite straightforward, there is a real danger, particularly on alternator systems, of damaging certain components if wrong connections are made. It is recommended, therefore, that no attempt be made to investigate faults in the charging system, unless the owner is reasonably experienced in the field. A qualified Honda Service Agent will have in his possession the necessary diagnostic equipment to effect an economical repair.

3 Charging system: checking the output

1   A defect in the charging system will produce poor headlamp performance, and probably, repeatedly discharged batteries. In order to check that the battery is receiving the correct charge, the following procedure should be adopted:

2   Obtain a 0 – 10 volt dc voltmeter, and connect this between the two battery terminals. Disconnect the battery positive lead (red and white) from the battery, and connect an ammeter capable of measuring 0 – 4 amps at least, and connect this between the positive battery terminal and the lead.

3   Start the engine, and check the charging characteristics with the following figures:

Switch position		Initial charge	@ 4000 rpm	@ 8000 rpm
Ignition	Lighting			
On	Off	6·3v @ 1000 rpm max	8·5v, 2·0 amp minimum	8·8v, 3·7 amp maximum
On	On	6·3v @ 1500 rpm max	8·0v, 0·8 amp minimum	8·5v, 2·0 amp maximum

4   While it is essential that the battery is in good condition and fully charged for the results of this test to be accurate, if the readings obtained differ widely from those given the battery should be checked first to ensure that it is not at fault. Check the generator coils as shown in Fig. 6.2, and check also that the rectifier is in good condition, as described in Section 4. Always have your findings checked by an expert using the correct test equipment before attempting repairs or renewing components.

4 Rectifier: checking for malfunction

1   The rectifier, as mentioned previously, changes the alternator output from ac to dc. It takes the form of a small sealed unit, mounted in a rubber sleeve at the front of the battery case. It is easily dismounted for examination, if suspected of malfunctioning.

2   Test the unit using a pocket multimeter set on the resistance scale. Place one lead from the meter on each terminal, and note the reading given. Now transpose the leads, and note the second reading. If all is well, no resistance will be found in one position, and infinite resistance in the other. If this is not so, the chances are that the unit is in need of renewal. A Honda Service Agent will be able to verify this, and supply a new component.

3.2a Stator can be removed for testing if required

3.2b Check condition of oil seal and O-ring prior to reassembly

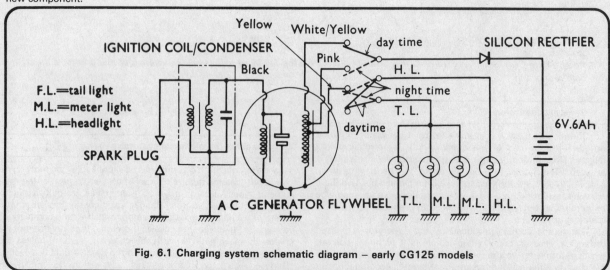

Fig. 6.1 Charging system schematic diagram – early CG125 models

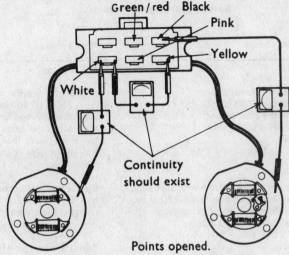

Fig. 6.2 Checking the generator stator

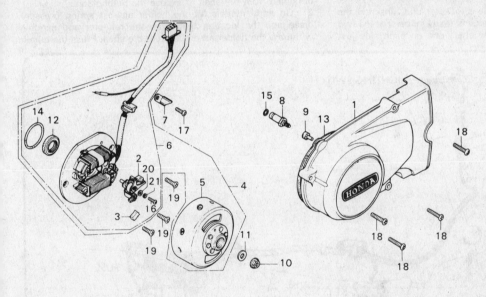

Fig. 6.3 Flywheel generator
and left-hand cover

1   Left-hand outer cover
2   Contact breaker assembly
3   Lubricating wick
4   Generator complete
5   Flywheel rotor
6   Stator assembly
7   Cable guide
8   Neutral switch body
9   Neutral switch support
    rubber
10 Flywheel centre nut
11 Plain washer
12 Oil seal
13 Gasket
14 O ring
15 O ring
16 Screw
17 Screw
18 Screw – 4 off
19 Screw – 3 off
20 Plain washer
21 Spring washer

3   Symptoms of a damaged rectifier; a persistent flat battery or persistent overcharging. Note that if the battery is connected up incorrectly, a damaged rectifier is very likely to result.

5   Battery: charging procedure and maintenance

1   Whilst the machine is in normal use it is unlikely that the battery will require attention other than routine maintenance because the generator will keep it fully charged. However, if the machine is used for a succession of short journeys only, mainly during the hours of darkness when the lights are in full use, it is possible that the output from the generator may fail to keep pace with the heavy electrical demand. Under these circumstances it will be necessary to remove the battery from time to time to have it charged independently.

2   The battery is located behind the left-hand side panel. It is secured by a strap which, when released, will permit the battery to be withdrawn after disconnection of the leads. Remember that the machine has a negative earth system.

3   The normal off-machine charge rate is 0·6 amp. A more rapid charge up to 2 amps can be given in an emergency, but this should be avoided if possible because it will shorten the life of the battery. See accompanying table.

4   When the battery is removed from the machine, clean the battery top. If the terminals are corroded scrape them clean and cover them with Vaseline (not grease) to protect them from further attack. If a vent tube is fitted, make sure it is not obstructed and that it is arranged so that it will not discharge over any parts of the machine. If topping-up is necessary, use only distilled water to maintain the electrolyte level between the upper and lower level lines on the transparent casing.

5   If the machine is laid up for any period of time, the battery should be removed and given a 'refresher' charge every six weeks or so, in order to maintain it in good condition.

Battery charging instructions

	Normal charge	Rapid charge
Charging current rate	0.6 AH	2.0 AH max.
* Checking for full charge	(1) Specific gravity: 1.260 - 1.280 (20°C: 68° F) maintained constant (2) 0.2AH - 0.6AH (3) 7.5V - 8.3V	(1) Specific gravity: 1.260 - 1.280 maintained at 20° C (68°F) (2) Voltage: When large volume of gas is emitted from the battery (in about 2-3 hours for fully discharged battery), reduce charging rate to 0.2A. Battery is fully charged when a voltage of 7.5V is maintained.
Charging duration	By this method, a battery with specific gravity of electrolyte below 1.220 at 20°C (68°F) will be fully charged in approximately 12-13 hours.	By this method, battery with specific gravity of electrolyte below 1.220 at 20°C (68°F) will be fully charged approximately 1-2 hours.
Remarks		When the charging is urgent, quick charging method may be used, however the recommended charging current rate should be under 2.0A.

6 Headlamp: replacing bulbs and adjusting beam height

1   To remove the headlamp lens/reflector unit, unscrew the single screw at the bottom of the unit (early models) or the two screws which pass through the shell, one on each side just below the headlamp mounting bolts (CG125-C and E models). With the securing screw(s) removed, the headlamp unit can be detached from the shell to expose the bulbholders.

2   On early models lift the holder against spring pressure, disengage the locating tang from the reflector and carefully withdraw the holder assembly from the shell. Press the bulb in

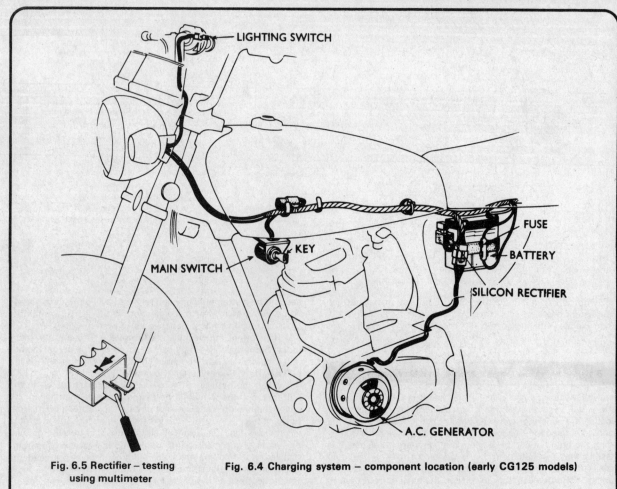

Fig. 6.5 Rectifier – testing using multimeter

Fig. 6.4 Charging system – component location (early CG125 models)

4.1 Rectifier is rubber-mounted to battery carrier

5.4 Maintain electrolyte between two level marks

and twist it anticlockwise to release it. On CG125-C and E models twist the holder anticlockwise to release it, and withdraw it, noting how the locating tangs must be engaged with the matching reflector cutouts if the holder is to be refitted correctly. Detach the bulb as described above. On refitting (all models) ensure that the bulb locating tangs engage with the matching bulbholder slots; never use force or the bulb will be broken.

3 On all except early CG125 models unplug the pilot lamp bulbholder from its rubber grommet, then press the bulb into the holder and twist it anticlockwise to release it. Reverse this procedure to fit the new bulb.

4 **Note:** on all models the lighting system voltage is regulated by the bulbs themselves; always ensure that all bulbs are of exactly the specified rating.

5 Headlamp beam height adjustment is made by slackening the mounting bolts and tilting the headlamp assembly to the required setting; tighten the bolts securely once the setting is correct.

6 To set the beam height the machine should be placed on level ground facing a wall 25 feet away. Measure the distance from the headlamp centre to the ground when the machine is standing on its wheels with the rider (and pillion passenger, if one is regularly carried) normally seated and the suspension and tyre pressures correctly set for the load carried. With the engine running and the headlamp switched to main beam the centre of the concentrated area of light should be at the same height on the wall as the headlamp is from the ground.

7 If the headlamp rim and reflector are to be dismantled at any time, note the location of the reflector before disturbing it, so that it can be refitted the correct way round. Wrap the assembly in a layer of rag and use a strong pair of needle-nose pliers to disengage each of the four W-clips in turn; note carefully exactly how these are engaged on the edge of the reflector and under the rim. On early models the reflector and glass are a single unit, but CG125-C and E models are fitted with separate glasses and reflectors, with a foam plastic gasket sealing the joint. In all cases note the small locating lug on the glass and/or reflector which must engage with the matching slot in the rim.

---

7 Tail and stop lamp: replacing bulbs

---

1 The combined tail and stop lamp is fitted with a double filament bulb having offset pins to prevent its unintentional reversal in the bulb holder. The lamp unit serves a two-fold purpose — to illuminate the rear of the machine and the rear number plate, and to give visual warning when the rear brake is applied.

2 To gain access to the bulb, remove the two screws holding the red plastic lens in position. The bulb is released by pressing inwards and with an anti-clockwise turning action; the bulb will now come out.

6.1 Lens/reflector unit is secured by screw through rim – early models

6.2 Bulb is mounted in spring-loaded holder – early models

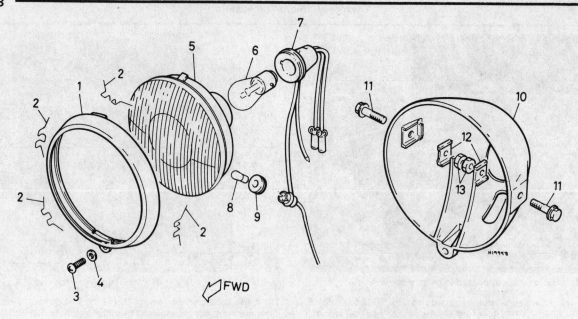

FWD

Fig. 6.6 Headlamp unit – CG125, CG125 K1 and B models

1 Rim	6 Headlamp bulb	11 Bolt – 2 off
2 W-clip – 4 off	7 Bulbholder	12 Washer – 2 off
3 Screw	8 Pilot lamp bulb*	13 Nut – 2 off
4 Washer	9 Grommet	
5 Reflector	10 Shell	*not fitted to early CG125 models

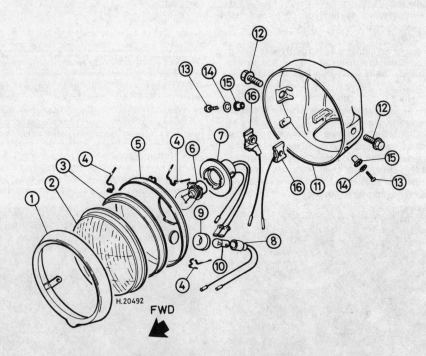

FWD

Fig. 6.7 Headlamp unit – CG125-C and E models

1 Rim	7 Bulbholder	12 Bolt – 2 off
2 Glass	8 Bulbholder	13 Screw – 2 off
3 Gasket	9 Grommet	14 Spring washer – 2 off
4 W-clip – 4 off	10 Pilot lamp bulb	15 Spacer – 2 off
5 Reflector	11 Shell	16 Nut – 2 off
6 Headlamp bulb		

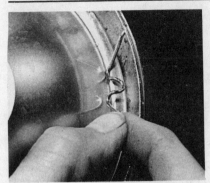

6.7 Note how W-clips are fitted before disturbing them

7.2 Tail lamp lens is retained by two screws

8.1 Brake switch can be adjusted by means of nut

8 Rear brake stop lamp switch: adjusting

1   To adjust the stop lamp switch hold the switch body and with the correct size spanner screw down the adjuster nut thus raising the rear brake light switch and making it operate sooner. Never adjust too tightly; the light should come on just as the first braking pressure is felt.

9 Front brake stop lamp switch: location and replacement

1   In order to give as much warning as possible to other road users of the braking of the machine, a front brake switch is incorporated in the front brake lever assembly.
2   There is no means of adjustment if it malfunctions, in which case the switch must be renewed.
3   To replace the switch, the headlamp reflector unit must be taken off and the wire from the switch disconnected. Take off the front brake lever and feed the switch and wires back out towards the lever pivot. Replace the new switch in the reverse order.

10 Instrument ilumination and warning lamps: replacing bulbs

1   The instrument illumination and warning lamp bulbs are retained by rubber bulbholders which are a push-fit in the base of the speedometer and/or warning lamp cluster, as appropriate. To renew speedometer-mounted bulbs, pull the bulbholder free, and remove the bulb by turning it anticlockwise. New bulbs are fitted by reversing the above procedure.
2   On CG125-C and E models it may be necessary to remove its mounting bolts and to lower the headlamp assembly so that the two screws can be removed which secure the cluster housing to the bracket; the housing can then be raised sufficiently for the bulbholders to be unplugged. These bulbs are of the capless type and are pressed into their sockets; be careful not to damage the fine wire terminals on fitting the new bulb.

11 Flashing indicator lamps

1   The forward facing indicator lamps are connected to 'stalks' which are attached to the headlamp brackets. The hollow stalks carry the leads to the lens unit. The rear facing lamps are mounted on similar, shorter stalks, at a point immediately to the rear of the dualseat.
2   In each case, access to the bulb is gained by removing the plastic lens cover, which is retained by two screws. Bayonet fitting bulbs of the single filament type are used.

12 Flasher unit: location and replacement

1   The flasher relay unit is located under the dualseat, being rubber-mounted to the frame top tube.
2   If the flasher unit is functioning correctly, a series of audible clicks will be heard when the indicator lamps are in action. If the unit malfunctions and all the bulbs are in working order, the usual symptom is one initial flash before the unit goes dead; it will be necessary to replace the complete unit if the fault cannot be attributed to any other cause.
3   Take great care when handling the unit because it is easily damaged if dropped.

13 Headlamp dip switch

1   The headlamp dip switch is incorporated in the handlebar controls and is used to dip the main headlamp beam to avoid dazzling oncoming traffic.
2   Should this unit malfunction it is necessary to fit a new replacement since repairs are usually impracticable. A sudden failure when changing from one beam to the other can plunge the lighting system into darkness, with disastrous consequences.

10.1 Instrument bulb holders are a push-fit in base

11.2 Remove lens to change bulb – check condition of seal

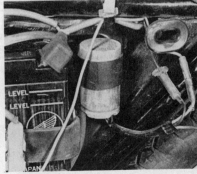

12.1 Flasher unit is rubber-mounted to rear of battery

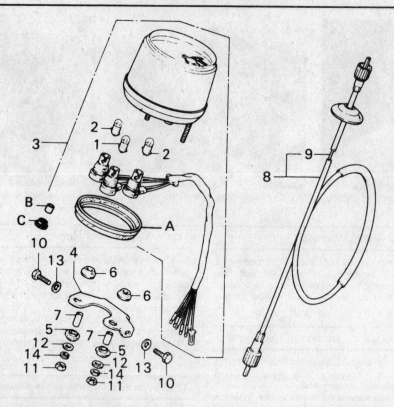

Fig. 6.8 Speedometer – early models (later models similar)

1 Bulb (6v 3w)	7 Spacer – 2 off	13 Washer – 2 off
2 Bulb (6v 1.7w) – 2 off	8 Speedometer cable complete	14 Spring washer – 2 off
3 Speedometer assembly	9 Inner cable	A Seat
4 Mounting bracket	10 Bolt – 2 off	B Spacer
5 Rubber ring – 2 off	11 Nut	C Rubber ring
6 Rubber washer – 2 off	12 Washer – 2 off	

14 Horn push and horn: adjustment

1 The horn push button is incorporated in the handlebar control and must be replaced if it malfunctions.

2 The horn is situated below the petrol tank at the front and has an adjustment screw inset into the rear. This is a volume screw which may need adjustment from time to time to compensate for wear inside the horn.

3 To adjust the horn, depress the horn button (with the ignition on) and screw the adjuster in or out to obtain maximum horn volume. Turn off the ignition when adjustment is correct.

15 Fuse: location and replacement

1 The fuse is incorporated in the red lead wire from the battery, enclosed in a nylon case. It is incorporated to protect the wiring and electrical components from accidental damage should a short circuit occur.

2 If the electrical system will not operate, a blown fuse should be suspected, but before the fuse is replaced the electrical system should be inspected to trace the reason for the failure of the fuse. If this precaution is not observed the replacement will almost certainly blow as well.

3 The fuse is rated at 10 amps and at least one spare should be carried at all times. In an extreme emergency and only when the cause of the failure has been rectified and no spare is available, a get-you-home repair can be made by wrapping silver paper around the blown fuse and re-inserting it in the fuse holder. It must be stressed that this is only an emergency

measure and the fuse should be replaced at the earliest possible opportunity, as it affords no protection at all to the electrical system when bridged in this fashion.

16 Ignition switch: location and replacement

1 On early models the ignition switch is secured to a bracket rubber-mounted to the frame top tube, underneath the front left-hand side of the petrol tank. If the switch is to be renewed the tank must be removed so that the switch wires can be disconnected; unscrew the plated retaining ring to release the switch from its bracket. On refitting, use a hammer and a small punch to tighten the ring without marking it.

2 On CG125-C and E models the switch is mounted in the warning lamp cluster, next to the speedometer. Remove the headlamp rim and reflector unit (see Section 6), then trace and disconnect the switch wires. Remove the headlamp shell mounting bolts and allow the shell to hang down on the wiring. Remove the two screws which secure the cluster housing to its bracket, unplug the warning lamps and withdraw the housing. Use an electrical screwdriver or similar to disengage the clips which secure the switch to the housing. On refitting align the switch with the housing and press it into position from above until the clips snap into place.

17 Resistor: function and testing

1 Except for early CG125 models, all models are fitted with a resistor which is bolted to the front fork lower yoke. It's function

14.2 Horn is located here

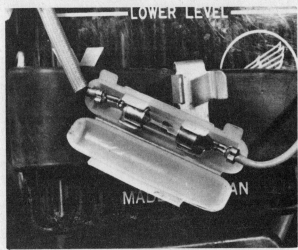

15.1 Main fuse holder clips to battery case

15.2 Spare fuses should be kept in holder inside panel

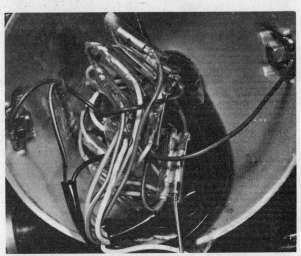

17.2 Wiring is colour-coded to facilitate tracing of faults

is to drain off excess power generated when only the side lights are in use and to convert it to heat which is dissipated by the air stream. When the main headlamp is in use, the resistor is switched out of the circuit so that full current is available to meet the increased electrical demand.

2 If the pilot light burns out with recurring frequency but the headlamp is unaffected, the resistor should be suspected. Because it is a sealed unit a new replacement should be fitted. For those with the necessary equipment the resistor can be tested. Connect a multimeter, set to the most sensitive resistance function, between the brown wire terminal and earth. The correct resistance for the unit fitted to CG125-C and E models is 2 ohms; a similar reading can be expected from the unit fitted to earlier models. If the reading obtained is significantly different, the resistor must be considered faulty and renewed.

18 Wiring: layout and examination

1 The cables of the wiring harness are colour-coded and will correspond with the accompanying wiring diagrams.

2 Visual inspection will show whether any breaks or frayed outer coverings are giving rise to short circuits which will cause the main fuse to blow. Another source of trouble is the snap connectors and spade terminals, which may make a poor connection if they are not pushed home fully.

3 Intermittent short circuits can sometimes be traced to a chafed wire passing through, or close to, a metal component, such as a frame member. Avoid tight bends in the cables or situations where the cables can be trapped or stretched, especially in the vicinity of the handlebars or steering head.

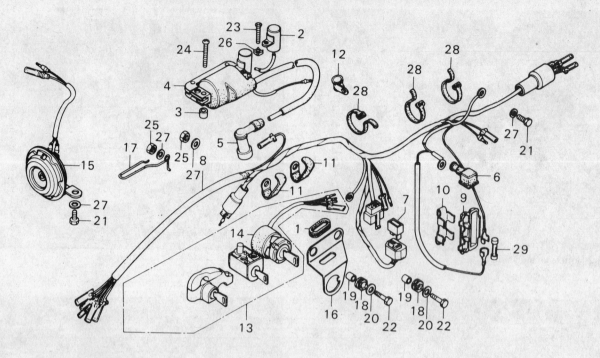

Fig. 6.9 Electrical system component parts – CG125, CG125 K1 and B models

1 Grommet	11 Wiring clip – 2 off	21 Bolt – 2 off
2 Condenser	12 HT cable guide	22 Bolt – 2 off
3 Distance piece – 2 off	13 Key and locking components	23 Screw
4 Ignition coil	14 Ignition switch	24 Screw
5 Plug cap	15 Horn	25 Nut – 2 off
6 Insulating cover	16 Switch bracket	26 Spacer
7 Rectifier unit	17 Cable guide	27 Washer – 4 off
8 Wiring harness	18 Rubber mounting – 2 off	28 Cable clip – 3 off
9 Fuse holder	19 Collar – 2 off	29 Fuse
10 Fuse holder clip	20 Washer – 2 off	

19 Fault diagnosis : electrical system

Symptom	Cause	Remedy
Complete electrical failure	Blown fuse	Check wiring and electrical components for short circuit before fitting new 10 A fuse.
	Isolated battery	Check battery connections, also whether connections show signs of corrosion.
Dim lights, horn inoperative	Discharged battery	Recharge battery with battery charger and check whether generator is giving correct output.
Constantly 'blowing' bulbs	Vibration, poor earth connection	Check whether bulb holders are secured correctly. Check earth return or connections to frame.

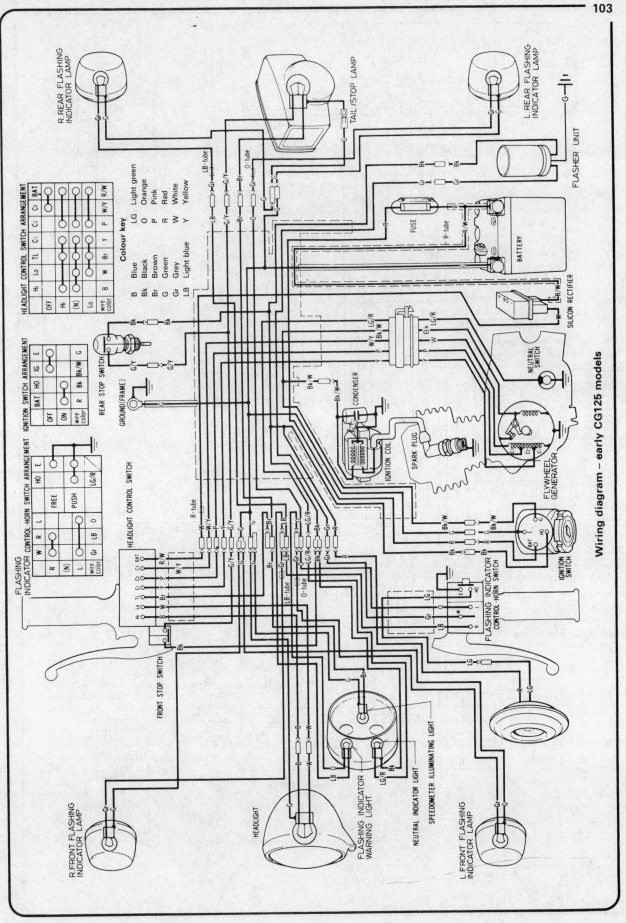

Wiring diagram – early CG125 models

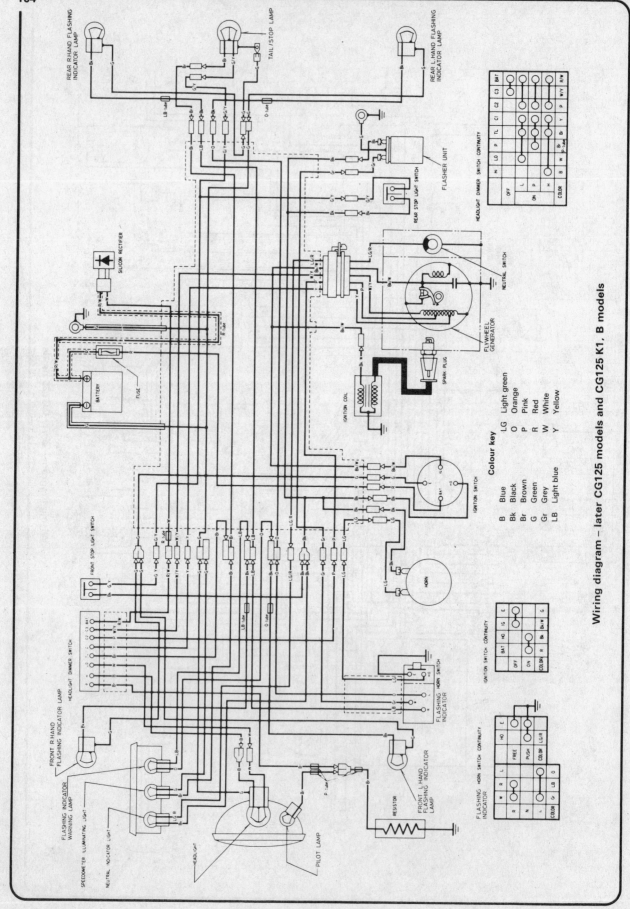

Colour key

B	Blue	LG	Light green
Bk	Black	O	Orange
Br	Brown	P	Pink
G	Green	R	Red
Gr	Grey	W	White
LB	Light blue	Y	Yellow

Wiring diagram – later CG125 models and CG125 K1, B models

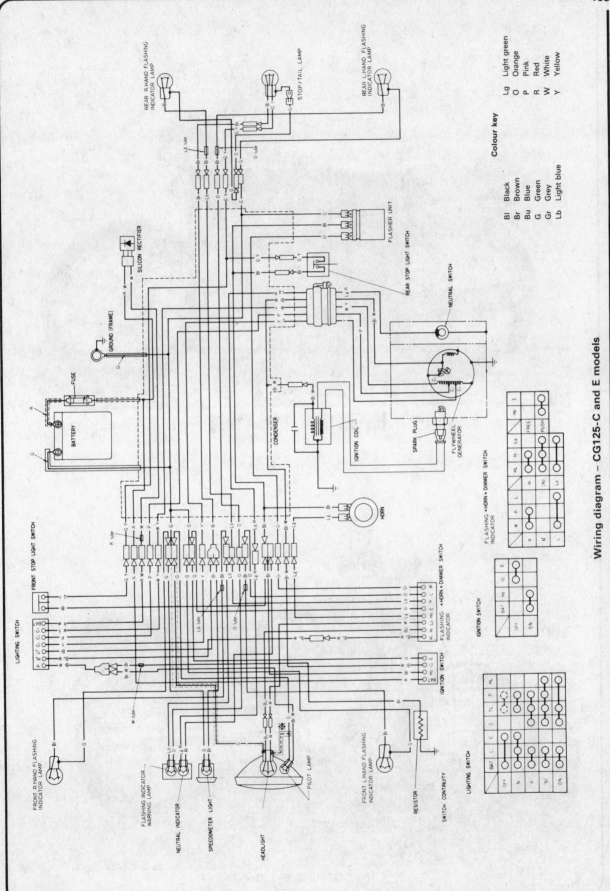

Wiring diagram – CG125-C and E models

The CG125 (BR)-E/F model

The CG125 (BR)-J model

Chapter 7 The 1985-on models

Contents

Specifications

Note: *The following specifications apply to the CG125 BR-E/F, BR-J, BR-K, BR-S/T, ES-4, ES-7 (Brazilian-built) and W, M-1 (Turkish-built) models imported from April 1985 onwards. Information is given only where different from that applicable to the CG125-E (Japanese-built) model described in Chapters 1 to 6 of this manual.*

Model dimensions and weight

	CG125 BR-E/F, J	CG125 BR-K
Overall length	1936 mm (76.2 in)	1985 mm (78.1 in)
Overall width	745 mm (29.3 in)	735 mm (28.9 in)
Overall height	1050 mm (41.3 in)	1040 mm (40.9 in)
Wheelbase	1280 mm (50.4 in)	1295 mm (51.0 in)
Seat height	760 mm (29.9 in)	770 mm (30.3 in)
Ground clearance	150 mm (5.9 in)	150 mm (5.9 in)
Dry weight	99 – 101 kg (218 – 223 lb)	105 kg (232 lb)

Model dimensions and weight

	CG125 BR-S/T	CG125-W
Overall length	1985 mm (78.1 in)	2000 mm (78.7 in)
Overall width	730 mm (28.7 in)	730 mm (28.7 in)
Overall height	1038 mm (40.8 in)	1040 mm (40.9 in)
Wheelbase	1300 mm (51.2 in)	1300 mm (51.2 in)
Seat height	Not available	770 mm (30.3 in)
Ground clearance	150 mm (5.9 in)	135 mm (5.3 in)
Dry weight	107 kg (236 lb)	116 kg (256 lb)

Model dimensions and weight

	CG125M-1	CG125ES-4, ES-7
Overall length	2000 mm (78.7 in)	2035 mm (80.1 in)
Overall width	730 mm (28.7 in)	740 mm (29.1 in)
Overall height	1040 mm (40.9 in)	1060 mm (41.7 in)
Wheelbase	1300 mm (51.2 in)	1295 mm (51.0 in)
Seat height	770 mm (30.3 in)	780 mm (30.7 in)
Ground clearance	135 mm (5.3 in)	175 mm (6.9 in)
Dry weight	110 kg (242.5 lb)	114 kg (251 lb)

Quick glance maintenance data

Spark plug type – CG125 BR-K, S/T, CG125-W,
CG125M-1, CG125ES-4, CG125ES-7 models ....   NGK DPR8EA-9 or ND X24EPR-U9
Front fork leg oil capacity – per leg:
CG125 BR-E/F and J models ....   85 cc (2.99 Imp fl oz)
CG125 BR-K and S/T models ....   82.5 ± 2.5 cc (2.90 ± 0.09 Imp fl oz)
CG125-W and CG125M-1 models ....   88 cc (3.10 Imp fl oz)
CG125ES-4 and CG125ES-7 models ....   74.5 ± 1.0 cc (2.6 ± 0.04 Imp fl oz)
Front brake lever free play – CG125 BR-K, S/T,
CG125-W and CG125M-1 models ....   10 – 20 mm (0.4 – 0.8 in) at tip
Final drive chain free play – CG125-W, CG125M-1,
CG125ES-4 and CG125ES-7 models ....   10 – 20 mm (0.4 – 0.8 in)

Specifications relating to Chapter 1

Engine (general)
Compression ratio:
CG125-W model 9.0:1
CG125M-1 model 9.2:1
CG125ES-4 and CG125ES-7 models 9.5:1

Valves

Valve timing – CG125M-1, CG125ES-4 and CG125ES-7 models:
Inlet valve opens at ....   11° BTDC
Inlet valve closes at ....   29° ABDC
Exhaust valve opens at ....   41° BBDC
Exhaust valve closes at ....   1° ATDC
Valve spring free length – CG125ES-4 and CG125ES-7 models:
Standard – inlet and exhaust ....   38.94 mm (1.533 in)
Wear limit – inlet and exhaust ....   36.4 mm (1.43 in)
Valve stem diameter – CG125ES-4 and CG125ES-7 models:
Inlet – standard ....   4.975 – 4.990 mm (0.1959 – 0.1965 in)
Inlet – wear limit ....   4.92 mm (0.194 in)
Exhaust – standard ....   4.955 – 4.970 mm (0.1951 – 0.1957 in)
Exhaust – wear limit ....   4.90 mm (0.193 in)
Valve guide bore diameter – CG125ES-4 and CG125ES-7 models:
Inlet and exhaust – standard ....   5.000 – 5.012 mm (0.1969 – 0.1973 in)
Inlet and exhaust – wear limit ....   5.02 mm (0.198 in)
Rocker arm ID service limit
CG125 BR-S/T models ....   12.04 mm (0.474 in)
CG125M-1 models ....   Not available
CG125ES-4 and CG125ES-7 models ....   12.05 mm (0.474 in)
Rocker arm shaft OD service limit
CG125 BR-S/T models ....   11.95 mm (0.470 in)
CG125M-1 models ....   Not available
CG125ES-4 and CG125ES-7 models ....   11.75 mm (0.463 in)

Cam and followers – CG125-W, CG125M-1, CG125ES-4 and CG125ES-7 models

Cam follower bore diameter ....   12.000 – 12.018 mm (0.4724 – 0.4731 in)
Wear limit ....   12.03 mm (0.474 in)
Cam follower shaft diameter ....   11.979 – 11.994 mm (0.4715 – 0.4722 in)
Wear limit ....   11.96 mm (0.471 in)
Cam gear shaft diameter ....   14.033 – 14.044 mm (0.5525 – 0.5543 in)
Wear limit ....   14.017 mm (0.5518 in)
Cam gear bore diameter ....   14.060 – 14.078 mm (0.5535 – 0.5543 in)
Wear limit ....   14.123 mm (0.5560 in)
Gear to shaft clearance ....   0.016 – 0.045 mm (0.0006 – 0.0018 in)
Wear limit ....   0.106 mm (0.0042 in)

Piston
Skirt OD wear limit ....   56.40 mm (2.2205 in)
Note: *Piston OD must be measured at 10 mm (0.4 in) from the bottom of piston skirt at 90° to the gudgeon pin holes*
Gudgeon pin bore ID – standard
CG125 BR-E/F, J, K, S/T, CG125-W and CG125M-1 models ...   15.002 – 15.008 mm (0.5906 – 0.5909 in)
CG125ES-4 and CG125ES-7 models ....   13.002 – 13.008 mm (0.5119 – 0.5121 in)
Gudgeon pin bore ID – wear limit
CG125 BR-E/F, J, K, S/T, CG125-W and CG125M-1 models ..   15.04 mm (0.592 in)
CG125ES-4 and CG125ES-7 models ....   13.04 mm (0.513 in)
Gudgeon pin OD – standard
CG125 BR-E/F, J, K, S/T, CG125-W and CG125M-1 models ..   14.994 – 15.000 mm (0.5903 – 0.5906 in)
CG125ES-4 and CG125ES-7 models ....   12.994 – 13.000 mm (0.5116 – 0.5118 in)
Gudgeon pin OD – wear limit
CG125 BR-E/F, J, K, S/T, CG125-W and CG125M-1 models ..   14.96 mm (0.589 in)
CG125ES-4 and CG125ES-7 models ....   12.96 mm (0.510 in)
Piston to gudgeon pin maximum clearance ....   0.020 mm (0.0008 in)

Piston rings

Ring to groove clearance:
Top –
CG125 BR-E/F, J, K, CG125-W and CG125M-1 models ...   0.015 – 0.050 mm (0.0006 – 0.0020 in)
CG125 BR-S/T, CG125ES-4 and CG125ES-7 models ....   0.015 – 0.045 mm (0.0006 – 0.0018 in)
Second – all models ....   0.015 – 0.045 mm (0.0006 – 0.0018 in)
Wear limit – both rings ....   0.090 mm (0.0035 in)
End gap (installed) – CG125 BR-E/F, J, K, CG125-W and CG125M-1 models:
Top and second ring ....   0.15 – 0.35 mm (0.006 – 0.014 in)
Wear limit ....   0.5 mm (0.02 in)
Oil scraper ring side rails ....   0.20 – 0.90 mm (0.008 – 0.035 in)
End gap (installed) – CG125 BR-S/T models:
Top ring ....   0.10 – 0.25 mm (0.004 – 0.010 in)
Wear limit ....   0.40 mm (0.016 in)
Second ring ....   0.25 – 0.40 mm (0.010 – 0.016 in)
Wear limit ....   0.55 mm (0.022 in)
Oil scraper ring side rails ....   0.20 – 0.70 mm (0.008 – 0.028 in)
End gap (installed) – CG125ES-4 and CG125ES-7 models:
Top and second ring ....   0.05 – 0.20 mm (0.002 – 0.008 in)
Wear limit ....   0.5 mm (0.02 in)
Oil scraper ring side rails ....   0.20 – 0.70 mm (0.008 – 0.028 in)
Note: *Piston ring installed end gap must be measured at 10 mm (0.4 in) above bottom of cylinder bore*
Thickness ....   Not available

Cylinder bore

Gasket surface maximum warpage ....   0.100 mm (0.0039 in)
Piston to cylinder clearance ....   0.010 – 0.040 mm (0.0004 – 0.0016 in)
Wear limit ....   0.100 mm (0.0039 in)
Cylinder compression pressure:
CG125-W model ....   12.0 kg/cm^2 (171 psi)
CG125M-1 model ....   13.5 kg/cm^2 (192 psi)
CG125ES-4 and CG125ES-7 models ....   13.2 kg/cm^2 (188 psi)

Cylinder head

Gasket surface maximum warpage ....   0.100 mm (0.0039 in)

Crankshaft

CG125 BR-E/F, J, K, S/T, CG125-W and CG125M-1 models:
Connecting rod small-end bore ID ....   15.010 – 15.028 mm (0.5909 – 0.5917 in)
Wear limit – CG125 BR-E/F, J, K, CG125-W and CG125M-1 .   15.060 mm (0.5929 in)
Wear limit – CG125 BR-S/T ....   15.080 mm (0.5937 in)
CG125ES-4 and CG125ES-7 models:
Connecting rod small-end bore ID ....   13.010 – 13.028 mm (0.5122 – 0.5129 in)
Wear limit ....   13.06 mm (0.514 in)
Connecting rod big-end side clearance – wear limit
CG125 BR-E/F, J, K, S/T and CG125-W ....   0.05 mm (0.002 in)
CG125M-1, CG125ES-4 and CG125ES-7 ....   0.5 mm (0.02 in)
Big-end bearing maximum radial play ....   0.05 mm (0.002 in)
Crankshaft maximum runout ....   0.80 mm (0.032 in)

Clutch

CG125ES-4 and CG125ES-7 – outer friction plate thickness
Standard ....   3.62 – 3.70 mm (0.143 – 0.146 in)
Wear limit ....   3.3 mm (0.13 in)

Gearbox

Reduction ratios:
Primary drive – CG125 BR-E/F, J, K 3.333:1 (21/70T)
Primary drive – CG125 BR-S/T, CG125M-1, CG125ES-4 and
CG125ES-7 ....   3.333:1 (18/60T)
Primary drive – CG125-W 4.055:1 (18/73T)
CG125 BR-E/F, J, K, S/T and CG125M-1:
1st 2.769:1 (13/36T)
2nd 1.882:1 (17/32T)
3rd 1.400:1 (20/28T)
4th 1.130:1 (23/26T)
5th 0.960:1 (25/24T)
CG125ES-4 and CG125ES-7:
1st 2.769:1 (13/36T)
2nd 1.722:1 (18/31T)
3rd 1.273:1 (22/28T)
4th 1.041:1 (24/25T)
5th 0.884:1 (26/23T)
Final drive – all CG125 BR models 2.929:1 (14/41T)
Final drive – CG125-W 2.400:1 (15/36T)
Final drive – CG125M-1 ....   3.071:1 (14/43T)
Final drive – CG125ES-4 and CG125ES-7 ....   3.214:1 (14/45T)

Gearbox (continued)

Selector fork claw end minimum thickness:

All CG125 BR models, CG125M-1, CG125ES-4 and CG125ES-7 .	4.50 mm (0.1772 in)
CG125-W	4.60 mm (0.1811 in)
Selector fork shaft diameter	11.976 – 11.994 mm (0.4715 – 0.4722 in)
Wear limit	11.96 mm (0.4709 in)

Torque wrench settings

Component	kgf m	lbf ft
Cylinder head cover bolts	0.8 – 1.2	6 – 9
Rocker assembly mounting bolts:		
CG125 BR-E/F and J models	1.5 – 2.0	11 – 14.5
CG125 BR-K model	2.1	15
CG125 BR-S/T models	2.6	18
CG125-W models	1.8	13
Rocker arm shaft bolt		
CG125 BR-S/T models	2.6	18
CG125ES-4 and CG125ES-7 models	1.2	9
Special bolt into cam follower pivot:		
CG125 BR-E/F and J models	1.5 – 2.0	11 – 14.5
CG125 BR-K, S/T, CG125-W models	2.1	15
Cylinder head sleeve bolt:		
CG125 BR-E/F and J models	2.3 – 2.8	16.5 – 20
CG125 BR-K and S/T models	3.3	23
CG125-W, CG125M-1, CG125ES-4 and CG125ES-7 models .	3.3	24
Cylinder head bolt		
CG125-W models	2.1	15
CG125M-1, CG125ES-4 and CG125ES-7 models	2.0	14
Crankcase and crankcase cover screws	0.8 – 1.2	6 – 9
Selector drum camplate bolt	1.0 – 1.6	7 – 11.5
Selector drum stopper arm bolt	0.8 – 1.2	6 – 9
Generator rotor nut:		
CG125 BR-S/T models	5.5	39
CG125-W model	6.5	47
Generator rotor bolt:		
CG125M-1, CG125ES-4 and CG125ES-7 models	7.5	54
Generator stator screws:		
CG125 BR-E/F, BR-J, BR-K models	0.8 – 1.2	6 – 9
CG125 BR-S/T, CG125-W models	Not available	
CG125M-1, CG125ES-4 and CG125ES-7 models	0.5	4
Starter clutch mounting bolts	1.6	12
Centrifugal oil filter slotted nut		
CG125-W, CG125M-1, CG125ES-4 and CG125ES-7 models .	5.5	40
Oil pump mounting screws		
CG125M-1, CG125ES-4 and CG125ES-7 models	1.0	7
Gearbox sprocket mounting bolts	1.0 – 1.6	7 – 11.5
Endfloat plug mounting bolt	1.0 – 1.6	7 – 11.5
Engine oil drain plug (where fitted)	2.0 – 3.0	14.5 – 22
Oil filter gauze cap:		
CG125 BR-E/F and J models	1.0 – 3.5	7 – 25
CG125 BR-K, S/T, CG125-W, CG125M-1, CG125ES-4 and CG125ES-7 models	1.5	11
Engine mounting bolts:		
CG125 BR-K model	3.5	25
CG125 BR-S/T, CG125-W and CG125M-1 models	2.7	20
CG125ES-4 and CG125ES-7 models		
Front mounting bolts	3.3	24
Rear mounting bolts	4.5	33
Footrest bar mounting bolts:		
CG125 BR-E/F and J models	1.8 – 2.5	13 – 18
CG125 BR-K, S/T, CG125-W, CG125M-1, CG125ES-4 and CG125ES-7 models	2.7	20

Specifications relating to Chapter 2

Fuel tank capacity

Overall:

All CG125 BR models	12 litres (2.6 Imp gal)
CG125-W and CG125M-1 models	12.7 litres (2.8 Imp gal)
CG125ES-4 and CG125ES-7 models	13.5 litres (3.0 Imp gal)
Including reserve of:	
CG125 BR-E/F, J, K models	2.6 litres (0.6 Imp gal)
CG125 BR-S/T, CG125-W and CG125M-1 models	2.3 litres (0.5 Imp gal)
CG125ES-4 and CG125ES-7 models	2.5 litres (0.55 Imp gal)

Carburettor

	CG125 BR-E/F, J	CG125 BR-K
ID number	PD47C-A or D-A	PD47F-A
Main jet	90 (95*)	95
Pilot (slow) jet	38	35
Needle jet	E2052J (E2352H*)	Not available
Needle jet clip position – grooves from top	4th (2nd*)	Not available
Pilot screw – turns out from fully closed	1 3/8	1 1/2
Float height	14.0 mm (0.55 in)	14.0 mm (0.55 in)
Idle speed	1400 ± 100 rpm	1400 ± 100 rpm

See Section 14 for details of modified specifications denoted by the asterisk

Carburettor

	CG125 BR-S/T	CG125-W
ID number	PD47K-A	PDC4A-A
Main jet	110	80
Pilot (slow) jet	35	35
Needle jet	Not available	Not available
Needle jet clip position – grooves from top	Not available	3rd
Pilot screw – turns out from fully closed	1 1/2	1 3/4
Float height	14.0 mm (0.55 in)	14.0 mm (0.55 in)
Idle speed	1400 ± 100 rpm	1400 ± 100 rpm

Carburettor

	CG125M-1	CG125ES-4, ES-7
ID number	PDC4B	PDCAA
Main jet	Not available	90
Pilot (slow) jet	Not available	38
Needle jet	Not available	Not available
Needle jet clip position – grooves from top	3rd	-
Pilot screw – turns out from fully closed	Not available	1 7/8
Float height	14.0 mm (0.55 in)	14.0 mm (0.55 in)
Idle speed	1400 ± 100 rpm	1400 ± 100 rpm

Carburettor heater resistance

CG125-W and CG125M-1 models	13 – 15 ohms
CG125ES-4 and CG125ES-7 models	7.25 – 13.25 ohms

Oil pump

All CG125 BR and CG125-W models:	
Outer rotor to pump body clearance	0.30 – 0.36 mm (0.0118 – 0.0142 in)
CG125M-1 models:	
Outer rotor to pump body service limit	0.40 mm (0.016 in)
Rotor tip clearance – service limit	0.20 mm (0.008 in)
Rotor endfloat – service limit	0.25 mm (0.010 in)
CG125ES-4 and CG125ES-7 models:	
Outer rotor to pump body service limit	0.35 mm (0.014 in)
Rotor tip clearance – service limit	0.20 mm (0.008 in)
Rotor endfloat – service limit	0.15 mm (0.006 in)

Torque wrench settings

Component	kgf m	lbf ft
Petrol tap filter bowl	0.3 – 0.5	2 – 3.5
Engine oil drain plug (where fitted)	2.0 – 3.0	14.5 – 22
Oil filter gauze cap:		
CG125 BR-E/F and J models	1.0 – 3.5	7 – 25
CG125 BR-K, S/T, CG125-W, CG125M-1, CG125ES-4		
and CG125ES-7 models	1.5	11
Centrifugal oil filter slotted nut		
CG125-W, CG125M-1, CG125ES-4 and CG125ES-7 models .	5.5	40
Oil pump mounting screws		
CG125M-1, CG125ES-4 and CG125ES-7 models	1.0	7

Specifications relating to Chapter 3

Ignition system – CG125 BR-E/F, J and K models

Ignition timing:	
Initial – F mark aligned	15° BTDC static or at idle speed
Advance starts at	1800 ± 150 rpm
Full advance at	35 ± 1.5° BTDC @ 3800 ± 150 rpm
Ignition HT coil spark gap	6 mm (0.24 in) minimum
Condenser capacity	0.25 ± 10% microfarad

Ignition system – CG125 BR-S/T, CG125-W and CG125M-1 models

Ignition timing	15° BTDC @ idle speed
Ignition HT coil primary resistance	0.18 – 0.24 ohms
Ignition HT coil secondary resistance:	
With plug cap	6.45 – 9.75 K-ohms
Without plug cap	2.7 – 3.5 K-ohms

Ignition system – CG125 BR-S/T, CG125-W and CG125M-1 models (continued)

Ignition HT coil primary peak voltage – CG125M-1models only . . . . 100V minimum
Ignition source coil resistance . . . . 300 – 700 ohms
Ignition source coil peak voltage – CG125M-1models only . . . . . 100V minimum
Ignition pick-up coil resistance . . . . 180 – 280 ohms
Ignition pick-up coil peak voltage – CG125M-1models only . . . . 0.7V minimum

Ignition system – CG125ES-4 and CG125ES-7 models

Ignition timing . . . . 15° BTDC @ idle speed
Ignition HT coil primary peak voltage . . . . 100V minimum
Ignition pick-up coil peak voltage . . . . 0.7V minimum

Spark plug

CG125 BR-K, S/T, CG125-W, CG125M-1, CG125ES-4
and CG125ES-7 models . . . . NGK DPR8EA-9 or ND X24EPR-U9

Torque wrench settings

Component	kgf m	lbf ft
Generator stator screws:		
CG125 BR-E/F, BR-J, BR-K models	0.8 – 1.2	6 – 9
CG125 BR-S/T, CG125-W models	Not available	
Alternator stator bolts:		
CG125M-1, CG125ES-4 and CG125ES-7 models	0.5	4
Ignition pick-up coil bolts		
CG125M-1, CG125ES-4 and CG125ES-7 models	0.5	4
Generator rotor nut:		
CG125 BR-S/T models	5.5	39
CG125-W model	6.5	47
Alternator rotor bolt – CG125M-1, CG125ES-4 and		
CG125ES-7 models	7.5	54

Specifications relating to Chapter 4

Front forks

Travel:
All CG125 BR models . . . . 115 mm (4.53 in)
CG125-W models . . . . 102 mm (4.02 in)
CG125M-1 models . . . . 120 mm (4.72 in)
CG125ES-4 and CG125ES-7 models . . . . 115 mm (4.72 in)
Spring free length:
Standard – all BR models . . . . 457 mm (17.9921 in)
Wear limit – BR-E/F, J, K models . . . . 448 mm (17.6378 in)
Wear limit – BR-S/T models . . . . 445 mm (17.5197 in)
Standard – CG125-W and CG125M-1 models . . . . 461 mm (18.1496 in)
Wear limit – CG125-W and CG125M-1 models . . . . 452 mm (17.7952 in)
Standard – CG125ES-4 and CG125ES-7 models . . . . 462 mm (18.2 in)
Wear limit – CG125ES-4 and CG125ES-7 models . . . . 453 mm (17.8 in)
Stanchion maximum warpage . . . . 0.2 mm (0.0079 in)
Oil capacity – per leg:
CG125 BR-E/F and J models . . . . 85 cc (2.99 Imp fl oz)
CG125 BR-K and S/T models . . . . 82.5 ± 2.5 cc (2.90 ± 0.09 Imp fl oz)
CG125-W and CG125M-1 models . . . . 88 cc (3.10 Imp fl oz)
CG125ES-4 and CG125ES-7 models . . . . 74.5 ± 1.0 cc (2.6 ± 0.04 cc Imp fl oz)

Rear suspension

Travel:
CG125 BR-E/F and J models . . . . 64 mm (2.52 in)
CG125 BR-K, S/T, CG125-W, CG125ES-4 and
CG125ES-7 models . . . . 80 mm (3.15 in)
CG125M-1 models . . . . 75 mm (2.95 in)

Suspension unit spring free length:	Standard	Wear limit
CG125 BR-E/F, J, K models	197.7 mm (7.7835 in)	194.0 mm (7.6378 in)
CG125 BR-S/T models	198.4 mm (7.8110 in)	190.7 mm (7.5079 in)
CG125-W, CG125M-1, CG125ES-4 and CG125ES-7 models . .	Not available	

Note: Springs must be fitted with closer-pitched coils at the top

Torque wrench settings

Component	kgf m	lbf ft
Steering stem nut:		
All CG125 BR models and CG125-W models	6.0 – 7.0	43 – 50.5
CG125M-1, CG125ES-4 and CG125ES-7 models	7.5	54
Steering head bearing adjuster nut:		
CG125-W, CG125M-1, CG125ES-4 and CG125ES-7 models		
Initial setting	2.8	20
Final setting	0.3	2.2
Top yoke pinch bolts:		
All CG125 BR models	1.0 – 1.2	7 – 9
CG125-W, CG125M-1, CG125ES-4 and CG125ES-7 models	2.7	20

Torque wrench settings (continued)

Component	kgf m	lbf ft
Lower yoke pinch bolts:		
CG125 BR-E/F and J models	2.0 – 2.5	14.5 – 18
CG125 BR-K, S/T, CG125-W, CG125M-1, CG125ES-4		
and CG125ES-7 models	3.3	24
Handlebar clamp bolts:		
CG125 BR-E/F and J models	0.9 – 1.1	6.5 – 8
CG125 BR-K, S/T, CG125-W, CG125M-1, CG125ES-4		
and CG125ES-7 models	1.2	9
Fork top bolt:		
CG125 BR-E/F and J models	4.0 – 5.0	29 – 36
CG125 BR-K model	3.5	25
CG125 BR-S/T, CG125-W and CG125M-1 models	4.5	33
CG125ES-4 and CG125ES-7 models	2.2	16
Damper rod Allen screw:		
All CG125 BR models, CG125-W and CG125M-1 models	0.8 – 1.2	6 – 9
CG125ES-4 and CG125ES-7 models	2.0	15
Swinging arm pivot bolt nut:		
CG125 BR-E/F and J models	3.5 – 5.0	25 – 36
CG125 BR-K, S/T, CG125-W, CG125M-1, CG125ES-4		
and CG125ES-7 models	9.0	65
Rear suspension unit mounting nuts	3.0 – 4.0	22 – 29
Rear suspension unit top mounting eye locknut	1.5 – 2.0	11 – 14.5
Footrest bar mounting bolts:		
CG125 BR-E/F, J models	1.8 – 2.5	13 – 18
CG125 BR-K, S/T, CG125-W, CG125M-1, CG125ES-4		
and CG125ES-7 models	2.7	20

Specifications relating to Chapter 5

Wheels

Rim size:		
Front	1.60 x 18	
Rear	1.85 x 18	

Brakes

Front brake drum inside diameter:	
All CG125BR models, CG125-W and CG125M-1 models	
Standard	130 mm (5.1181 in)
Wear limit	131 mm (5.1575 in)
Front brake disc thickness – CG125ES-4 and CG125ES-7 models:	
Standard	4.0 mm (0.16 in)
Wear limit	3.5 mm (0.14 in)
Brake disc warpage limit	0.15 mm (0.006 in)
Rear brake drum inside diameter – CG125ES-4 and CG125ES-7 models:	
Standard	130 mm (5.1181 in)
Wear limit	131 mm (5.1575 in)

Tyres

	Front	Rear
Sizes:		
CG125 BR-E/F and J models	2.75 – 18 42P	90/90 – 18 51P
CG125 BR-K, S/T, CG125-W, CG125M-1, CG125ES-4		
and CG125ES-7 models	2.75 – 18 42P	90/90 – 18 57P
Pressures – tyres cold:		
Solo	25 psi (1.75 kg/cm^2)	28 psi (2.00 kg/cm^2)
Pillion	25 psi (1.75 kg/cm^2)	32 psi (2.25 kg/cm^2)

Torque wrench settings

Component	kgf m	lbf ft
Front wheel spindle nut:		
Castellated nut – with split pin	4.0 – 5.0	29 – 36
Self-locking nut	5.0 – 7.0	36 – 50.5
CG125M-1, CG125ES-4 and CG125ES-7 models	6.3	46
Drum brake (front and rear) actuating arm pinch bolts	0.8 – 1.2	6 – 9
Disc brake caliper pad pins – CG125ES-4 and CG125ES-7 models .	1.8	13
Disc brake caliper mounting bolts – CG125ES-4 and		
CG125ES-7 models	2.7	20
Brake hose union banjo bolts	3.5	25
Disc brake caliper slider pins – CG125ES-4 and CG125ES-7 models	2.2	16
Brake disc mounting nuts	1.5	11
Rear wheel spindle nut:		
Castellated nut – with split pin	5.0 – 7.0	36 – 50.5
Self-locking nut	8.0 – 10.0	58 – 72
CG125M-1, CG125ES-4 and CG125ES-7 models	9.0	65
Rear brake torque arm mountings	1.8 – 2.5	13 – 18

Specifications relating to Chapter 6

Electrical system

Voltage	12V
Generator/alternator output	94W @ 5000 rpm

Battery

All CG125 BR models and CG125-W models:

Make and type	Yuasa Yumicron YB2.5L-A
Capacity	2.5Ah

Charging rate:

Normal	0.25 amp
Maximum	0.40 amp

CG125M-1, CG125ES-4 and CG125ES-7 models:

Capacity	4.0Ah

Charging rate:

Normal	0.4 amp (5 – 10 hours)
Maximum	4.0 amp (30 minutes maximum)

Note: CG125ES-4 and CG125ES-7 models are fitted with a maintenance-free (MF) type battery

Fuse

CG125M-1, CG125ES-4 and CG125ES-7 models	15A

Charging system – BR-E/F, BR-J and BR-K models

Charge starts at	1500 rpm maximum

Output:

@ 4000 rpm	0.9 amp minimum/17.8 volt
@ 8000 rpm	3.0 amp maximum/18.1 volt

Note: Test conducted with lights switched on, to main beam

Charging system – BR-S/T and W models

Current leakage	0.01mA (max)
Voltage output – no-load	14.0 – 15.0V @ 5000 rpm
Voltage output – with lights on	10.5 – 14.0V @ 5000 rpm

Generator coil resistance

Charging coil	0.3 – 1.1 ohm
Lighting coil	0.2 – 1.0 ohm

Resistor:

CG125 BR-S/T models	6.7 ohms
CG125-W model	5.9 ohms

Charging system – CG125M-1 models

Current leakage	0.01mA (max)
Voltage output – no-load	15.5V @ 5000 rpm
Voltage output – with lights on	12.6 – 13.6V @ 5000 rpm

Generator coil resistance

Charging coil	0.3 – 1.1 ohm
Lighting coil	0.2 – 1.0 ohm

Charging system – CG125ES-4 and CG125ES-7 models

Current leakage	0.5mA (max)
Voltage output – no-load	15.5V @ 5000 rpm
Generator coil resistance	0.1 – 1.0 ohm

Fuel level sensor resistance – CG125ES-4 and CG125ES-7 models

Full position	4 – 10 ohms
Empty position	90 – 100 ohms

Bulbs

Headlamp	12V, 35/35W

Pilot lamp:

All CG125 BR models	12V, 3.4W
CG125-W, CG125M-1, CG125ES-4 and CG125ES-7 models	12V, 4W
All instrument illuminating and warning lamp bulbs	12V, 3W or 3.4W
Instrument panel illuminating lamp bulbs – GG125ES-4 and CG125ES-7	12V, 2W

Flashing indicator lamps

All BR models	12V, 18W or 21W*
CG125-W and CG125M-1models	12V, 10W
CG125ES-4 and CG125ES-7 models	12V, 16W
Stop/tail lamp	12V, 21/5W
Licence plate light	12V, 5W

*Check flasher unit rating and bulbholder marking to ensure correct bulb wattages are used

1.7a Chain enclosure is secured by three bolts at the rear on BR-E/F and BR-J models . . .

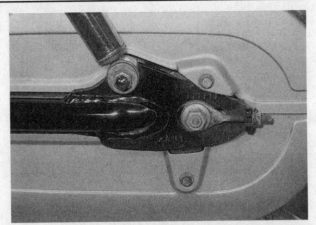

1.7b . . . and by two bolts at the rear on all later models

1   Introduction

1 The first six Chapters of this Manual describe the Japanese-built CG125 models imported into the UK from June 1976 to April 1985. This Chapter describes the models imported from that date, built in Honda's subsidiary factories in Brazil and in Turkey.

2 With the exception of the information on the (T)PFC/(Transient) Power Fuel Control carburettor, which was also fitted to the Japanese-built CG125C and E models, all information in this Chapter relates specifically to the Brazilian- and Turkish-built models. Information is given only where different from that given for the Japanese-built CG125E model described in Chapters 1 to 6.

3 If working on one of the Brazilian or Turkish models, first check the relevant part of this Chapter. If no information is given it can be assumed that the procedure or specification is unchanged from that given in the relevant part of Chapters 1 to 6.

4 As with their Japanese predecessors, the models covered in this Chapter have appeared in a number of slightly different versions. Each can be identified as follows:

CG125 BR-E/F

5 The first model from the Brazilian factory was imported from April 1985 to April 1988 and is referred to as the CG125 BR-E or F; either suffix letter may be used. Its frame numbers began with CG125BR–8100001 and its engine numbers with CG125BRE–8100001. Models are finished in red or black.

6 The Brazilian models differ from their Japanese predecessors chiefly in the appearance of their cycle parts and bodywork, the engine unit being largely identical. A 12 volt electrical system is fitted and the speedometer and warning lamp cluster are mounted in a single panel. A larger front brake is fitted inside a conical shaped hub and the tank, seat, rear mudguard and side panels have been redesigned to give an updated appearance.

7 Amongst other detail differences, the pillion passenger footrest mountings have been modified, the rear chain enclosure halves are secured by five bolts instead of four on BR-E/F and BR-J models (reverted to four bolts on later models), a grab rail is fitted as standard and new handlebar switches are fitted.

CG125 BR-J

8 Imported from April 1988 to September 1991. Frame numbers start at CG125BR–8106211 to 8115880 (engine numbers are not available). Finished in red, blue or white, it can be easily identified by its plastic front mudguard as opposed to the chrome-plated steel item fitted to all earlier models.

CG125 BR-K

9 Imported from September 1991 to April 1995. Frame numbers start at JC18-1000002 and engine numbers at JC18E5000006. Colours available were red or blue. Apart from minor modifications to its cycle parts the UK market version can be distinguished from its predecessor by its tail fairing and the large CG graphic on the fuel tank.

CG125 BR-S/T

10 Imported from April 1995 to November 1997 and referred to as the BR-S or BR-T; either suffix may be used. Frame numbers start at 9C2JC1821-RRO10001 and engine numbers at JC18E-5004601. The most significant difference from previous CG models is the use of CDI electronic ignition to replace the previous contact-breaker system. Colours available were grey, red or blue.

CG125-W

11 Manufactured in Turkey and imported for the production years 1998 to 2000. There are a number of subtle mechanical differences between the W and BR-S/T models, but for identification purposes the most obvious noticeable difference is its square headlamp and mirrors as opposed to the round items fitted to all earlier models and the HONDA name on the fuel tank instead of the previous CG decal. Initial engine and frame number details are not available. Colours available were red or blue.

CG125M-1

12 Manufactured in Turkey and imported for the production years 2001 to 2003. A major update is the fitting of an electric starter mounted on top of the crankcases behind the cylinder, although the kickstarter is retained. A new alternator is fitted, incorporating a starter clutch mechanism on the back of the rotor, and the alternator stator is mounted inside the left-hand engine cover. The clutch incorporates an anti-judder spring assembly and the cam gear is a two-piece spring-loaded unit to eliminate gear backlash. A safety circuit prevents the engine from starting unless the transmission is in neutral or the clutch lever is pulled in. Colours available were red, blue or black.

CG125ES-4

13 Manufactured in Brazil and imported for the production years 2004 to 2006. The styling is revised for a sleeker appearance, a hydraulic front disc brake is added and the rear chain enclosure is replaced by chainguard on the top run only. A new headlight, tail lamp and flashing indicators are fitted, the instrument panel incorporates a fuel gauge and an MF (maintenance-free) battery is used. The diameter of the rear drum brake is increased to 130 mm and an endless drive chain is fitted. The passenger footrests are mounted on cast aluminium brackets. The kickstarter and associated components are discontinued and the accelerator pump is no longer fitted to the carburettor. A new air filter element is fitted and a PAIR control valve introduces air into the exhaust port to promote burning of unburnt exhaust gasses and thus reduce the level of harmful exhaust emissions. Colours available were pearl red, pearl blue or silver metallic.

CG125ES-7

14 Apart from a minor modification to the gearbox, the ES-7 is unchanged from the ES-4 model and continues to be manufactured in Brazil. Colours available were force silver metallic, pearl carnival red or black.

2   Routine maintenance: schedule modifications

1 With reference to the Routine maintenance section at the front of this manual, note that the service schedules have been altered slightly.

CG125 BR-E/F, BR-J and BR-K models

2 The pre-ride (daily) check, the monthly/600 mile check and the three-monthly/1800 mile check remain unchanged. Note, however, that the battery is now retained by a metal strap which is secured by a single bolt.

3 The tasks described under the six-monthly/3600 mile check must be carried out at four-monthly intervals, or every 2500 miles/4000 km. They also include checking the petrol tap filter (Section 4) and checking the side stand (Section 7). Note also the revised procedure required for air filter cleaning, and checking brake wear. See Sections 4 and 5.

4 At every eight months, or 5000 miles/8000 km carry out all tasks listed under the four monthly heading (i.e. the previous six monthly check, plus two items above) then renew the spark plug and clean the engine oil centrifugal filter. Both of these items are given under the annual heading for earlier models.

5 Once annually, or every 7500 miles/12 000 km carry out all maintenance operations listed, then check the steering head bearings and change the front fork oil. **Note:** *When changing the fork oil the front of the machine must be supported securely so that the front wheel is clear of the ground before the fork top bolts are removed. Note also the different fork oil capacity.*

CG125 BR-S/T models

6 The pre-ride (daily) check remains unchanged from that given in *Routine maintenance* at the beginning of this manual.

7 Every 600 miles (1000 km) check the battery and the final drive chain (*Routine maintenance* section).

8 Every 900 miles (1500 km) change the engine oil and clean the filter gauze. See *Routine maintenance* and Section 3 of this Chapter.

9 Every 1850 miles (3000 km) check the air filter, spark plug, valve clearances, engine idle speed and throttle cable freeplay (fuel system), brakes, clutch, wheels, plus general checks and lubrication. Procedures can be found in *Routine maintenance*, but note also the new procedures in Sections 4 and 5 of this Chapter.

10 Every 3700 miles (6000 km) check the engine oil centrifugal filter, petrol tap filter, suspension and steering. Procedures can be found in *Routine maintenance*, but note also the new procedure for the petrol tap filter in Section 4 of this Chapter.

11 Every 5550 miles (9000 km) renew the front fork oil. See Sections 26 to 29 of this Chapter, noting that it is not necessary to dismantle the fork fully to change the oil, merely to remove the fork from the yokes (Section 26), then to remove the top bolt and spring and invert the fork to expel the oil (Section 27).

CG125-W models

12 The pre-ride (daily) check remains unchanged from that given in Routine maintenance at the beginning of this manual.

13 Every 600 miles (1000 km) check the final drive chain. See Section 5 of this Chapter.

14 Every 2500 miles (4000 km) or six months: change the engine oil and clean the filter gauze, check the battery, air filter, spark plug, valve clearances, fuel system, clutch, brakes, wheels, suspension and headlamp aim. Procedures can be found in *Routine maintenance*, but note also the new procedures in Sections 3, 4, and 5 of this Chapter. Refer to Section 44 of this Chapter for the headlamp aim checking procedure.

15 Every 5000 miles (8000 km) or annually: renew the spark plug and check the tightness of all major fasteners to ensure none have worked loose.

16 Every 7500 miles (12 000 km) or eighteen months: clean the engine oil centrifugal filter and check the steering head bearings. Procedures can be found in *Routine maintenance*.

CG125M-1 models

17 The pre-ride (daily) check remains unchanged from that given in Routine maintenance at the beginning of this manual.

18 Every 600 miles (1000 km) check the final drive chain. See Section 5 of this Chapter.

19 Every 2500 miles (4000 km) or six months: change the engine oil and clean the filter gauze, check the battery, air filter, spark plug, valve clearances, fuel system, clutch, brakes, wheels, suspension and headlamp aim. Procedures can be found in *Routine maintenance*, but note also the new procedures in Sections 3, 4, and 5 of this Chapter. Refer to Section 44 of this Chapter for the headlamp aim checking procedure.

20 Every 5000 miles (8000 km) or annually: renew the spark plug and check the tightness of all major fasteners to ensure none have worked loose.

21 Every 7500 miles (12,000 km) or eighteen months: clean the engine oil centrifugal filter and check the steering head bearings. Procedures can be found in *Routine maintenance*.

CG125ES-4 and ES-7 models

22 The pre-ride (daily) check remains unchanged from that given in Routine maintenance at the beginning of this manual with the additional need to check the front brake fluid level. See Section 5 of this Chapter.

23 Every 600 miles (1000 km) check the final drive chain. See Section 5 of this Chapter.

24 Every 2500 miles (4000 km) or six months: change the engine oil and clean the filter gauze, check the air filter, spark plug, valve clearances, fuel system, clutch, brakes, wheels, suspension and headlamp aim. Procedures can be found in *Routine maintenance*, but note also the new procedures in Sections 3, 4, and 5 of this Chapter. Refer to Section 44 of this Chapter for the headlamp aim checking procedure.

25 Every 5000 miles (8000 km) or annually: renew the spark plug and check the tightness of all major fasteners to ensure none have worked loose.

26 Every 7500 miles (12,000 km) or eighteen months: renew the air filter element, check the components of the secondary air supply system, clean the engine oil centrifugal filter and check the steering head bearings. Procedures can be found in *Routine maintenance* and in Sections 4 and 6 of this Chapter.

27 Every two years: renew the front brake fluid. See Section 5 of this Chapter.

3   Routine maintenance: changing the engine oil

1 Unlike previous models, there is no separate engine oil drain plug in the crankcase. Instead, the engine oil is drained by removing the large hexagon-headed cap which houses the oil filter gauze.

2 Refer to the procedure given in *Routine maintenance*, noting the revised torque setting for the oil filter gauze cap in this Chapter's specifications.

4   Routine maintenance: air filter and petrol tap

Cleaning the air filter element – all BR models

1 Although the filter element is still of the oil-damped polyurethane foam type, as found on earlier models, the servicing procedure is slightly modified as follows:

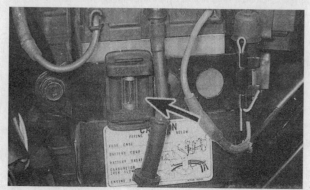

2.2 Modified battery retaining strap – note spare fuse location (arrow)

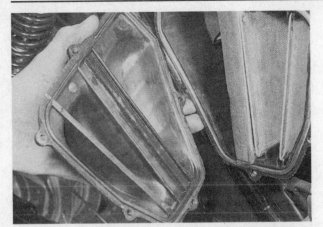

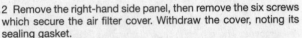

4.2 Air filter cover is retained by six screws – note sealing gasket

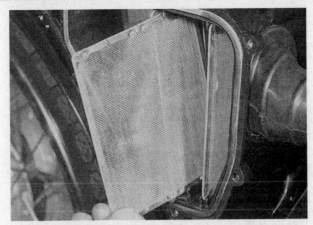

4.3 Note two flame traps – one is fitted next to filter element

2 Remove the right-hand side panel, then remove the six screws which secure the air filter cover. Withdraw the cover, noting its sealing gasket.

3 Note the presence of the two wire mesh flame traps fitted on the carburettor side of the filter casing; these should be withdrawn and cleaned in a high flash-point solvent. Although they should not get dirty or suffer any damage, they should be checked for the presence of any particles of foreign matter and should be renewed if they are split or torn.

4 The element itself consists of a foam block supported by a two-piece metal frame that slides into a groove in the filter casing, with one of the flame traps. Withdraw the assembly and remove the single retaining screw to separate the component parts.

5 Check the element for splits, tears or severe clogging and renew it if necessary. Clean the element as described in *Routine maintenance* and reassemble the element components. Refit them to the filter casing so that no unfiltered air can leak past, then refit the filter cover, with its sealing gasket, and the side panel.

Cleaning the air filter element – CG125-W and CG125M-1 models

6 Remove the right-hand side panel. Remove the four screws and withdraw the air filter cover and its seal if loose. Pull on the spring clip to release the filter from its housing. Slip the element off its support frame.

7 The foam element is a two piece assembly. Check the foam for splits, tears or severe clogging and renew it if necessary. Clean the element as described in *Routine maintenance* at the beginning of this manual, then refit it to the support frame. Install the filter back into the housing so that the shoulder at the front engages the neck of the carburettor hose, then slide in the spring clip to hold it in place.

8 Ensure the cover seal is in place, then refit the cover and secure it with the four screws. Install the side panel.

Checking the air filter element – CG125ES-4 and ES-7 models

9 Remove the right-hand side panel and the lower panel. Note the air filter housing drain and remove it for cleaning.

4.4a Withdraw element assembly . . .

4.4b . . . and remove single retaining screw to dismantle

4.6a Cover is retained by four screws (arrows)

4.6b Pull out the spring clip to release the filter

4.7 Foam air filter element is in two parts

4.9 Clean the air filter housing drain

4.10a Remove the four screws (arrows) . . .

4.10b . . . and pull out the filter element

10 Remove the four screws, lift off the cover and withdraw the air filter element. Tap the element on a hard surface or blow compressed air through it from the inside to remove any dust. If the element is damaged or heavily soiled, or at the specified service interval, renew the element.

11 Install the element in the housing, ensuring it seats correctly, then install the cover and secure it with the screws. Install the lower panel and the right-hand side panel.

Cleaning the petrol tap filters

12 Switch the tap to the 'Off' position and unscrew the filter bowl from the tap base, then remove the O-ring and filter gauze. Check the condition of the sealing O-ring and renew it if it is seriously compressed, distorted or damaged. Clean the filter gauze using a fine-bristled toothbrush or similar: remove all traces of dirt or debris and renew the gauze if it is split or damaged. Thoroughly clean the filter bowl; if excessive amounts of dirt or water are found in the petrol, follow the procedures in Steps 14 and 15.

13 Fit the filter gauze into the tap, ensuring that it is located correctly, then press the O-ring into place to retain it. Use only a close-fitting ring spanner to tighten the filter bowl, which should be secured by just enough to nip up the O-ring; do not over-tighten it as this will only damage the filter bowl, distort the O-ring and promote fuel leaks. The recommended torque setting is only 0.3 – 0.5 kgf m (2 – 3.5 lbf ft). If any leaks are found in the tap they can be cured only by the renewal of the tap assembly or the defective seal.

14 If excessive amounts of dirt or water are found in the petrol, or if the tap appears to be blocked, first remove tank (see Section 12). Empty the petrol into a clean container and remove the fuel tap by unscrewing its retaining gland nut. Remove the tubular filter gauze from the tap stack pipe, noting the presence of a small spacer and of the sealing O-ring, and clean it using a fine-bristled brush: if the gauze is split, twisted or damaged it

should be renewed. Flush the tank until all traces of dirt or water are removed. The tap cannot be dismantled further and must be renewed as a complete assembly if the lever is leaking or defective in any way. If its passages are blocked, use compressed air to blow them clear.

15 On reassembly, fit a new sealing O-ring if damaged or worn, then fit the spacer and filter gauze onto the stack pipe. Refit the assembly into the tank. Check that the tap is correctly aligned before tightening the gland nut; do not over-tighten the gland nut or its threads may be stripped, necessitating the renewal of the tap.

---

5   Routine maintenance: brakes and drive chain

Checking brake shoe wear – all BR models, CG125-W and CG125M-1 models, rear brake on CG125ES-4 and ES-7 models

1 Brake shoe wear can be checked by applying the brake firmly and looking at the wear indicator marks on the backplate. If the indicator pointer on the camshaft is aligned with, or has moved beyond, the fixed index mark cast on the backplate, the shoes are worn out and must be renewed as a pair.

2 This involves the removal of the wheel from the machine so that the brake components can then be dismantled, cleaned, checked for wear, and reassembled. It is important that moving parts such as the brake camshaft are lubricated with a smear of high melting-point grease on reassembly.

Checking front brake fluid level – CG125ES-4 and ES-7 models

3 Turn the handlebars until the top of the master cylinder reservoir is as level as possible. The fluid level is visible through

4.13a Ensure filter gauze is correctly located on refitting

4.13b Do not over-tighten filter bowl – note sealing O-ring

5.1 Wear indicators are fitted to permit quick check of brake shoe wear

the sightglass in the reservoir body – it must be above the LOWER level line.

4 If the fluid requires topping-up, wrap a rag around the reservoir to ensure any spillage does not come into contact with any painted surfaces, then undo the two cover screws and remove the cover, diaphragm plate and diaphragm. Top-up with new DOT 4 brake fluid until the level is just below the UPPER level line cast on the inside of the reservoir – do not overfill. Ensure that the diaphragm is correctly seated before installing the plate and cover, then tighten the cover screws securely.

5 If the fluid reservoir requires repeated topping-up this is an indication of a fluid leak somewhere in the system, which should be rectified immediately (see Section 36). Check the operation of the brake before riding the motorcycle; if there is evidence of air in the system (spongy feel to the lever) it must be bled as described in Steps 10 to 12.

Checking front brake pad wear – CG125ES-4 and ES-7 models

6 Inspect both brake pads to ensure the friction material is not worn down to the wear limit line – if the pads are dirty, displace the caliper and remove the pads to check them (see Section 36). Check that each pad is worn evenly – if not, the caliper is sticking and must be overhauled (see Section 36).

Checking the front brake hose – CG125ES-4 and ES-7 models

7 Twist and flex the hose while looking for cracks, bulges and seeping fluid. Check extra carefully around the each end of the hose where it connects to the union fittings, as these are common areas for hose failure. Inspect the union fittings for corrosion, cracks or damaged. If any defects are found, renew the hose (see Section 36). Inspect the union connections for leaking fluid. If they leak when tightened to the specified torque setting, unscrew the union bolt and fit new washers.

Brake fluid change and bleeding the brake system – CG125ES-4 and ES-7 models

8 To change the fluid you will need some new DOT 4 brake fluid, a suitable tool for siphoning the old fluid out of the master cylinder reservoir, a length of clear vinyl or plastic hose that fits tightly over the caliper bleed valve, a container partially filled with clean brake fluid, some rags and a spanner to fit the brake caliper bleed valve. Cover the fuel tank and other painted components to prevent damage in the event that brake fluid is spilled.

9 Pull the dust cap off the caliper bleed valve, then attach one end of the clear vinyl or plastic hose to the valve and submerge the other end in the brake fluid in the container. Remove the reservoir cover, diaphragm plate and diaphragm and siphon the old fluid out of the reservoir. Fill the reservoir with new brake fluid, then carefully pump the brake lever three or four times and hold it in while opening the bleed valve. When the valve is opened, brake fluid will flow out of the caliper into the clear hose and the lever will move toward the handlebars. If there is air in the system there will be air bubbles in the brake fluid coming out of the caliper. Retighten the bleed valve, then release the brake lever gradually. Keep the reservoir topped-up with new fluid at all times or air may enter the system and greatly increase the length of the task.

10 Repeat the process until new fluid can be seen emerging from the bleed valve without any bubbles – old brake fluid is invariably much darker in colour than new fluid, making it easy to see when all old fluid has been expelled from the system. On completion, disconnect the hose, tighten the bleed valve securely and install the dust cap. Top-up the reservoir, install the diaphragm, diaphragm plate and cover, then check the entire system for leaks.

11 Bleeding the brakes is simply the process of removing air from the brake fluid reservoir, the hose and the brake caliper. The procedure and materials are similar to those used for changing the fluid. Remove the reservoir top, diaphragm plate and diaphragm and slowly pump the brake lever a few times, until no air bubbles can be seen floating up from the holes in the bottom of the reservoir. Doing this bleeds the air from the master cylinder end of the line. Loosely refit the reservoir cover.

12 Pull the dust cap off the caliper bleed valve. Attach one end of the clear vinyl or plastic hose to the valve and submerge the other end in the brake fluid in the container. Carefully pump the brake lever three or four times and hold it in while opening the bleed valve. When the valve is opened, brake fluid will flow out of the caliper into the clear hose and the lever will move toward the handlebar. If there is air in the system there should be air bubbles in the brake fluid coming out of the caliper. Retighten

5.3 Brake fluid level must be above the LOWER level line

5.4a Remove the cover, plate and diaphragm . . .

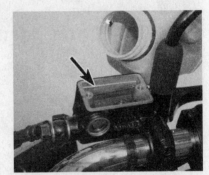

5.4b . . . and top-up to the UPPER level line

5.6 Inspect the brake pad friction material on both sides of the disc

5.9 Set-up for changing the brake fluid and bleeding air from the system

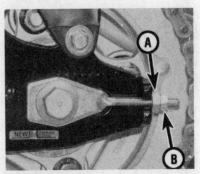

5.14 Chain adjuster nut (A) and locknut (B)

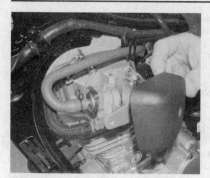

6.1a Remove the PAIR valve cover

6.1b Check the hoses on the front . . .

6.1c . . . and rear of the valve assembly

the bleed valve, then release the brake lever. Top-up the reservoir and repeat the process until no air bubbles are visible in the brake fluid leaving the caliper and the lever is firm when applied. On completion, disconnect the hose, then tighten the bleed valve securely and install the dust cap.

13 Check the operation of the brake before riding the motorcycle.

Final drive chain adjustment – CG125-W, CG125M-1, CG125ES-4 and ES-7 models

14 Follow the procedure in the 'Monthly' section of *Routine maintenance* at the beginning of this manual noting that the specified freeplay is 10 to 20 mm. Note also that the chain adjuster drawbolt locknuts must be backed off a couple of turns before making adjustment, then tightened against the adjusting nuts once the chain freeplay is correct.

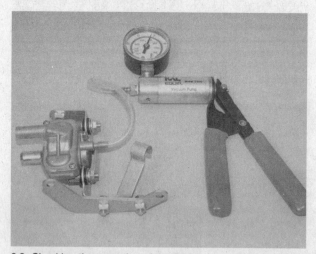

6.2 Checking the operation of the PAIR valve with a vacuum gauge

6　Routine maintenance: checking the secondary air supply system – CG125ES-4 and ES-7 models

1 Remove the petrol tank (see Section 12) then remove the cover from the pulse secondary air (PAIR) valve. Check the hoses between the PAIR valve and the cylinder head cover and the air filter housing, and the vacuum hose between the PAIR valve and the inlet stub. If they are damaged or deteriorated renew them; if the clips are corroded or loose fit, new ones.

2 If the valve is thought to be faulty, disconnect the hoses, then undo the two mounting bolts and remove it. First blow into the air filter housing hose union and ensure that air comes out the cylinder head cover hose union – the valve is open. Now apply a vacuum to the inlet stub hose union (specified vacuum 40 mmHg) and check that the valve has closed. If the valve does not function as described, or if it will not hold the vacuum, replace it with a new one.

3 To inspect the reed valve, undo the two screws and remove the cover, then lift out the reed valve, noting which way round it fits. If required, clean any carbon or gum off the reed and stopper plate with a suitable solvent, taking care not to distort the reed. Inspect the rubber seat – if it is damaged or deteriorated, renew the reed assembly. Hold the reed assembly up to the light and check that there is no gap between the reed and the seat. Ensure the reed assembly is installed the correct way round and tighten the cover screws securely.

7　Routine maintenance: checking the side stand

1 Examine the side stand for cracks or bending, and lubricate the pivot with a multi-purpose or graphite grease. The side stand pivots about a single shouldered bolt; check that its retaining nut is securely fastened. Check the return spring and renew it, if weak or strained: if the pivot is correctly lubricated and the spring sufficiently strong, a pull of 2 – 3 kg (4.4 – 6.6 lb) as measured with a spring balance hooked on to the stand foot,

6.3a Remove the cover . . .

6.3b . . . then lift out the reed valve noting how it fits

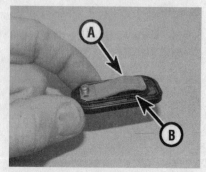

6.3c Note the arrangement of the stopper plate (A) and reed (B)

7.2 Side stand rubber pad must be renewed when worn to limit mark shown by arrow

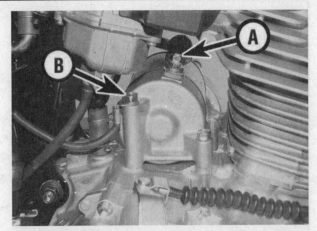

9.1 Disconnect the leads from the starter motor terminal (A) and rear mounting bolt (B)

should be required to retract the stand when it is in the 'down position (machine supported on centre stand).

2 Inspect the rubber pad on the side stand for wear, if it is worn down to or past the wear mark, it should be renewed. Renew with a pad marked 'Below 259 lb only'.

8 Compression test: all models

1 At regular intervals it is useful to check the compression pressure to gain some idea of the degree of engine wear that has taken place; if engine performance is faulty the compression test can be a useful diagnostic aid.

2 Engine compression pressure is tested using a compression gauge with an adapter suitable for a 12 mm spark plug thread. The engine must be fully warmed up, with the valve clearances accurately set and all cylinder head retaining nuts tightened to the correct torque settings. Open fully the throttle twistgrip and turn the engine over several times, noting the values recorded by the gauge.

3 If the readings obtained are significantly lower than those shown in the Specifications section of Chapter 1 (or of this Chapter – CG125-W, CG125M-1, CG125ES-4 and CG125ES-7 models), the engine is excessively worn and must be stripped for repair. The areas of wear are the piston/cylinder group, the head gasket, or the valves. The piston/cylinder group can be checked by removing the gauge, pouring a small amount of oil into the cylinder bore, then repeating the test. If the pressure recorded is significantly increased, the piston, piston rings or cylinder barrel are at fault; if the pressure remains unchanged, the head gasket or valves are faulty.

4 In the rare event of a pressure being recorded that is higher than that specified, this can be due only to an excessive build-up of carbon in the combustion chamber, which must be removed to restore full engine performance. However since it is extremely unlikely that an engine will run for long enough to build

up such excessive deposits without a proportionate amount of mechanical wear taking place, the cause of such an excessive build-up must be established and rectified.

9 Engine and clutch: modifications

Removing the engine/gearbox unit – CG125M-1, CG125ES-4 and CG125ES-7 models

1 Once the carburettor has been displaced, disconnect the lead from the starter motor terminal and disconnect the earth terminal from the rear starter motor mounting bolt.

2 Removes the gearchange pedal, then undo the two bolts securing the gearbox sprocket cover and lift off the cover. Note the location of the chain guide plate and remove it.

3 On CG125ES-4 and ES-7 models, trace the wires from the back of the alternator (left-hand) cover and disconnect them at the two multi-pin connectors. Free the wires from any clips or ties. Remove the PAIR valve from the cylinder head cover (see Section 6). The exhaust pipe is secured to the cylinder head studs by two nuts and a flange – there are no packing pieces behind the flange. The silencer is secured to the passenger footrest bracket by a single nut and bolt. An endless drive chain is fitted – loosen the chain adjuster nuts and the rear wheel spindle nut, then push the wheel forwards to allow the chain to be lifted off the gearbox sprocket. There is no upper engine mounting bolt connecting the cylinder head to the frame.

Cylinder head/rocker arms – CG125 BR-S/T

4 When removing and refitting the cylinder head, refer to Sections 7 and 39 of Chapter 1 noting the following differences:

a) Dowels are fitted to the two outer bolts of the rocker arm support bracket (see Fig. 7.1).

b) The pushrod guide bracket is no longer fitted.

c) As the cylinder head is lifted away, make note of the exact

9.2a Remove the sprocket cover . . .

9.2b . . . and remove the chain guide plate

9.3 Disconnect the multi-pin connectors as described

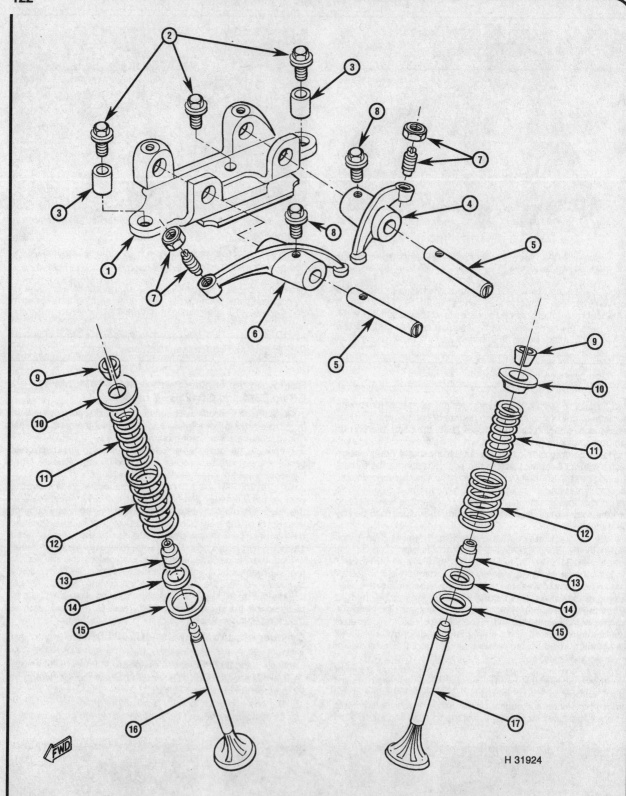

Fig. 7.1 Rocker arms and valves – CG125 BR-S/T models

1 Support bracket
2 Bolts
3 Dowels
4 Inlet rocker arm
5 Rocker arm shafts
6 Exhaust rocker arm
7 Valve clearance adjusters
8 Retaining bolts
9 Collets
10 Upper spring seats
11 Inner valve springs
12 Outer valve springs
13 Oil seals
14 Inner spring lower seats
15 Outer spring lower seats
16 Exhaust valve
17 Inlet valve

H 31924

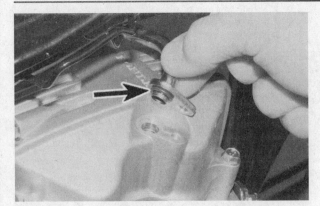

9.10a Note the O-ring on the pipe-to-cover joint

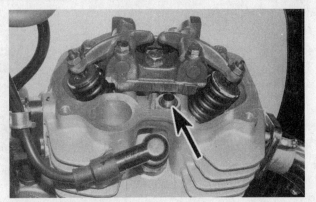

9.10b Note the O-ring and dowel in the top of the cylinder head

positions of any dowels fitted to the cylinder head studs and also whether there is an O-ring around the rear right-hand stud dowel, which is the oil feed line to the rocker assembly.

5 Note that the rocker arm assembly can be dismantled on these models, and individual replacement parts obtained if wear of the rockers or their shafts has occurred. Work on one rocker at a time to avoid interchanging the parts.

6 Remove the bolt which retains the shaft in the support bracket and slide out the shaft and rocker. Examine the shaft outside surface and rocker arm inside surface, plus the arm's contact point with the pushrod for wear. If the measuring equipment is available measure the rocker arm ID and shaft OD and compare them with the service limits given in the Specifications at the beginning of this Chapter.

7 When installing the rocker assembly, apply engine oil to the inside bore of the rocker arm, then slide the shaft through the support bracket and rocker arm so that the shaft hole aligns with the bolt hole; the slot in the end of the shaft should be vertical. Install the bolt and tighten it to the specified torque setting.

Cylinder head – CG125-W and CG125M-1

8 When removing and refitting the cylinder head refer to Sections 7 and 39 of Chapter 1, noting that there are two dowels between the cylinder head and barrel, fitted to the front left-hand stud and rear right-hand stud. The pushrod guide bracket is no longer fitted. On CG125-W models, check whether there is an O-ring fitted around the right-hand rear stud dowel (which is the oil feed line to the rocker assembly) and if so, ensure the O-ring is renewed on refitting.

9 On CG125M-1 models, dowels are fitted to the two outer bolts of the rocker arm support bracket (see Fig. 7.1). The rocker arm assembly can be dismantled on these models, and individual replacement parts obtained if wear of the rockers or their shafts has occurred (see Steps 6 and 7).

Cylinder head – CG125ES-4 and ES-7 models

10 When removing and refitting the cylinder head cover, first remove the PAIR valve (see Section 6). Undo the two bolts securing the pipe to the cylinder head cover and lift it off, noting the O-ring. Remove the three cover bolts and lift off the cover, noting the dowel and O-ring on the right-hand side of the cylinder head.

11 When removing and refitting the cylinder head, refer to Sections 7 and 39 of Chapter 1 noting the following differences:
  a) Dowels are fitted to the two outer bolts of the rocker arm support bracket (see Fig. 7.1).
  b) The pushrod guide bracket is no longer fitted.
  c) As the cylinder head is lifted away, note the dowel on the front left-hand cylinder head stud and the rear right-hand stud.

12 Note that the rocker arm assembly can be dismantled on these models, and individual replacement parts obtained if wear of the rockers or their shafts has occurred (see Steps 6 and 7). Tighten the rocker arm shaft bolts to the specified torque setting.

Valves – CG125 BR-S/T, CG125ES-4 and CG125ES-7 models

13 These models have a valve stem seal on each valve, not just the exhaust valve as on all other models. See Fig. 7.1.

14 On CG125ES-4 and ES-7 models, only one valve spring per valve is fitted.

Piston – all models

15 Note that the piston crown marking mentioned in Chapter 1, Section 39 is either AD or IN. Its purpose is the same; to identify the (larger) inlet valve cutaway which must face to the rear of the engine on reassembly.

Generator/alternator assembly – CG125 BR-S/T, CG125-W, CG125M-1, CG125ES-4 and CG125ES-7 models

16 Refer to the procedures in Section 41.

Cam gear and shaft – CG125M-1, CG125ES-4 and CG125ES-7 models

17 Refer to the procedures in Chapter 1 in this Chapter and remove the cylinder head, cylinder barrel and alternator rotor. The cam gear shaft is retained by a stopper plate; undo the bolt and remove the stopper plate, noting how it locates against the end of the shaft, then remove the small spring. Draw out the shaft, noting the O-ring, and lift out the cam gear. There is no thrust washer fitted to the shaft.

18 The cam gear is a two-piece spring-loaded assembly. To

9.17a Remove the stopper plate . . .

9.17b . . . and lift out the small spring

9.17c Draw out the shaft and lift out the cam gear

9.18a Remove the circlip and thrust washer (arrow)

9.18b Note how the pin locates in the hole (arrow)

9.19 Ensure the cam gear and crankshaft gear are fully meshed

9.21a Note slightly modified clutch release arm – extract roll pin to permit removal

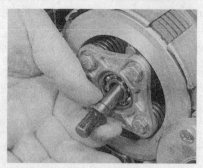

9.21b Clutch pushrod is now one-piece

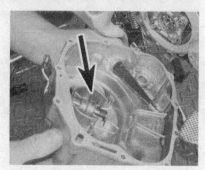

9.22   Note the location of the clutch pushrod inside the cover

renew the inner spring, first remove the circlip and thrust washer, then lift off the outer gear half – note how the pin in the gear locates in the hole in the end of the spring. On reassembly, align the pin and hole in the spring by inserting a screwdriver between the teeth of the two gear halves, then secure the assembly with the thrust washer and circlip.

19 On installation, follow the procedure in Section 41 and remove crankshaft oil seal holder to ensure the timing marks on the outer cam gear and crankshaft gear are aligned, then use a screwdriver to align the two halves of the cam gear so that the cam gear and crankshaft gear are fully meshed. Press the shaft into position. Install the small spring and stopper plate, ensuring the plate aligns correctly with the end of the shaft, then tighten the plate bolt securely.

Centrifugal oil filter

20 Follow the procedure in Chapter 1, Sections 10 and 36, noting that the part number for the Honda service tool has changed to 07716-0020100 for BR-E/F, BR-J, BR-K, W, M-1 and ES-4 models, and to 07716-0020400 for BR-S/T models. Note that no kickstarter is fitted to CG125ES-4 and ES-7 models.

Clutch – all BR and CG125-W models

21 The clutch release mechanism is very slightly modified on all BR models (see the accompanying photographs). On all BR models and the CG125-W, the four bolts which retain the clutch pressure plate are flanged and thus do not have plain washers under their heads.

Clutch – CG125M-1, CG125ES-4 and ES-7 models

22 The clutch pushrod is located in the crankcase right-hand cover.

23 The clutch is fitted with an anti-judder spring assembly. Follow the procedure in Chapter 1, Section 12, and remove the clutch thrust plate, springs and outer half of the clutch centre. There are no washers under the heads of the clutch pressure plate bolts. The anti-judder spring seat and spring may remain on the clutch centre or they may be inside the outer clutch friction plate. The spring seat locates against the clutch centre and the raised centre of the spring locates against the seat. Inspect the components for wear or fatigue and renew them if necessary. Note that the internal diameter of the outer friction plate is larger than the other friction plates. On CG125ES-4 and

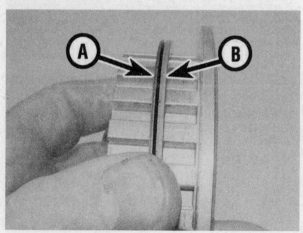

9.23a Location of the anti-judder spring (A) and spring seat (B)

9.23b Note the larger internal diameter of the outer friction plate

ES-7 models, the service limit for the outer plate is thicker than for the other friction plates.

24 On reassembly, ensure that the anti-judder spring and seat are installed the correct way round. Ensure that the clutch pushrod is fitted into the cover before it is installed.

Big-end bearings – CG125ES-7 model

25 Note that the con-rod, crankpin and big-end bearing are no longer available separately from the crankshaft.

Gearbox modification – CG125ES-7 model

26 When dismantling the gearbox layshaft, note that the 2nd gear pinion (item 23 in Fig 1.7 of Chapter 1) now has a removable bush in its centre. There is also a thrust washer between the 2nd and 5th gear pinions on the layshaft.

10 Dismantling and rebuilding the engine/gearbox unit: separating the crankcase halves

1 In Chapter 1 owners are instructed to lift off the crankcase right-hand half, leaving all internal components in the deeper left-hand casing.

2 For later models, work will be found much easier if the crankcase left-hand half is lifted off, leaving all components in the right-hand half. Note that on CG125ES-4 and ES-7 models, no kickstart shaft assembly or associated components are fitted.

3 On reassembly, therefore, mesh together the gearbox clusters and fit them to their bearings in the crankcase right-hand half. Ensure that all thrust washers are refitted and that both shafts rotate freely.

4 Refit the gear selector components as described in Section 11, then refit the kickstart shaft (if appropriate) and crankshaft as described in Chapter 1.

5 Fit a new gasket over the two locating dowels, lubricate all bearings and refit the crankcase left-hand half, following the instructions given in Chapter 1.

11 Gear selector mechanism: general

1 Although generally unchanged the selector mechanism has received a few detail modifications. Refer to Fig. 7.2 for details.

2 On removal, note that the selector fork shaft can be withdrawn as soon as the crankcase halves have been separated. Rotate the forks away from the selector drum, withdraw the drum and then lift out each fork in turn, making notes or marks as required to ensure correct identification of each fork and of which way up it is fitted.

3 On reassembly the right-hand fork should be refitted to the layshaft 3rd gear pinion, with its marking facing upwards (i.e. to the left). The centre fork is fitted to the mainshaft 4th gear pinion. The left-hand fork is fitted to the layshaft 5th gear pinion, with its marking facing downwards (i.e. towards the other forks).

4 Insert the selector drum so that the neutral switch contact aligns with the switch terminal and manoeuvre the fork guide pins into their respective grooves. Lubricate and insert the selector fork shaft, then rotate the drum to check that all gears can be selected, then return to the neutral position.

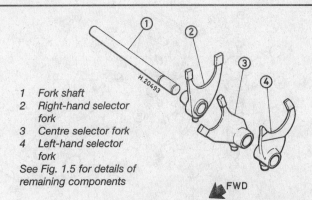

1 Fork shaft
2 Right-hand selector fork
3 Centre selector fork
4 Left-hand selector fork

See Fig. 1.5 for details of remaining components

FWD

Fig. 7.2 Modified gear selector mechanism components

12 Petrol tank: removal and refitting

1 Remove the side panels and seat (see Section 32 of this Chapter).

2 Turn the fuel tap to the OFF position and disconnect the fuel pipe from the tap stub. On CG125ES-4 and ES-7 models, trace the wiring from the fuel level sensor on the underside of the tank and disconnect it at the connector. On all models, remove the bolt with spacer from the tank rear mounting, then pull the tank rearwards and up off the frame.

3 When refitting the tank ensure that the channels in the front of the tank engage fully over the rubbers on the frame; apply a smear of liquid soap or silicone to the rubbers if necessary to help the tank slide into place. Make sure the tank's rear mounting point is settled correctly on the rubber damper, then install the spacer and mounting bolt.

4 Reconnect the fuel pipe to the tap and secure it with the wire clip. Turn the fuel tap ON and check that there are no leaks. On CG125ES-4 and ES-7 models, don't forget to reconnect the fuel level sensor wiring.

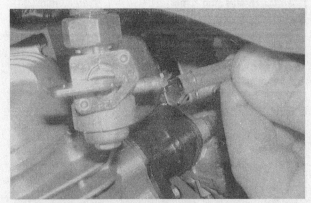

12.2a Pull the fuel pipe off the tap stub

12.2b Petrol tank rear mounting is secured by a single bolt (BR model fitment shown)

12.3a Ensure that the rubber damper is in place . . .

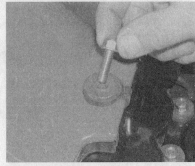

12.3b . . . then fit the spacer and retaining bolt (CG125-W shown)

Fig. 7.3 (T)PFC Carburettor

1 Rubber cover	16 Spring	30 O-ring
2 Cable adjuster	17 Carburettor cover	31 Float bowl
3 Carburettor top	18 Screw - 2 off	32 Drain screw
4 Gasket	19 Accelerator pump bracket	33 O-ring
5 Return spring	20 Screw	34 Screw - 3 off
6 Jet needle assembly	21 Accelerator pump free play	35 Drain pipe
7 Throttle valve	adjuster	36 Clip
8 Carburettor body	22 Accelerator pump cam assembly	37 Spring
9 Needle jet	23 Screw	38 Pump rod/diaphragm
10 Jet holder	24 Retaining plate	39 Rod gaiter
11 Main jet	25 Choke lever	40 Screw- 3 off
12 Pilot jet	26 Float	41 Accelerator pump cover
13 Pilot screw assembly	27 Float needle valve	42 Carburettor heater – CG125-W
14 O-ring	28 Float pivot pin	and M-1
15 Throttle stop screw	29 O-ring	43 Collar – CG125-W and M-1

13 (T)PFC carburettor: removal – CG125-C, E, all BR models, CG125-W and CG125M-1 models

1 Remove the petrol tank. Remove its two retaining screws and withdraw the carburettor cover. Pull the drain tube clear of the engine and frame. Remove the right-hand side panel for extra working space.

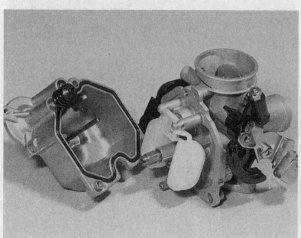

14.1a Float bowl can be removed complete with pump assembly

2 Slacken the screw clamp which secures the air filter hose to the carburettor. Slacken the adjuster locknut and unscrew the accelerator pump cable adjuster from its bracket, then disconnect the cable end nipple from the pump cam. On W models, trace the two wires from the heater unit screwed into the right-hand side of the carburettor body, and disconnect them at the two-pin connector.

3 Unscrew the two bolts securing the inlet stub to the cylinder head, then partially withdraw the carburettor assembly until the carburettor top can be unscrewed and the throttle valve withdrawn.

4 The throttle valve assembly can be dismantled as described in Chapter 2, Section 5.

5 The inlet stub can be detached by removing the two nuts which secure it to the carburettor. Examine the O-rings at each end of the stub; these must be renewed to prevent induction leaks if they are in any way flattened, worn, or damaged.

14 (T)PFC carburettor: overhaul – CG125-C, E, all BR models, CG125-W and CG125M-1 models

1 The float bowl can be detached complete with the accelerator pump diaphragm and rod assembly in place, if required. All other components of the carburettor are the same as the later type of carburettor described in Chapter 2; refer, therefore, to that Chapter for all information unless shown below. Do not disturb the accelerator pump linkage unless absolutely necessary; it is pre-set at the factory and will not require adjustment in normal use unless disturbed.

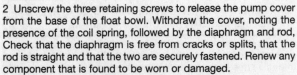

14.1b Do not dismantle accelerator pump linkage unless absolutely necessary

14.2a Pump cover is retained by three screws – note coil spring and valve in centre of cover

2 Unscrew the three retaining screws to release the pump cover from the base of the float bowl. Withdraw the cover, noting the presence of the coil spring, followed by the diaphragm and rod, Check that the diaphragm is free from cracks or splits, that the rod is straight and that the two are securely fastened. Renew any component that is found to be worn or damaged.

3 Remove the float bowl as described in Chapter 2 and examine the rod gaiter; renew it if it is split or damaged.

4 There are two spring-loaded one-way ball valves in the pump system. The first is situated in the pump feed, in the centre of the pump cover, while the second is on the delivery side, screwed into the float bowl mating surface. Always dismantle these two valves separately to avoid any risk of interchanging components. Each is removed by unscrewing the jet, whereupon the coil spring and ball can be tipped out. Blow clear the passageways with compressed air, clean the valve components in petrol and

reassemble. Note the springs should be fitted inside the jets before the jets are screwed into place.

5 If the pump linkage must be dismantled, slacken the adjuster locknut and unscrew the adjuster screw until the pump cam arm is released, then remove its retaining screw and withdraw the bracket. The components can then be withdrawn, noting carefully how each engages with the other and with the return spring. Renew any component that is worn or damaged.

6 On reassembling the linkage lubricate all bearing surfaces with molybdenum disulphide-based grease. When all components are in place check the pump operation to ensure correct installation and smooth return under spring pressure. Use the cam arm adjuster to eliminate all clearance between the cam and arm, and between the arm and rod as a preliminary setting for final adjustment (see Section 16).

7 As described above, all other carburettor components are

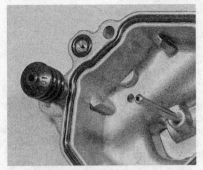

14.2b Check pump diaphragm for splits and rod for straightness

14.3 Check that rod gaiter is undamaged – note pump delivery valve in gasket surface

14.4a Carefully clean components of pump one-way valves . . .

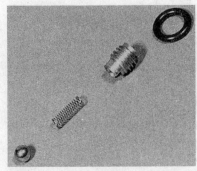

14.4b . . . and be careful not to mix them up – note sealing O-ring fitted to delivery valve

14.5 If linkage must be dismantled note how components are fitted before removal

14.6 Use cam arm adjuster to eliminate clearance on reassembly – initial setting

14.7a Carburettor jets are the same as earlier models – note removable pilot jet

14.7b Check choke assembly is correct – note simple detent mechanism

serviced according to the instructions given in Chapter 2. On reassembly, fit all components in the reverse of the dismantling procedure, noting the general instructions given in Chapter 2.

8 A modified main jet and needle jet are fitted to CG125 BR-J models from frame number 8107614 to cure poor running as a result of hesitation at certain throttle positions. If this problem is experienced on earlier CG125 BR models it is possible to fit the later components (see specifications) which are available from an authorised Honda dealer.

9 On W models the carburettor heater can be unscrewed from the body if required. Note its collar.

15   (T)PFC carburettor: refitting – CG125-C, E, all BR models, CG125-W and CG125M-1 models

1 Refit the throttle valve assembly ensuring that the groove in the valve engages with the locating pin set in the carburettor body, and that the needle enters correctly into the jet, then tighten the carburettor top securely. Check that the valve opens and closes smoothly.

2 Ensuring that new sealing O-rings are used if necessary, refit the inlet stub to the carburettor and the carburettor assembly to the cylinder head. Tighten the mounting nuts and bolts securely, but do not overtighten them.

3 Connect the accelerator pump cable end nipple to the pump cam, then fit the cable adjuster to the bracket. Refit the air filter hose and tighten its clamp screw securely. Refit the right-hand side panel. Route the drain tube correctly to the rear of the engine/gearbox unit. Reconnect the carburettor heater wires (W model). Refit the petrol tank.

4 Check that the throttle and accelerator cables are adjusted with reasonable accuracy, but leave them slightly slack until final adjustment, as described in the next Section.

16   (T)PFC carburettor: adjustment – CG125-C, E, all BR models, CG125-W and CG125M-1 models

1 The procedure for setting the float height, idle mixture setting and idle speed are exactly as described in Chapter 2, but note the different settings specified in this Chapter. Note also that if a plastic float assembly is fitted the float height can be corrected only by renewing the faulty component; no adjustment is possible.

2 To adjust the throttle cable, note that the twistgrip adjuster should be used to eliminate slack from the upper cable (twistgrip to junction box) while the carburettor top adjuster (where fitted) is used to eliminate slack from the lower cable.

Note that individual machines will vary considerably due to production tolerances in cable component length and to the different rates of 'stretch' that must be expected; correct adjustment, therefore, may well be obtained only by using both adjusters to achieve a compromise setting. This is simplified on later models which have only the twistgrip adjuster. The throttle cable must have 2 – 6 mm (0.08 – 0.24 in) free play measured in terms of twistgrip rotation. When the throttle cable is correctly set, tighten the (twistgrip) adjuster locknut, refit the rubber sleeve over both adjusters and check that the idle speed remains steady after the throttle has been opened and closed several times, and at all handlebar positions.

3 When the idle speed and throttle cable setting are correct, adjust the accelerator cable so that the reference mark etched in the pump cam aligns exactly with the index mark cut in the linkage bracket when the throttle is fully open (engine switched off). Tighten the locknut and re-check the setting. Set the required amount of free play in the pump linkage by slackening its adjuster locknut and screwing the adjuster screw in through ½ to 1 turn while holding the adjuster holding nut steady. Retain

16.1 If float assembly is one-piece plastic item, incorrect float height can be cured only by renewing worn components

16.2a Presence of junction block may complicate throttle cable adjustment

16.2b Adjusting idle speed – throttle stop screw is reached via hole in cover

16.3 With throttle fully open, marks on pump linkage cam and bracket should align

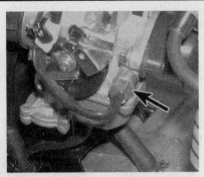

18.1a Carburettor heater unit (arrow) . . .

18.1b . . . and thermoswitch (arrow)

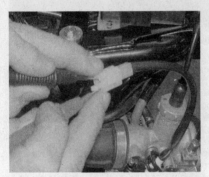

18.2 Heater unit test

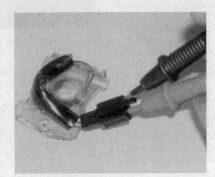

18.3 Thermoswitch test

19.1 Note tachometer drive worm – not used on UK models

the setting while the locknut is tightened securely, then refit the carburettor cover. Check the correct operation of the pump linkage.

4 Note that if the carburettor has been completely dismantled the pump passages may require priming before they function normally, and that they may, therefore, take some time to fill after the machine has been started and run for the first time.

17 Carburettor: CG125ES-4 and ES-7 models

1 The procedure for removing and installing the carburettor is the same as for the pre (T)PFC type described in Chapter 2, Section 5 (see Fig. 2.2). Note that this carburettor has a heater – remove the heater cover on the right-hand side and disconnect the two wires.

2 To detach the jet needle from the throttle valve, turn the jet needle holder anti-clockwise, then lift out the holder, small spring and jet needle. Ensure that the small spring is installed on reassembly and turn the needle holder clockwise until it is felt to click into place.

3 Carburettor overhaul is the same as described in Chapter 2, with reference to the Specifications at the beginning of this Chapter. If required, the carburettor heater can be unscrewed from the body – note its collar wiring terminal.

4 Note that since a plastic float assembly is fitted the float height can be corrected only by renewing the faulty component; no adjustment is possible.

18 Carburettor heater: location and testing – CG125-W, CG125M-1, CG125ES-4 and CG125ES-7 models

1 An electrical heater element is fitted to the right-hand side of the carburettor body. Its purpose is to warm the carburettor body when temperatures are low and thus prevent carburettor

icing. A thermostatically operated switch mounted either under the petrol tank or the seat controls the switching of the heater.

2 To test the heater, on CG125-W and CG125M-1 models, trace the wires from the heater to the 2-pin connector and disconnect it. Using a test meter set to the ohms x 100 range, connect its probes to the yellow/brown and brown/black wires on the heater side of the connector and measure the resistance. On CG125ES-4 and ES-7 models, disconnect the wires from the heater terminals and connect the meter probes across the terminals. Compare the result to the Specifications at the beginning of this Chapter. If the reading differs widely from the specification, especially if an open circuit (high resistance) is indicated, the heater is faulty and must be renewed.

3 To test the thermo switch, trace the wires from the switch to the 2-pin connector and disconnect it. Using a test meter set to the ohms x 100 range, connect its probes to the terminals on the switch side of the connector. At normal temperature (approx. 20°C/68°F) the meter should indicate no continuity (high, infinite resistance). If continuity is shown at this temperature the thermo switch is faulty and must be renewed.

4 Pack the thermo switch in ice and make the same test at 7°C/45°F, or lower. At this temperature the thermo switch will have closed and continuity should be indicated on the meter. If no continuity is indicated, the thermo switch has failed and should be renewed.

19 Oil pump: general

On servicing the oil pump, note that on some models a tachometer worm drive has been incorporated in the assembly. The drive fits into an extended housing and replaces the pump spindle shown in Chapters 1 and 2; however, servicing procedures remain the same. When checking the oil pump note the additional Specifications in this Chapter, as well as those given in Chapter 2.

20 Condenser: general – CG125 BR-E/F, BR-J and BR-K models

Note that while the condenser is mounted as described in Chapter 3, it is no longer listed as a separate item and can only be purchased (as a genuine Honda replacement part) as part of the ignition HT coil assembly.

21 Ignition system: general description – CG125 BR-S/T, CG125-W, CG125M-1, CG125ES-4 and CG125ES-7 models

1 These models have a fully electronic CDI (Capacitor Discharge Ignition) system. The system dispenses with the contact breaker arrangement used previously and, with the exception of regular spark plug checks, is virtually maintenance-free.
2 The CDI system comprises an ignition source coil built into the generator stator, a pick-up coil mounted next to the generator rotor, the CDI unit itself which is mounted under the left-hand side panel on S/T models and under the petrol tank on all other models, the ignition HT coil and the spark plug. The CDI unit is powered from the ignition source coil. As the crankshaft rotates, a trigger on the generator rotor periphery induces a current in the pick-up coil each time it passes the coil. The signal in the pick-up coil is passed to the CDI unit which then provides the necessary power to the ignition coil to provide a spark at the plug at precisely the correct time. The CDI unit contains in-built circuitry to advance the spark in relation to engine speed, thus obviating the need for a mechanical means of advance. Note that on CG125M-1, CG125ES-4 amd CG125ES-7 models, the CDI unit performs additional tasks and is more correctly termed the ignition control module (ICM).
3 Because of its lack of moving parts, there are no regular checks required of the ignition system. The only exception to this is the spark plug, which should be cleaned/re-gapped and renewed at the specified service intervals.

22 Ignition system: testing – CG125 BR-S/T and CG125-W models

1 If an ignition fault is suspected, first check that there is a spark at the plug. Pull the HT lead off the spark plug and connect it to a known good spark plug. Lay the spark plug on the cylinder head, with the threads of the plug in contact with the engine. It is important that the plug is earthed against the engine, otherwise the ignition system components could be damaged if they are isolated when checking for a spark. Don't hold the spark plug with your fingers, use a tool with insulated handles if the plug needs to be held in position.
2 Turn the ignition ON and operate the kickstarter whilst watching for a spark at the plug. If the ignition is in good condition a regular, fat blue spark should be evident at the plug electrodes. If the spark is thin or yellowish, or is non-existent, further investigation will be required.

20.1 Condenser location – not listed as a separate part

3 The ignition timing can be checked, but not adjusted. Run the engine until it reaches normal operating temperature, then turn the ignition OFF. Refer to Section 41 and remove the engine left-hand cover. Connect a stroboscopic timing light to the engine, then start the engine and aim the timing light at the timing marks on the top of the generator rotor. At idle speed the line next to the F on the rotor should align with the cut-out in the stator plate. Gradually increase the engine speed up to 4500 rpm (only hold it at this speed briefly) and observe the rotor marking in relation to the cut-out. If the ignition system is advancing correctly, the two scribed lines on the rotor should now align with the cut-out. Stop the engine and disconnect the timing light when the check is complete. There is no provision for timing adjustment, but any deviation from the specified settings indicates a problem with the CDI unit.
4 Ignition faults can be divided into two categories, namely those where the ignition system has failed completely, and those which are due to a partial failure. The likely faults are listed below, starting with the most probable source of failure. Work through the list systematically, referring to the relevant sub-sections for test procedures.
  a) Faulty spark plug. Clean and re-gap or renew the plug.
  b) Loose, corroded or damaged wiring connections, broken or shorted wiring between the ignition system components.
  c) Faulty ignition switch.
  d) Faulty ignition HT coil, HT lead or spark plug cap.
  e) Faulty ignition source coil.
  f) Faulty ignition pick-up coil.
  g) Faulty CDI unit.
5 If the fault cannot be traced by carrying out the following procedures, refer to a Honda dealer equipped with a peak voltage tester. This equipment will enable the system components to be tested under load.

Ignition switch test

6 Make sure that the ignition switch is OFF, then remove the left-hand side panel and disconnect the battery negative lead. This

22.1 Checking for a spark

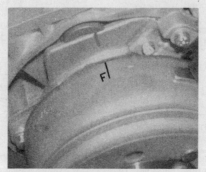

22.3a Timing mark at idle speed

22.3b Full advance timing marks

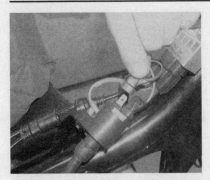

22.11a Disconnect the two primary wires from the HT coil

22.11b HT coil is retained by a single bolt – note the earth connection

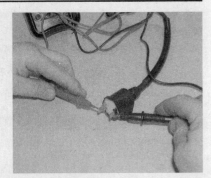

22.12 Primary winding test

is important to prevent the risk of short circuits when testing the ignition switch.

7 Trace the ignition switch wiring from the base of the instruments to the multi-connector (BR-S/T models) or the single connectors (W models) and disconnect the black, black/white, green and red wires; the connector(s) will be located either inside the headlamp shell or along the frame top tube under the petrol tank. Make the following tests on the switch side of the wire connectors.

8 Using a multimeter set to the resistance or continuity test range, or a continuity tester, connect its probes between the black/white and green wire terminals; continuity should be indicated when the ignition key is in the OFF position and no continuity when turned to the ON position. Now connect the probes between the black and red wire terminals; continuity should be indicated when the ignition key is in the ON position and no continuity when turned to the OFF position.

9 If the switch does not function as described and the fault is not due to corroded or damaged wiring or connectors, the switch should be renewed.

Ignition HT coil test

10 Remove the petrol tank (see Section 12).

11 Disconnect the two wires from the coil having taken note of which terminals they connect to; the coil terminals should be colour-coded to match the wire colour. Pull the spark plug cap off the spark plug. Free the HT lead from its clip, then remove the coil's mounting bolt and move the HT coil to the bench for testing.

12 Using a multimeter set to the ohms x 1 scale, measure the resistance across the coil's two primary terminals. Compare the

reading with the primary resistance specified at the beginning of this Chapter. Disconnect the test meter.

13 Switch the multimeter to the K-ohms range and connect one probe to the terminal inside the plug cap and the other probe to one of the coil's primary terminals. Compare the reading with the secondary resistance specified at the beginning of this Chapter. Now unscrew the plug cap from the HT lead and make the same test, but this time connecting the probe to the end of the HT lead. Again compare the value obtained with that given in the specifications. Disconnect the test meter and screw the plug cap back onto the lead.

14 If the primary or secondary readings differ widely from that specified the coil is most likely faulty. If the secondary resistance was inside the specified figure with the plug cap removed yet incorrect with it fitted, then only the plug cap requires renewal.

15 When refitting the coil, take care that the primary wires are connected to their original terminals, and that the earth lead is secured by the coil mounting bolt.

Ignition source coil test

16 Make sure the ignition is switched off. Remove the left-hand side panel and locate the wiring connectors from the generator which will be under a plastic sleeve. Disconnect the 6-pin multi-connector and the single connector on the black/red wire.

17 Using a multimeter set to the ohms x 100 scale, connect its probes between the black/red and green wire pins on the generator side of the connector. If the coil is in good condition the reading should be within the range given in the specifications at the beginning of this Chapter. If infinite resistance is indicated (i.e. no continuity) the coil is open-circuit, however check first that the wiring is sound between the connector and generator

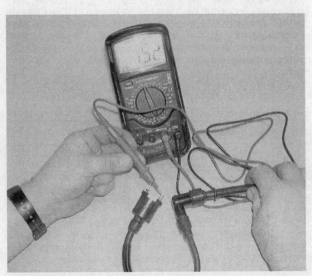

22.13a Secondary winding test with cap in place

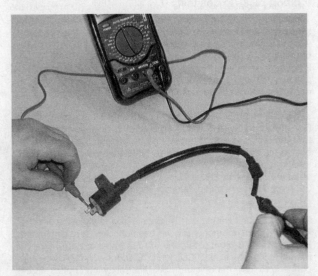

22.13b Secondary winding test without cap

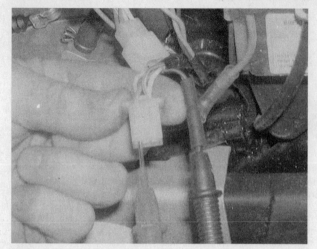

22.17 Source coil resistance test

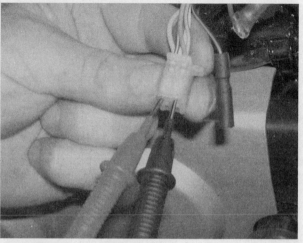

22.20 Pick-up coil resistance test

22.22a CDI unit location (BR-S/T models)

22.22b CDI unit location (W model)

before the coil is confirmed faulty. Note that the source coil is integral with the generator stator and cannot be obtained as a separate part.

18 If renewal is required, refer to Section 41.

Ignition pick-up coil test

19 Make sure the ignition is switched off. Remove the left-hand side panel and locate the wiring connectors from the generator which will be under a plastic sleeve. Disconnect the 6-pin multi-connector.

20 Using a multimeter set to the ohms x 100 scale, connect its probes between the blue/yellow and green wire pins on the generator side of the connector. If the coil is in good condition the reading should be within the range given in the specifications at the beginning of this Chapter. If infinite resistance is indicated (i.e. no continuity) the coil is open-circuit, however check first that the wiring is sound between the connector and generator before the coil is confirmed faulty. Note that the pick-up coil is sold as an assembly with the generator stator and cannot be obtained as a separate part.

21 If renewal is required, refer to Section 41.

CDI unit test

22 The CDI unit should only be considered faulty once all other ignition system components have been checked and eliminated. Remove the left-hand side panel (S/T models) or petrol tank (W model) to access the CDI unit. Disconnect the two wire connectors from the unit and make the following checks on the wiring harness side of these connectors.

23 With the ignition OFF and the meter set to the ohms x 100

range, connect its probes between the black/red and green wires; 300 to 700 ohms should be indicated (i.e. the source coil value). Now connect the probes between the blue/yellow and green wires; 180 to 280 ohms should be indicated (i.e. the pick-up coil value). Reset the meter to the ohms x 1 range and connect its probes between the black/yellow and green wires; 0.18 to 0.24 ohm should be shown (i.e. the ignition HT coil primary value).

24 Finally, use the multimeter or a continuity tester to check that continuity exists between the green wire and earth (i.e. the frame).

25 If the results to all checks are satisfactory, yet the ignition system still malfunctions, the CDI unit is probably faulty.

23 Ignition system: testing – CG125M-1 models

1 The procedure for testing the ignition system is the same as for previous models as described in Section 22, noting that if the electric starter is used the battery and starter system components must be in good working order (see Sections 51 and 53).

2 The alternator is of a different design to that fitted to earlier models. To check to ignition timing, follow the procedure in Section 24. Also note that the wiring connectors for the alternator charging and ignition systems are separate – refer to the appropriate wiring diagram at the end of this Chapter.

3 To confirm the peak voltage ignition system specifications at the beginning of this Chapter you will require either

an Imrie diagnostic tester or a digital multimeter (impedance 10 M-ohms/DCV minimum) together with a peak voltage adapter (Honda service tool part number 07HGJ-0020100). The procedure for these tests is described in Section 24.

24 Ignition system: testing – CG125ES-4 and ES-7 models

Note: *to confirm the peak voltage ignition system specifications at the beginning of this Chapter you will require either an Imrie diagnostic tester or a digital multimeter (impedance 10 M-ohms/DCV minimum) together with a peak voltage adapter (Honda service tool part number 07HGJ-0020100).*

1 The procedure for testing the spark plug is the same as for previous models as described in Section 22, noting that if the machine's battery must be fully charged and the electric starter system components must be in good working order (see Sections 51 and 53).

2 The ignition timing can be checked, but not adjusted. Run the engine until it reaches normal operating temperature, then turn the ignition OFF. Unscrew the timing inspection plug from the engine left-hand cover. The timing mark on the alternator rotor which indicates the firing point at idle speed is a line with the letter F above it. The static timing mark with which this should align is the notch in the top of the timing inspection hole. Connect a stroboscopic timing light to the engine, then start the engine and aim the timing light at the static timing mark. At idle speed the line next to the F on the rotor should align with the static timing mark. Stop the engine and disconnect the timing light when the check is complete. There is no provision for timing adjustment, consequently any deviation from the specified setting indicates a problem with one of the ignition system components .

3 Refer to the list of ignition faults in Section 22 and work through the relevant procedures as described below.

Ignition and starter switch test

4 Make sure that the ignition switch is OFF, then remove the left-hand side panel and disconnect the battery negative lead. Remove the headlamp from its shell, then trace the wiring from the switch and disconnect it at the connector. Using an ohmmeter or continuity tester, test for continuity between the connector terminals (see *Wiring diagrams* at the end of this Chapter). Continuity should exist between the terminals connected by a solid line on the diagram when the switch is in the indicated position. Use the same procedure for testing the starter switch.

5 If the switch does not function as described and the fault is not due to corroded or damaged wiring or connectors, the switch should be renewed.

Ignition HT coil primary peak voltage test

6 Ensure that the machine's battery is fully charged. Pull the HT lead off the spark plug and connect it to a known good spark plug. Lay the spark plug on the cylinder head, with the threads of the plug in contact with the engine as in the spark test. Remove the left-hand side panel. Connect the negative (-) test equipment probe to the HT coil black/yellow wire terminal and the positive (+) probe to earth. Ensure that the transmission is in

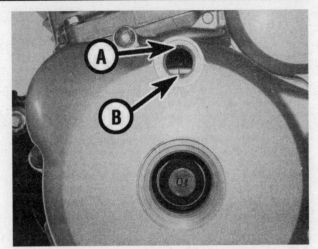

24.2 Static timing mark (A) and F mark on rotor (B)

neutral and turn the ignition ON. Turn the engine over on the starter motor and note the peak voltage. If the result is lower than the standard value, either the ignition coil or the ignition control module (ICM) is faulty. The only way to confirm a component fault is to substitute a known good component.

7 If no peak voltage is recorded, check for a loose connector at the ICM, a damaged red/black wire between the ICM, the ignition switch and the fuse box, or a damaged green wire between the ICM and earth. Test the ignition pick-up coil. If all the components are good, it is likely that the ICM is faulty.

8 If the peak voltage is correct but there is no spark at the plug, then either the HT lead, plug cap or the ignition coil is at fault.

Ignition pick-up coil peak voltage test

9 Ensure that the machine's battery is fully charged. Remove the petrol tank and disconnect the ICM wiring connector. Connect the positive (+) test equipment probe to the blue/yellow wire terminal in the connector and the negative (-) probe to earth. Ensure that the transmission is in neutral and turn the ignition ON. Turn the engine over on the starter motor and note the peak voltage. If the result differs from the standard value, first check the wiring between the ICM connector and the alternator connector. If the wiring is good it is likely that the pick-up coil is faulty – the pick-up coil is integral with the alternator stator and is not available as a separate item (see Section 41).

25 Handlebar: mountings

When installing the handlebars, align the handlebar punch marks with the upper edge of the top yoke mounting, then fit the clamps with their punch-marked ends to the front. Tighten the front clamp bolts first, to the specified torque setting, then tighten the rear clamp bolts, also to the specified setting. Do not try and overtighten the bolts to close the gap between the clamp rear ends and the top yoke.

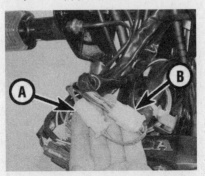

24.4 Ignition switch (A) and instrument cluster (B) wiring connectors

24.6 Ignition HT coil location (ES-4 and ES-7 models)

24.9 Ignition control module (ICM) location (ES-4 and ES-7 models)

26 Front fork legs: removal

1 Position the machine on its centre stand and support it under the crankcase to prevent it toppling when the front wheel is removed. Remove the front wheel and mudguard – for CG125ES-4 and ES-7 models refer to Section 34. Unscrew the two reflectors from the bottom yoke cover (if fitted) and remove the two cover mounting bolts to release the cover. On CG125ES-4 and ES-7 models, undo the two brake caliper mounting bolts and displace the caliper – secure it to the machine with a cable tie to avoid straining the brake hose. Do not operate the front brake while the caliper is off the disc.

2 Slacken fully the top yoke pinch bolts; if the fork legs are going to be dismantled, slacken the fork leg top bolts while the legs are still clamped in the bottom yoke. Slacken fully the bottom yoke pinch bolts and withdraw each leg by pulling it downwards out of the yokes. If corrosion obstructs removal of the leg, apply a liberal quantity of penetrating fluid, allow time for it to work, then release the leg by rotating it in the yoke as it is pulled downwards. In extremely stubborn cases, tap smartly on the top of each bolt using a hammer and a wooden drift; take great care not to damage the bolts. Alternatively, if care is used it is permissible to open up the split clamp of each yoke slightly by removing the pinch bolt and working the flat blade of a screwdriver into the clamp. Exercise extreme caution when doing this, as the clamps can be overstressed and broken easily.

27 Front fork legs: dismantling and overhaul

1 Dismantle and rebuild the fork legs separately, and store the components of each leg in separate, clearly marked containers, so that there is no risk of exchanging components, thus promoting undue wear.

2 First slacken the damper rod Allen bolt at the bottom of each lower leg. If the damper rod is not locked, in this case by the pressure of the fork spring, it will rotate with the bolt. Tap smartly on the bolt head with a hammer and a suitable drift, then unscrew it. If it breaks free and can be unscrewed do not remove it completely at this stage; if it breaks free but merely rotates with the rod try compressing the fork leg against a solid object to apply more spring pressure. If all else fails proceed with the dismantling and use the more positive method of damper rod locking described below.

3 Remove the fork top bolt. If this was not slackened while still in the machine, as described in the previous Section, clamp the stanchion upper end in a vice using padded jaw covers to prevent scratching. Unscrew the bolt carefully; place a thickly wadded piece of rag over the bolt before it is finally removed. The bolts are under some pressure from the fork spring and may be ejected with considerable force; use firm hand pressure to counter this until the bolt threads are released.

4 Remove the fork spring noting carefully which way up it was fitted. Invert the leg over a container and tip out the fork oil;

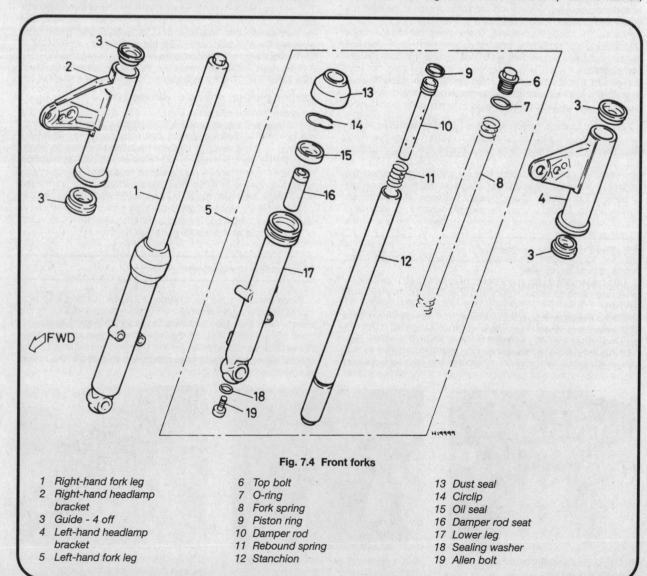

Fig. 7.4 Front forks

1 Right-hand fork leg	6 Top bolt	13 Dust seal
2 Right-hand headlamp bracket	7 O-ring	14 Circlip
3 Guide - 4 off	8 Fork spring	15 Oil seal
4 Left-hand headlamp bracket	9 Piston ring	16 Damper rod seat
5 Left-hand fork leg	10 Damper rod	17 Lower leg
	11 Rebound spring	18 Sealing washer
	12 Stanchion	19 Allen bolt

27.2 Unscrew damper rod Allen screw to release stanchion from lower leg

27.4 Remove dust seal from lower leg

27.6 Ease out the circlip to permit removal of fork oil seal

depress the leg slowly to expel as much oil as possible. Carefully prise the dust seal off the lower leg.

5 Remove the damper rod Allen bolt. If this has broken free from the lower leg but will not unscrew from the damper rod, obtain a piece of hardwood dowel of the same length and diameter as the fork spring(s) and grind a coarse taper on one end. Compress the stanchion fully into the lower leg and insert the dowel into the stanchion so that its tapered end engages with the head of the damper rod. Either rest the dowel outer end against a solid object so that the maximum pressure can be applied to lock the damper rod, clamp it in a vice, or clamp a self-locking wrench on to it so that an assistant can apply pressure and prevent rotation at the same time.

6 Remove the stanchion from the lower leg and invert it to tip out the damper rod and rebound spring, then invert the lower leg to tip out the damper rod seat. Ease the wire circlip out of the top of the lower leg to avoid scratching the metal, then prise out the oil seal using a large flat-bladed screwdriver which has had any sharp edges ground off: be very careful not to damage the top edge or to scratch the seal housing when using this method. Do not apply excessive pressure; if the seal proves difficult to remove, pour boiling water over the outside of the lower leg to expand the alloy sufficiently to release its grip on the seal. Note that on CG125ES-4 and ES-7 models a large washer is fitted under the seal.

7 All components can be checked for wear and renewed if necessary following the general instructions given in Chapter 4. If the damping action has deteriorated renew the damper rod piston ring and be very careful to clean all components.

28 Front fork legs: reassembly

1 On reassembly, all components should have been checked for wear and renewed as necessary and should be completely clean and dry.

2 Clamp the lower leg vertically in a vice by its spindle lug. Coat the inner and outer diameters of the new seal with the recommended fork oil and push the seal squarely into the bore of the fork lower leg by hand – on CG125ES-4 and ES-7 models remember to install the large washer first. Ensure that the seal is fitted squarely, then tap it fully into position, using a hammer and a suitably sized drift such as a socket spanner, which should bear only on the seal's hard outer edge. Tap the seal into the bore of the lower leg just enough to expose the circlip groove. Refit the retaining circlip securely in its groove.

3 Refit the damper rod assembly to the stanchion, pushing it down with the spring or wooden dowel, then place the damper rod seat over the damper rod end, using a smear of grease to stick it in place. Smear the sliding surface of the stanchion with a light coating of fork oil and carefully insert the stanchion into the lower leg, taking great care not to damage the sealing lips of the oil seal. Check that the threads of the damper rod bolt are clean and dry, apply a few drops of thread locking compound and fit the damper rod bolt. Do not forget the sealing washer fitted under the head of the bolt. Tighten the bolt only partially at first, using an Allen key of suitable size. Maintain pressure on the head of the damper rod and push the stanchion firmly as far down into the lower leg as possible to centralise the damper rod in the stanchion. The damper rod bolt can then be tightened to the specified torque setting and the dowel or spring removed.

28.3a Fit rebound spring and piston ring to damper rod . . .

28.3b . . . and insert damper assembly into top of stanchion

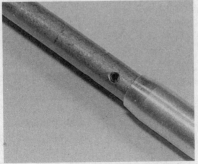

28.3c When damper rod projects from stanchion lower end, fit damper rod seat

28.3d Take care not to damage oil seal as stanchion is refitted to lower leg

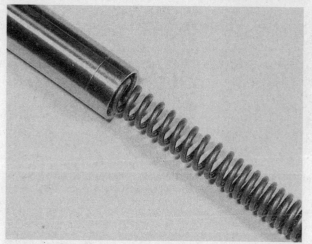

28.5a Fork springs are refitted with closer-pitched coils at the top

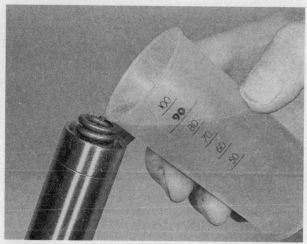

28.5b Refill fork leg with exactly the correct amount of oil

4 Pack grease above the seal for additional protection and press the dust seal firmly into place.
5 Refill the fork leg with the correct amount of the specified type of fork oil, then install the spring – on all BR models the closer-pitched coils should be at the top, on CG125-W, M-1, ES-4 and ES-7 models the closer-pitched coils should be at the bottom. Refit the fork leg top bolt: tighten it to its specified torque setting when the stanchion is held either in a vice with padded jaws or in the machine's fork yokes.

29 Front fork legs: refitting

1 On refitting, check that the upper length of each stanchion is clean and polished, and that all traces of dirt and corrosion have been removed. Apply a thin smear of grease to ease the passage of the stanchion through the yokes and to prevent corrosion. When the stanchion is in position, i.e. with its top end flush with the upper surface of the top yoke so that the fork top bolt is standing proud, tighten the yoke pinch bolts just enough to retain the leg. Unless tightened prior to inserting the legs in the yokes, tighten the fork top bolts to the specified torque setting.
2 Refit the mudguard and tighten lightly the mounting bolts.
3 Refit the front wheel but before final tightening of the various fasteners, push the machine off its stand and bounce the front suspension a few times to settle the fork components. Tighten to the specified torque settings the front wheel spindle nut, followed by the mudguard mounting bolts and the bottom and top yoke pinch bolts in that order. It is essential to tighten the fasteners from the wheel spindle upwards so that the front forks are clamped securely but without stress.
4 Complete the refitting of the front wheel, then adjust the front drum brake. On CG125ES-4 and ES-7 models, install the disc brake caliper (see Section 36), then apply the brake a few times to bring the pads back into contact with the disc.
5 Check that the front wheel is free to rotate, that the speedometer functions correctly, and that the front brake and front forks are working efficiently before taking the machine out on the road. Don't forget to refit the bottom yoke cover and reflectors.

30 Steering stem: removal and refitting – CG125ES-4 and ES-7 models

1 The headlamp bracket is bolted to the fork top yoke; after removing the instrument panel (see Section 43) undo the two bolts securing the bracket to the yoke and lift it off, noting how it locates in the bottom yoke.
2 Undo the bolt securing the front brake hose to the bottom yoke.

31 Swinging arm: check, removal and refitting

Check

1 With the machine on its centre stand, grasp both swinging arm ends and attempt to move them from side to side. if a significant amount of side play exists the bearings should be renewed.

Removal and refitting

2 Remove the rear wheel and chainguard as described in Chapter 5 (having referred first to Section 34 of this Chapter). Disconnect the chain. The torque arm should be disconnected from the swinging arm.
3 Detach the rear suspension units from their bottom mountings and lower the swinging arm to the ground.
4 Remove the nut and washer from the end of the swinging arm pivot shaft and pull the shaft out of the swinging arm and frame mountings. The swinging arm can now be pulled free. Note that on CG125ES-4 and ES-7 models, it is not necessary to remove the pillion footrest brackets.
5 Pull the caps off the swinging arm pivot bosses and slide out the bearing sleeves. If the headed bushes are in need of renewal, they are best withdrawn using a slide-hammer with an internally expanding adapter. If using a drift to remove the old bushes, move it around the inner face to ensure that the bush leaves the housing squarely.
6 Clean the housing thoroughly before installing the new bushes. Each bush should be installed with care to prevent damage to its head – the use of a drawbolt and suitably-sized plain washers is advised to ensure that each bush enters its housing squarely.
7 Grease each bearing sleeve and insert them into the bushes. Apply grease to the inner face or the caps and fit them to each side of the housings. Grease the pivot shaft, then offer up the swinging arm and insert the pivot shaft fully. Install the plain washer and nut and tighten the nut to the specified torque setting. Check that the swinging arm is able to move freely and that there is no discernible side play in the pivot.
8 Refit all disturbed components in a reverse of the removal procedure.

32 Side panels, seat and tail fairing: removal and refitting

Side panels

1 On the BR-E/F and BR-J models, the side panels are secured by a lock at their lower front mounting points. To release the lock, insert the ignition key into the lock and rotate it until it unlocks. Reverse the procedure on refitting.
2 On the CG125 BR-K, BR-S/T, CG125-W and CG125M-1

32.3a Lift the side panels off carefully to avoid damaging the fixings

32.3b CG125ES-4 and ES-7 lower right-hand panel is secured by a lock

32.4 Press latch on each side to release seat (all BR models)

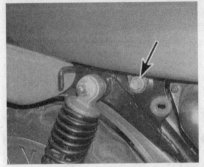

32.5a Seat is retained by a bolt on each side (CG125-W)

32.5b Engage the hook with the bracket (arrows)

32.6 Note the location of the seat mounting brackets (CG125ES-4 and ES-7)

models, the side panels are secured by a screw at the lower mounting point. Remove the screw and pull the panel stubs out of their mounting grommets to release.

3 On CG124ES-4 and ES-7 models, the left-hand side panel is secured by a lock – insert the ignition key to release it. The right-hand side panel is secured by a screw. Pegs on the inside of the panels press into grommets on the lower edge of the petrol tank. The left-hand panel is retained by an additional hook on the frame, the right-hand panel by an additional peg and grommet. The lower right-hand panel is secured by a lock – insert the ignition key to release it.

Seat – all BR models

4 The seat is removable to allow easy access to the toolbox, and on BR-K and S/T models to the small storage box in the tail fairing. The seat is secured by two latches, one on each side at the rear end, just behind the suspension unit top mountings. Note that the tail fairing will obscure the latches on later models. Press each latch to the rear to release, and where applicable, unlock the helmet lock to release the wire clip. On refitting, hook the seat front mounting under its locating bracket and press the

seat down at the rear so that its two latches snap into engagement. Where fitted, slip the wire clip into the helmet lock to provide a measure of security.

Seat – CG125-W and CG125M-1 models

5 Remove both side panels. Remove the mounting bolt on each side at the front of the seat, then pull the seat forwards and upwards to release it. On refitting, engage the hook on the rear underside of the seat with the bracket on the frame. Refit the two bolts and tighten them securely. Install the side panels.

Seat – CG125ES-4 and ES-7 models

6 The seat is secured by two bolts, one on each side underneath the rear mudguard. Remove the bolts and pull the seat rearwards to release the tab that locates under the rear petrol tank mounting.

Tail fairing – CG125 BR-K models

7 Remove the seat as described above, then release the grab rail by removing its four mounting bolts. Remove the six tail fairing mounting bolts and manoeuvre it free of the frame.

32.7a Remove grab rail (four bolts), then two rear bolts (arrows) . . .

32.7b . . . followed by four bolts (arrows) to free tail fairing

32.9 Tail fairing/grab rail bolts (arrows)

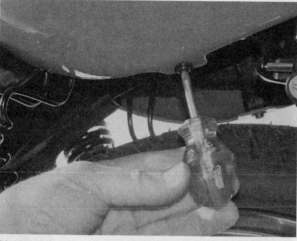

32.10a Undo the screw on both sides . . .

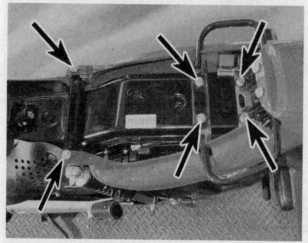

32.10b . . . followed by the six bolts (arrows)

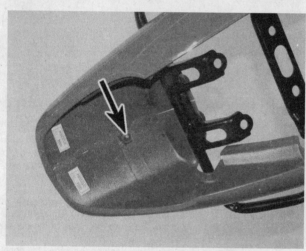

32.10c Tail fairing halves are joined by single screw

8 Reverse the removal procedure to refit the tail fairing, noting that a plain washer, damping rubber and spacer must be fitted to each grab rail bolt.

Tail fairing – CG125 BR-S/T, CG125-W and CG125M-1 models

9 Remove both side panels and the seat (see above). The tail fairing is removed as a complete unit with the grab rail; remove the six bolts and carefully ease the assembly off the frame. If required the individual components can be separated by removing the four screws on the underside.

Tail fairing – CG125ES-4 and ES-7 models

10 Remove both side panels and the seat (see above). The tail fairing is removed as a complete unit with the grab rail; undo the screw on the underside of each side of the fairing, then remove the six bolts and lift the unit off. If required the individual components can be separated by removing the grab rail and the single screw on the underside.

33 Speedometer: removal and refitting

1 The speedometer is mounted in a panel with the ignition switch and warning lamp cluster. To remove the complete assembly, first remove the headlamp shell. Trace the wiring from the instruments and ignition switch to the connectors and disconnect it. Disconnect the speedometer drive cable.
2 Unscrew the two bolts which secure the panel to the top yoke and lift it off.
3 On all models except the CG125ES-4 and ES-7 models, unplug

the bulbholders, then withdraw the bolts which retain the mounting bracket, noting the arrangement of washers and damper rubbers.
4 On CG125ES-4 and ES-7 models, remove the small screws which secure the bottom cover and lift it off.
5 Remove all the small screws which secure the panel top and bottom halves and separate them. The speedometer head is secured by two screws. When all screws have been released the various components can be separated.
6 Reassembly is the reverse of the dismantling procedure.

33.1 Disconnect the speedometer drive cable

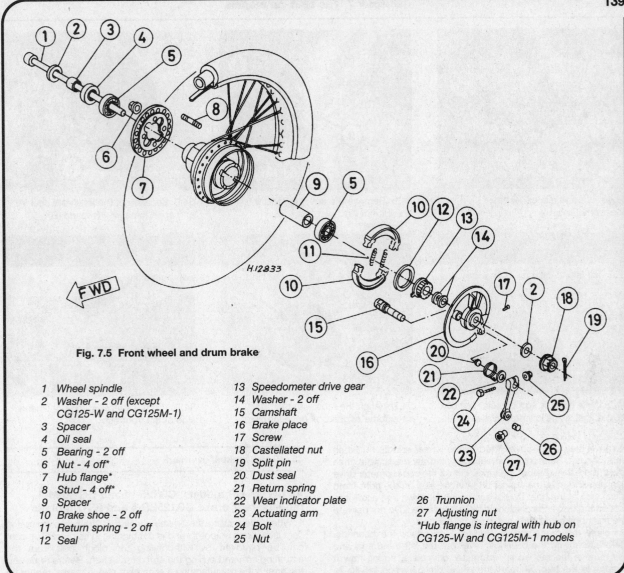

Fig. 7.5 Front wheel and drum brake

1 Wheel spindle	13 Speedometer drive gear	
2 Washer - 2 off (except CG125-W and CG125M-1)	14 Washer - 2 off	
3 Spacer	15 Camshaft	
4 Oil seal	16 Brake place	
5 Bearing - 2 off	17 Screw	
6 Nut - 4 off*	18 Castellated nut	
7 Hub flange*	19 Split pin	
8 Stud - 4 off*	20 Dust seal	
9 Spacer	21 Return spring	
10 Brake shoe - 2 off	22 Wear indicator plate	26 Trunnion
11 Return spring - 2 off	23 Actuating arm	27 Adjusting nut
12 Seal	24 Bolt	*Hub flange is integral with hub on CG125-W and CG125M-1 models
	25 Nut	

34   Wheels: removal, inspection and refitting

All CG125 BR models, CG125-W and CG125M-1 models

1 In spite of its different appearance, the front wheel is the same in layout as those of the earlier models described in Chapter 5. Detail changes are shown in Fig. 7.5.

2 The rear wheel differs only in rim size. Servicing procedures, therefore, remain the same, although note that the direction of fitting of the rear wheel spindle varies according to model; on all BR models the spindle is inserted from the left-hand side, whereas on CG125-W and CG125M-1 models it is inserted from the right-hand side. Note that there is no dust cover fitted on the left-hand (sprocket) side of the hub on CG125-W and CG125M-1 models.

3 When removing and refitting wheels, note that some later models are fitted with self-locking spindle nuts instead of having castellated nuts and split pins. Ensure that the appropriate torque setting is used on refitting (see Specifications).

CG125ES-4 and ES-7 models

4 These models are fitted with a disc front brake. If required, before removing the wheel, displace the brake caliper – refer to Section 36. Undo the small screw securing the speedometer

cable in the drive gearbox and pull out the cable, noting how it fits.

5 With the machine supported on the centre stand, block the stand and crankcase to raise the wheel clear of the ground.

34.4a Undo the small screw . . .

34.4b . . . and disconnect the speedometer cable

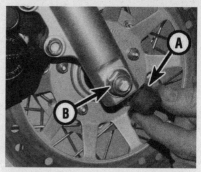

34.5 Remove the cover (A) and the spindle nut (B)

34.6 Location of the left-hand seal (A) and speedometer driveplate (B)

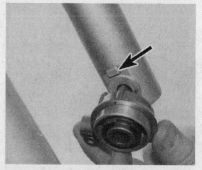

34.7a Note how the speedometer gearbox locates against the lower leg (arrow)

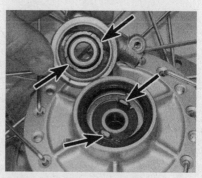

34.7b Align the tabs with the speedometer gearbox drive (arrows)

34.7c Fit the spacer in the right-hand side of the front hub

Remove the rubber cover fitted to the wheel spindle nut, then undo the nut. Support the wheel and withdraw the spindle, then lower the wheel clear of the forks. Lift off the speedometer drive gearbox and note the spacer fitted in the seal on the right-hand (disc) side of the hub. Do not lay the wheel down and allow it to rest on the disc – the disc could become warped. Do not operate the front brake while the caliper is off the disc.

6 Follow the procedure in Chapter 5 to check the bearings. Before removing the bearings, lever out the left-hand seal and the remove the tabbed speedometer driveplate, noting how it locates in the hub. Support the wheel rim on wood blocks to protect the disc when driving out the right-hand bearing. Fit new seals to both sides of the hub on reassembly.

7 Before refitting the front wheel, note how the speedometer drive gearbox locates against the tab on the inside of the left-hand fork lower leg. Install the gearbox in the left-hand side of the hub, ensuring the driveplate tabs engage in the gearbox drive, and don't forget to fit the spacer in the right-hand side.

8 If the brake caliper is in place, ensure the brake pads fit either side of the disc when the wheel is installed, then push the spindle through from the left-hand side. Tighten the spindle nut to the specified torque setting and refit the nut cover. If displaced, follow the procedure in Section 36 to install the brake caliper.

9 Apply the brake a few times to bring the pads back into contact with the disc. Check that the front wheel is free to rotate, that the speedometer functions correctly.

10 Check the operation of the front brake before taking the machine out on the road.

11 These models are fitted with an endless drive chain. Before removing the rear wheel it is necessary to loosen the chain adjuster nuts and the wheel spindle nut, then push the wheel forwards until these is enough slack in the chain to lift it off the rear sprocket. Note that the chainguard does not have to be removed before removing the rear wheel.

12 Servicing procedures for the rear wheel remain the same as for earlier models. Note that there is no dust cover fitted on the left-hand (sprocket) side of the hub, a large washer is fitted under the circlip that retains the rear sprocket and there are two bearings fitted in the right-hand side of the hub. The rear wheel spindle is inserted from the left-hand side.

35 Drum brakes: overhaul

All CG125 BR models, CG125-W and CG125M-1 models, rear brake CG125ES-4 and ES-7 models

1 When overhauling the brakes check that the brake operating cam is working smoothly and is not binding in its pivot. The cam can be removed by withdrawing the pinch bolt from the actuating arm and pulling the arm off the shaft. Before removing the arm, if the manufacturer's alignment punch marks cannot be seen, it is advisable to mark its position in relation to the shaft so that it can be relocated correctly with the wear indicator pointer.

2 Remove any deposits of hardened grease or corrosion from the bearing surface of the brake cam and shoe by rubbing it lightly with a strip of fine emery paper or by applying solvent with a piece of rag. Lightly grease the length of the shaft and the face of the operating cam prior to reassembly. Clean and grease the pivot stub which is set in the backplate.

3 On the front brake only, check the condition of the felt seal which prevents the escape of grease from the end of the camshaft. If it is in any way damaged or too dirty to be of further use, it must be renewed before the shaft is relocated in the backplate. Dip the seal in clean engine oil before refitting it, pack grease into the backplate passage and refit the camshaft. Hook the return spring inner end into the backplate hole.

4 On front and rear brakes, fit the wear indicator to the camshaft, aligning the indicator inner tab with the matching slot in the camshaft splines. Check that the camshaft is rotated to its correct position then refit the actuating arm, aligning its punch mark with that of the camshaft. On front brakes only, hook the return spring outer end over the arm. Tighten the arm pinch bolt to the specified torque setting, then refit the brake shoes.

5 On all models, note that the brake operating mechanism is at its most efficient when, with the brake correctly adjusted and applied fully, the angle between the cable or rod and the actuating arm on the brake backplate does not exceed 90°. This can be adjusted by removing the actuating arm from the brake camshaft and rotating it by one or two splines until the angle is correct. Ensure that all components are correctly secured on reassembly.

36.1a Loosen the pad pins . . .

36.1b . . . then undo the caliper mounting bolts

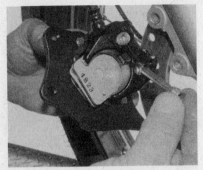

36.1c Remove the pad pins . . .

36.1d . . . the lift the pads out of the caliper

36.1e Note the location of the pad shim

36.1f Note the location of the pad spring

36 Disc brake: overhaul – front brake CG125ES-4 and ES-7 models

Brake pads – removal, inspection and refitting

1 To remove the brake pads, first loosen the pad pins, then undo the caliper mounting bolts and draw the caliper off the disc. Remove the pad pins and lift out the pads, noting the location of the shim on the back of the outer pad. Note the location of the pad spring inside the caliper. Renew the pad pins and the pad spring if they are badly corroded or worn. Do not operate the brake lever while the pads are out of the caliper.

2 Inspect the surface of each pad for contamination and check that the friction material has not worn down level with or beyond the wear limit line in the pad edge. If either pad is worn down to, or beyond, the wear limit, is fouled with oil or grease, or heavily

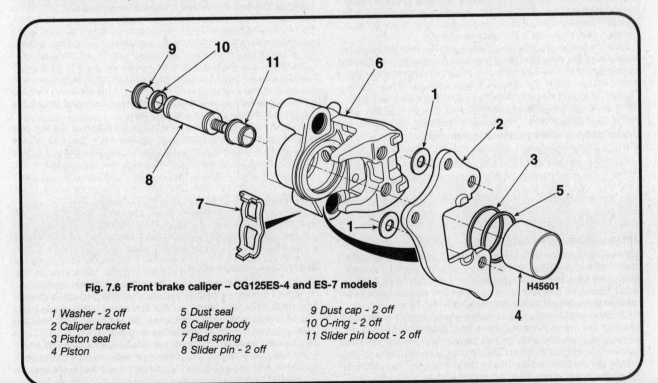

Fig. 7.6 Front brake caliper – CG125ES-4 and ES-7 models

H45601

1 Washer - 2 off
2 Caliper bracket
3 Piston seal
4 Piston

5 Dust seal
6 Caliper body
7 Pad spring
8 Slider pin - 2 off

9 Dust cap - 2 off
10 O-ring - 2 off
11 Slider pin boot - 2 off

36.2 Brake pad wear limit indicator line

36.18 Measuring the brake disc thickness

scored or damaged by dirt and debris, both pads must be renewed as a set. **Note:** *It is not possible to degrease the friction material; if the pads are contaminated in any way they must be renewed.* Check that each pad has the same amount of wear as the other. If uneven wear is noticed, the caliper is probably sticking, in which case it must be overhauled (see Steps 9 to 16).
3 If the pads are in good condition clean them carefully, using a fine wire brush which is completely free of oil and grease, to remove all traces of road dirt and corrosion. Clean out the grooves in the friction material and dig out any embedded particles of foreign matter carefully. Any areas of glazing may be removed using emery cloth.
4 Check the condition of the brake disc (see Step 17).
5 If new pads are being installed, push the piston as far back into the caliper as possible. A good way of doing this is to insert one of the old pads between the disc and the piston, then push the caliper against the pad and disc using hand pressure. Due to the increased friction material thickness of new pads, it may be necessary to remove some fluid from the master cylinder reservoir (see Section 5).
6 Smear the backs of the pads and the shanks of the pad pins lightly with copper-based grease, making sure that none gets on the pad friction material. Ensure that the shim is in place on the back of the outer pad and that the pad spring is in place inside the caliper, then insert the pads into the caliper so that the friction material faces the disc. Push up on the pads to align the holes in the pads with the holes in the caliper and install the pad pins.
7 Slide the caliper onto the disc, making sure the pads sit squarely each side of the disc, then apply a suitable non-permanent thread locking compound to the caliper mounting bolts and tighten them to the torque setting specified at the beginning of this Chapter. Tighten the pad pins to the specified torque. Apply the brake a few times to bring the pads into contact with the disc. Check the operation of the brake before riding the motorcycle.

Brake caliper – removal and installation

8 If the brake caliper is being displaced, remove the caliper mounting bolts and slide the caliper off the disc. Secure the caliper to the machine with a cable tie to avoid straining the brake hose. Do not operate the brake lever while the caliper is off the disc. On installation, apply a suitable non-permanent thread locking compound to the caliper mounting bolts and tighten them to the torque setting specified at the beginning of this Chapter.

Brake caliper – overhaul

9 If the brake caliper indicates the need for an overhaul (usually due to leaking fluid or sticky operation), all old brake fluid should be flushed from the system. Before you start, read through the entire procedure first and make sure that you have obtained all the new parts required, including some new DOT 4 brake fluid.
10 Before removing the caliper, note the alignment of the brake hose on the caliper, then unscrew the hose union bolt and separate the hose from the caliper. **Note:** *If you are planning to overhaul the caliper and don't have a source of compressed air to blow out the piston, the hydraulic system can be used to force the piston out of the body once the pads have been removed.*

Disconnect the hose once the piston has been displaced. Clamp the hose or wrap a plastic bag tightly around it to prevent fluid spills and stop dirt entering the system. Discard the sealing washers as new ones must be used on installation.
11 Follow the procedure in Step 1 and remove the caliper and brake pads. Remove the pad spring. Pull the caliper off the caliper bracket, noting how it fits on the slider pins. Clean the exterior of the caliper with denatured alcohol or brake system cleaner. Make sure all old grease is removed from the slider pins. Displace the piston from its bore as far as possible using either low pressure compressed air directed into the fluid inlet, or by carefully operating the brake lever to pump it out. If the piston is being displaced hydraulically, it may be necessary to top-up the fluid reservoir during the procedure. Have some clean rag ready to catch any spilled brake fluid when the piston reaches the end of its bore.
Warning: Never place your fingers in front of the piston in an attempt to catch or protect it when applying compressed air, as serious injury could result.
12 Using a wooden or plastic tool, remove the dust and piston seals from the caliper bore. Discard them as new ones must be used on installation. Clean the piston and bore with clean brake fluid or brake system cleaner. If compressed air is available, use it to dry the parts thoroughly (make sure it's filtered and unlubricated).
Caution: Do not, under any circumstances, use a petroleum-based solvent to clean brake parts.
13 Inspect the caliper bore and piston for signs of wear and corrosion; if surface defects are present, the caliper assembly must be renewed. Renew the slider pins if they are badly corroded or worn. When fitting new slider pins, apply a suitable non-permanent thread locking compound and tighten them to the specified torque setting.
14 Lubricate the new piston and dust seal with clean brake fluid and install them in their grooves in the caliper bore. Lubricate the piston with clean brake fluid and install it closed-end first into the caliper bore. Push the piston all the way in, making sure it enters the bore squarely. Fit the pad spring, then apply a smear of copper-based grease to the slider pins and slide the caliper onto the bracket.
15 Follow the procedure in Steps 6 and 7 to install the pads and caliper.
16 Connect the brake hose using new sealing washers on each side of the union. Align the hose as noted on removal and tighten the union bolt to the torque setting specified at the beginning of this Chapter. Top-up the master cylinder reservoir with new DOT 4 brake fluid and bleed the brake system (see Section 5).

Brake disc – inspection

17 Inspect the surface of the disc for score marks and other damage. Light scratches are normal after use and won't affect brake operation, but deep grooves and heavy score marks will reduce braking efficiency and accelerate pad wear. If the disc is badly grooved it must be machined or renewed.
18 The disc must not be machined or allowed to wear down to a thickness less than the service limit listed in this Chapter's Specifications and as marked on the disc itself. The thickness of the disc can be checked with a micrometer. If the thickness of

**Fig. 7.7 Front brake master cylinder
– CG125ES-4 and ES-7 models**

1 Reservoir cover
2 Diaphragm plate
3 Diaphragm
4 Union bolt
5 Sealing washers - 2 off
6 Brake hose
7 Spring
8 Piston/seals
9 Washer
10 Circlip
11 Dust boot
12 Lever pivot bolt
13 Brake lever
14 Nut
15 Brake light switch

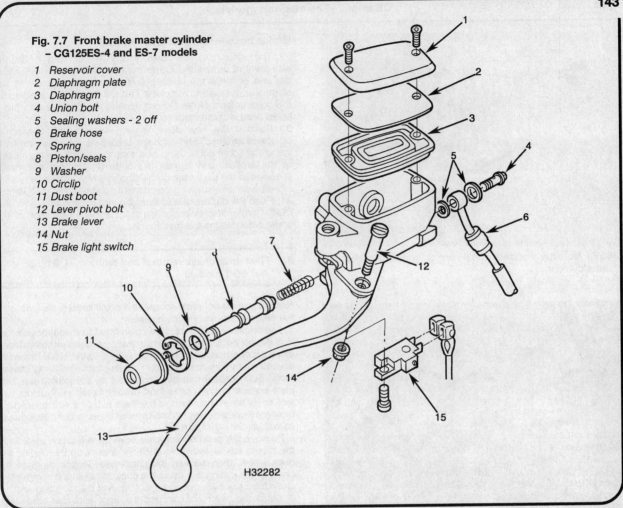

H32282

the disc is less than the service limit, it must be renewed. When fitting a new disc, tighten the nuts in a criss-cross pattern evenly and progressively to the torque setting specified at the beginning of this Chapter. Remove any protective coating from the disc's working surfaces and clean it with brake system cleaner. After the wheel has been installed, apply the brake a few times to bring the pads into contact with the disc. Check the operation of the brake before riding the motorcycle.

Brake master cylinder – overhaul

19 If the brake lever does not feel firm when the brake is applied, and the hydraulic hose is in good condition and bleeding the brake does not help (see Section 5), or if the master cylinder is leaking fluid, then master cylinder overhaul is recommended. Before you start, read through the entire procedure first and make sure that you have obtained all the new parts required, including some new DOT 4 brake fluid. To prevent damage to the paint from spilled brake fluid, always cover the petrol tank when working on the master cylinder.
20 Remove the rear view mirror, disconnect the wiring connectors from the brake light switch and remove the front brake lever.
21 Unscrew the brake hose union bolt and separate the hose from the master cylinder, noting its alignment. Discard the sealing washers as they must be renewed. Wrap a plastic bag tightly around the end of the hose to stop dirt entering the system and secure the hose in an upright position to prevent fluid spills.
22 Unscrew the master cylinder clamp bolts, remove the back of the clamp, then lift the master cylinder away from the handlebar. Unscrew the reservoir cover retaining screws and lift off the cover, the diaphragm plate and the diaphragm. Drain the brake fluid from the reservoir into a suitable container. Wipe any remaining fluid out of the reservoir with a clean rag. Inspect the

reservoir cover rubber diaphragm and renew it if it is damaged or deteriorated.
22 Remove the dust boot from the end of the piston, then, using circlip pliers, remove the circlip. Withdraw the washer, piston assembly and spring, noting how they fit. If they are difficult to remove, apply low pressure compressed air to the fluid outlet.
23 Inspect the master cylinder bore for signs of wear and corrosion; if surface defects are present, the master cylinder must be renewed. Ensure that the fluid inlet and outlet ports in the master cylinder are clear.
24 The dust boot, circlip, washer, piston assembly and spring are all included in the master cylinder overhaul kit. Use all of the new parts, regardless of the apparent condition of the old ones. Install the new spring in the master cylinder, wide end first. Lubricate the new piston assembly with clean brake fluid and install it in the master cylinder, making sure it is the correct way round. Press the piston in and install the new washer and circlip, making sure the circlip locates in its groove, then install the dust boot.
25 Attach the master cylinder to the handlebar and fit the clamp with its UP mark facing up, then tighten the bolts to the torque setting specified at the beginning of this Chapter. Connect the brake hose to the master cylinder, using new sealing washers on each side of the union, and aligning the hose as noted on removal. Tighten the union bolt to the specified torque setting.
26 Install the brake lever, then fill the fluid reservoir with new DOT 4 brake fluid and bleed the brake system (see Section 5). Fit the diaphragm, diaphragm plate and cover onto the master cylinder reservoir and tighten the cover screws securely.
27 Connect the brake light wiring and install the rear view mirror.
28 Check the operation of the brake before riding the motorcycle.

36.29a Note the alignment of the hose union (arrow) with the master cylinder . . .

36.29b . . . and with the brake caliper

Brake hose – removal and refitting

29 The brake hose has banjo unions on each end – note the alignment of the unions. Cover the surrounding area with clean rag and unscrew the union bolt, then free the hose from any clamps or guides and remove it. Discard the sealing washers on the hose unions. **Note:** *Do not operate the brake lever while a brake hose is disconnected.*

30 Position the new hose, making sure it isn't twisted or otherwise strained, and align the unions as noted on removal. Install the union bolts, using new sealing washers on both sides of the unions, and tighten the bolts to the torque settings specified at the beginning of this Chapter. Make sure the hose is routed clear of all moving components and reinstall the clamps.

31 Flush the old brake fluid from the system and refill with new DOT 4 brake fluid (see Section 5). Check the operation of the brake before riding the motorcycle.

37   Final drive chain: removal and refitting – CG125ES-4 and ES-7 models

Note: *If you do not have access to a chain riveting tool, have the chain fitted by a Honda dealer.*

1 The original equipment drive chain fitted to these models has a staked-type joining link which can be disassembled using either Honda service tool, Pt. No. 07HMH-MR10103, or one of several commercially-available drive chain breaking/staking tools. Such chains can be recognised by the joining link side plate's identification marks (and usually its different colour), as well as by the staked ends of the link's two pins which look as if they have been deeply centre-punched, instead of peened over as with all the other pins.

2 Remove the gearbox sprocket cover (see Section 9). Locate the joining link in a suitable position to work on by rotating the back wheel, then slacken the chain (see Section 5). Split the chain at the joining link using the chain breaker and remove the chain from the bike, noting its routing over the swinging arm.

3 Install the new chain around the front and rear sprockets, leaving the two ends in a convenient position to work on. Insert the new joining (soft) link from the inside with the O-rings correctly located between the link plates. Install the new side

37.2a Tighten the chain breaker to push the pin out of the link . . .

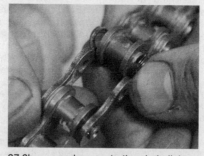

37.2b . . . and separate the chain link

37.3a Insert the new soft link, with O-rings, through the chain ends . . .

37.3b . . . and install the O-rings over the pin ends . . .

37.3c . . . followed by the side plate

37.3d Press the side plate into position using a clamp

37.4 Assemble the chain riveting tool over one pin at a time and tighten it fully

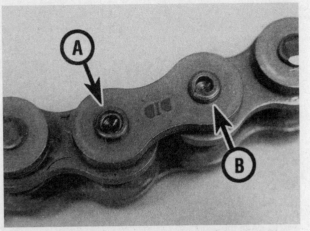

37.5 Pin end correctly riveted (A) and pin end unriveted (B)

plate with its identification marks facing out, then press it into position and measure the amount that the joining link pins project from the side plate – the projection should be 1.1 mm (0.04 in).

4 Stake the new link using the breaking/staking tool. DO NOT re-use old joining link components.

5 After staking, check the joining link and staking for any signs of cracking. If there is any evidence of cracking, the joining link, O-rings and side plate must be renewed. Measure the diameter of the staked ends in two directions and check that they are evenly staked and within the measurements specified – 4.8 mm (0.19 in).

6 Install the gearbox sprocket cover, then adjust and lubricate the chain following the procedure described in Section 5.

38 Regulator/rectifier unit: location and testing – CG125 BR-E/F, BR-J and BR-K models

1 The 12 volt electrical system fitted to these models uses a combined regulator/rectifier unit to replace the rectifier and resistor fitted to the earlier models described in Chapter 6.

2 The unit is fitted either under the seat, in front of the rear mudguard, or under the petrol tank immediately behind the steering head. Remove the seat (and petrol tank, if necessary) to gain access to it. The unit is a heavily finned sealed metal unit; on later models it is rubber-mounted to the frame top tube and is covered by a rubber sheath.

3 The regulator side of the unit can be tested only by a general check of the charging system output, as described in Chapter 6, Section 3. If the results obtained differ widely from those specified in this Chapter then one or more components of the

system is faulty. While basic tests of the generator coils can be made as described in Chapter 6, if a charging system fault is suspected the machine should be taken to a Honda Service Agent for testing by an expert. The only way of curing a faulty regulator/rectifier unit is to renew it; owners are advised to have their findings confirmed by an expert using the correct test equipment before condemning a component.

4 The rectifier side of the unit can be checked by measuring the resistances each way across the red and white wire terminals, as described in Chapter 6, Section 4. If the rectifier diode is faulty, the complete unit must be renewed.

5 Always ensure that the unit's connections are clean and securely fastened and that its mountings are secure.

39 Charging/lighting system: checking the output – CG125 BR-S/T, CG125-W and CG125M-1 models

Note: *Prior to making checks of the charging or lighting system components, ensure that the battery is fully charged and in good condition.*

Voltage output check

Note that the voltage output check described relates to the CG125-W and M-1 models. No data is available on the BR-S/T models although it should be possible to gain a good indication of the charging system's condition using this procedure.

1 Start the engine and warm it up to normal operating temperature, then stop the engine. Remove the left-hand side panel.

2 Start the engine and allow it to idle. Connect a multimeter set to the 0 – 20 volts DC scale (voltmeter) across the terminals of the battery (positive (+ve) probe to battery positive (+ve)

38.2 Location of regulator/rectifier unit – BR-K model shown

39.2 Voltage output test

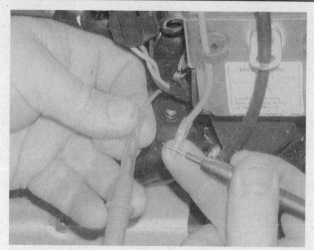

39.6 Checking for current leakage

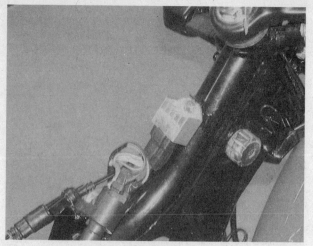

39.13 Regulator/rectifier unit location

terminal, negative (-ve) probe to battery negative (-ve) terminal). Slowly increase the engine speed to 5000 rpm and note the reading obtained, then stop the engine and turn the ignition OFF; do not allow the engine to overheat. The regulated voltage should be as specified at the beginning of the Chapter. If the voltage is outside these limits, check the generator coils and the regulator (see below).

3 Remove the two screws from the base of the headlamp shell and ease the headlamp out of the shell – leave the bulb wiring connected. Identify the blue and green wires to the headlamp bulb, then connect a multimeter set to the 0 – 20 volts DC scale (voltmeter) between the wires, positive (+ve) probe to the blue wire and negative (-ve) probe to the green; do not disconnect the wires for this test, insert the meter probes into the back of the connectors. Start the engine and switch the lights onto main beam (HI). Slowly increase the engine speed to 5000 rpm and note the reading obtained, then stop the engine and turn the lights and ignition OFF; do not allow the engine to overheat.

4 The voltage should be as specified at the beginning of this Chapter. If the voltage is outside these limits, check the generator coils and the regulator (see below).

Current leakage check

Caution: Always connect an ammeter in series, never in parallel with the battery, otherwise it will be damaged. Do not turn the ignition ON or operate the starter motor when the ammeter is connected – a sudden surge in current will blow the meter's fuse.

5 Turn the ignition switch OFF and disconnect the lead from the battery negative (-ve) terminal.

6 Set the multimeter to the Amps function and connect its negative (-ve) probe to the battery negative (-ve) terminal, and positive (+ve) probe to the disconnected negative (-ve) lead. Always set the meter to a high amps range initially and then bring it down to the mA (milli Amps) range; if there is a high current flow in the circuit it may blow the meter's fuse. On no account turn the ignition ON during this test.

7 If the current leakage indicated exceeds the amount specified

at the beginning of this Chapter, there is probably a short circuit in the wiring. Disconnect the meter and reconnect the negative (-ve) lead to the battery, tightening it securely,

8 If leakage is indicated, use the wiring diagram at the end of this book to systematically disconnect individual electrical components and repeat the test until the source is identified.

Generator coil check

9 Make sure the ignition is switched off. Remove the left-hand side panel and locate the wiring connectors from the generator which will be under a plastic sleeve. Disconnect the 6-pin multi-connector. Make the following checks on the generator side of the connector (see photo 20.20).

10 To check the charging coil, connect a test meter set to the ohms x 1 range between the white and green wire pins of the connector. Compare the reading obtained with that given in the specifications at the beginning of this Chapter.

11 To check the lighting coil, connect the meter between the yellow and green wire pins and compare the reading with the specified value.

12 If the values are similar to those specified the charging and lighting coils are sound. If, however, infinite (very high) resistance is indicated the coil is open-circuit and the generator stator assembly must be renewed.

Regulator/rectifier check

13 The regulator/rectifier unit is mounted to the frame top tube; remove the petrol tank for access (see Section 12).

14 On CG125 BR-S/T models, the regulator/rectifier internal circuitry can be tested, although note that this is not always conclusive and you should be sure that the fault does not lie elsewhere in the charging system before purchasing a new unit. Remove the regulator/rectifier from the frame having disconnected its wire connector and move it to the bench for testing. Make the checks shown in Fig. 7.8 using a good quality ohmmeter set to the K-ohms scale.

15 No test data is available on CG125-W and M-1 models for testing of the regulator/rectifier internal circuitry. If the voltage output check indicates overcharging or the battery doesn't

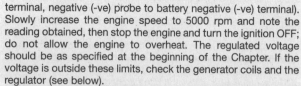

− \ +	White	Yellow	Red	Green
White		∞	3 to 50 KΩ	∞
Yellow	∞		∞	5 to 100 KΩ
Red	∞	∞		∞
Green	∞	5 to 100 KΩ	∞	

Fig. 7.8 Regulator/rectifier test table – CG125 BR-S/T models (∞ = infinity)

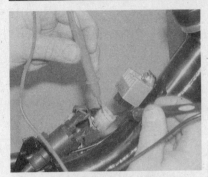

39.16 Regulator/rectifier power supply test

39.20a Resistor location – CG125 BR-S/T models

39.20b Resistor location – CG125-W models

receive a charge at all, yet the charging coil is confirmed good, the regulator/rectifier could be at fault.

16 Ensure the ignition is OFF, then pull off the wire connector and check that the terminals are clean, dry and free from corrosion. Check for battery voltage (12V) between the red wire of the connector (+ve probe of voltmeter, set to the 0-20 dc volts range) and the green wire (-ve probe).

17 Now use an ohmmeter to measure the resistance between the yellow and green wire terminals of the connector – the charging coil value should be shown. Similarly measure the resistance between the white and green wire terminals to obtain the lighting coil value. If either of these two checks show infinite (very high) resistance, yet the generator coil check results were good, there will be a break in the wiring between this point and the generator 6-pin connector.

18 Finally check the earth connection by checking for continuity between the green wire and the frame or engine.

Resistor check

Note: *This check does not apply to CG125M-1 models*

19 The function of the resistor is to drain off excess electrical power when only the side light (pilot light) is in use and convert this to heat to be dissipated by the air stream. When the headlamp switch is in the ON position the resistor is no longer in circuit.

20 The resistor is located on the rear of the frame, bolted to the left-hand side of the tail lamp bracket on BR-S/T models, and between the bracket and tail lamp on CG125-W models; remove the tail fairing for access on all models.

21 Connect a meter set to the ohms x 1 range between the resistor's pink wire connector and earth on its bracket. The value should be as given in the Specifications at the beginning of this Chapter. If the resistor's value differs widely from that specified and especially if pilot bulb failure has been experienced, the resistor should be renewed.

40 Charging/lighting system: checking the output – CG125ES-4 and ES-7 models

Note: *Prior to making checks of the charging or lighting system components, ensure that the battery is fully charged and in good condition.*

Voltage output check

1 Follow the procedure in Section 39, Steps 1 and 2. If the regulated voltage is outside the specified limits, check the charging system as follows. The regulator/rectifier is located underneath the front of the petrol tank on the right-hand side; remove the left-hand side panel, then trace the wiring from the regulator/rectifier and disconnect it at the two-pin connector. Use a multimeter to check for battery voltage between the red/white wire terminal on the loom side of the connector and earth. Now check for continuity between the green wire terminal and earth.

2 Disconnect the alternator three-pin (black) connector and check the stator resistance between the yellow wire terminals on the alternator side of the connector – make three tests. Compare the readings obtained with those given in the Specifications at the beginning of this Chapter. If any of the results are outside the specified limits it is likely the alternator stator is faulty and must be renewed. If the results of the all the above tests are as specified and no faults can be found in the wiring or the connectors, it is likely the regulator/rectifier is faulty.

41 Generator/alternator: removal and refitting

CG125 BR-S/T and CG125-W models
Removal

1 Mark the position of the gearchange lever in relation to the end of the gearchange shaft, then remove its pinch bolt and pull

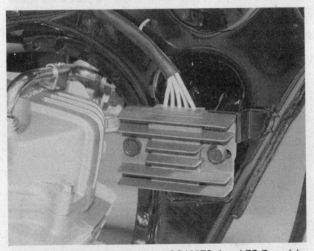

40.1a Regulator/rectifier location – CG125ES-4 and ES-7 models

40.1b Regulator/rectifier connector (A) and alternator connector (B)

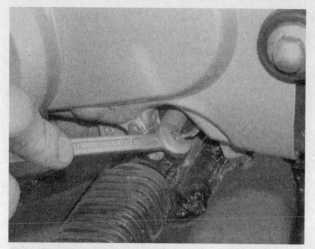

41.1a Remove the gearchange lever . . .

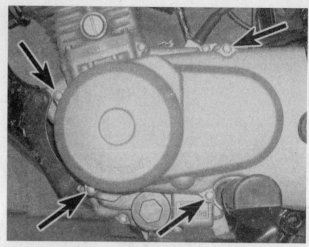

41.1b . . . and the engine cover (four bolts arrowed)

the lever off the shaft. Remove the four bolts and withdraw the engine left-hand cover.

2 Refer to Chapter 1, Section 8, paragraphs 1 and 2 to remove the rotor nut and pull the rotor off the tapered end of the crankshaft. Whichever method is used, take care not to damage the ignition pick-up coil or its trigger set in the rotor periphery. Remove the Woodruff key from its crankshaft slot if it is loose.

3 Trace the wiring up from the generator and disconnect it at the connectors under the left-hand side panel (see photo 22.20). Also free the wiring from any clips and ties and ease the wiring grommet out of the casing. Free the wire from the neutral switch.

4 At this point, either drain the engine oil or be prepared to catch the oil from the crankcase as the stator plate is released. Remove the three bolts and withdraw the stator plate. On W models, if necessary, the coil assembly can be separated from the stator backing plate.

Refitting

5 Prior to refitting the stator plate, check the condition of the oil seal and O-ring in its rear face. It is good practice to renew these as a matter or course. If the stator plate was dismantled on W models, reassemble the coils on the plate, tightening their screws securely.

6 Check that the small spring remains in position in the end of the cam gear shaft, then fit the stator plate, taking care not to damage the oil seal as the stator passes over the crankshaft end; the stator plate has a flat on its top edge which engages the cut-out in the cam gear shaft. Install the three retaining screws and tighten them securely. Seat the wiring grommet in position and reconnect the neutral switch wire. Check that all wiring is routed correctly and secured by any clamps provided. Reconnect the generator wiring connectors.

41.2a Using a holding tool whilst slackening the rotor nut

41.2b Using a puller to draw the rotor off the crankshaft

41.4 Stator plate is retained by three bolts (arrows)

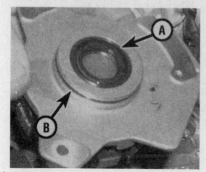

41.5 Renew the oil seal (A) and O-ring (B) set in the rear face of the stator plate

41.6a Install the small spring in the cam gear shaft end

41.6b Ensure that the wiring grommet is seated in the casing

41.7a Install the Woodruff key in its slot

41.7b Install the rotor and washer . . .

41.7c . . . followed by the nut

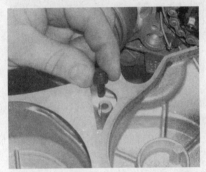
41.8 Insert the neutral switch bung in the cover

41.10a Remove the reduction gear cover . . .

41.10b . . . then draw out the shaft and the gear

7 If the Woodruff key was removed from the crankshaft, refit it into its slot. Wipe the inside of the generator rotor clean and install the rotor on the crankshaft taper aligning its slot with the Woodruff key. Install the washer (if the washer has OUTSIDE stamped in one face, ensure this faces outwards) and thread the nut onto the crankshaft end to draw the rotor down onto the taper. Using one of the methods used on removal to hold the rotor, tighten the nut to the specified torque setting.

8 Make sure that the neutral switch bung is in place in the engine left-hand cover, then position a new gasket on the cover and fit the cover to the engine, securing it with the four bolts. Realign the gearchange lever using the previously made marks, and tighten its pinch bolt. Check the engine oil level and top-up if necessary. Run the engine for a few minutes, then recheck the oil level.

CG125M-1, CG125ES-4 and CG125ES-7 models

Removal

Note: *To remove the alternator rotor you will require Honda service tool Pt. No. 07733-0020001 or a similar commercially-available puller.*

9 Follow the procedure in Section 9 to remove the gearbox sprocket cover and disconnect the alternator and ignition pick-up coil wiring connectors.

10 Remove the starter reduction gear cover, noting the cover O-ring, then draw out the gear shaft and reduction gear.

11 Remove the alternator wiring guide and disconnect the wire from the neutral switch terminal.

12 Remove the seven bolts securing the left-hand crankcase cover – note that one bolt is inside the opening for the starter reduction gear. Note where the bolts fit as they are of different

41.11a Remove the wiring guide (arrow) . . .

41.11b . . . and disconnect the neutral switch wire

41.12a Remove the engine cover bolts . . .

41.12b . . . and lift off the cover, noting the dowels (arrows)

41.12c Draw out the idler gear and shaft

41.13a Undo the rotor centre bolt . . .

41.13b . . . and remove the bolt and large washer

41.13c Using a special puller to draw the rotor off the crankshaft

41.13d The starter driven gear is on the back of the rotor

41.13e Remove the Woodruff key (arrow) if it is loose

41.14 Oil seal holder is secured by two bolts

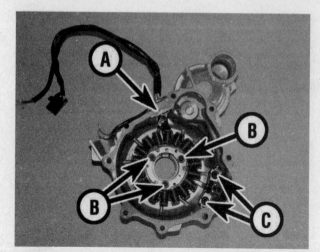

41.15 Wiring grommet (A), stator bolts (B) and pick-up coil bolts (C)

lengths. Tap the cover smartly with a soft-faced mallet to break the seal and lift it off, noting the location of the two cover dowels. Be prepared to catch any residual oil when the cover is removed. Draw out the starter idler gear and shaft.

13 Hold the rotor to prevent it turning, then undo the centre bolt – note the large washer on the bolt. Thread the puller carefully all the way into the internal threads in the rotor centre, then hold the rotor and strike the pulley sharply to draw the rotor off the crankshaft taper. Lift off the rotor – the starter driven gear will come off with it. Turn the driven gear anti-clockwise to release it from the starter clutch on the back of the rotor. Note the location of the Woodruff key in the crankshaft and remove it if is loose.

14 If required, undo the two bolts securing the crankshaft oil seal holder and carefully draw it off.

15 To remove the alternator stator from inside the crankcase cover, first lift out the wiring clamp and grommet, then undo the bolts securing the stator and ignition pick-up coil and lift the assembly out.

Refitting

16 Position the stator assembly in the crankcase cover. Clean the threads of the ignition pick-up coil mounting bolts and apply

41.17 Note which way round the crankshaft seal is fitted in the holder

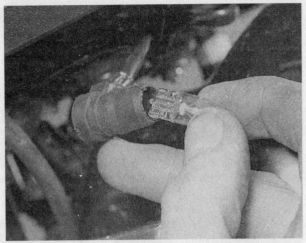

43.1 Instrument panel bulbs are of capless type – remove and refit as described for earlier models

a suitable non-permanent thread locking compound to the bolts, then tighten them to the specified torque setting. Install the stator mounting bolts and tighten them to the specified torque. Apply sealant to the wiring grommet and install it and the wiring clamp in the cover.

17 Install a new seal in the crankshaft seal holder, making sure it is fitted the right way round, then lubricate the seal and slide it carefully over the shaft. Tighten the seal holder bolts securely. If the Woodruff key was removed from the crankshaft, refit it into its slot.

18 Install the starter driven gear into the starter clutch on the back of the alternator rotor, turning it anti-clockwise. To check the operation of the starter clutch, it should rotate freely anti-clockwise, but lock when turned clockwise. If there is a fault with the starter clutch, refer to Section 52.

19 Install the rotor on the crankshaft taper aligning its slot with the Woodruff key. Apply clean engine oil to the threads of the rotor bolt, then fit the washer and thread the bolt onto the crankshaft end. Hold the rotor and tighten the bolt to the specified torque setting.

20 Install the starter idler gear and shaft. Ensure the cover dowels are in place, fit a new gasket onto the cover and fit the cover to the engine. Secure the cover with the seven bolts, tightening them evenly in a criss-cross pattern.

21 Install the starter reduction gear and shaft, then smear the cover O-ring with oil and install the cover.

22 Ensure the alternator wiring is correctly routed, then fit the wiring guide and connect the neutral switch wire to the terminal.

23 Connect the alternator and ignition pick-up coil wiring

connectors and install the gearbox sprocket cover (see Section 9).

24 Check the engine oil level and top-up if necessary. Run the engine for a few minutes, then recheck the oil level.

42 Ignition switch: removal and refitting

Note that the ignition switch is mounted in the instrument panel and is secured in the same way as described in Chapter 6 for CG125-C and E models. It will be necessary to remove the complete panel and dismantle it, as described in Section 33, to gain access to the switch mounting,

43 Instrument panel bulbs: removal and refitting

1 Although the instrument panel is very different in appearance from that fitted to earlier models, the instrument and warning lamp bulbholders and bulbs are fitted in the same way as described in Chapter 6. Note that it may be necessary to remove the two mounting bolts and to lift the instrument panel upwards to gain access to an awkwardly placed bulbholder, or to remove the headlamp shell.

2 On CG125ES-4 and ES-7 models, follow the procedure in Section 33 and remove the instrument panel, then remove the three small screws which secure the bottom cover and lift it off. Unplug the bulbholders and pull the bulb out carefully; the bulbs are of the capless type.

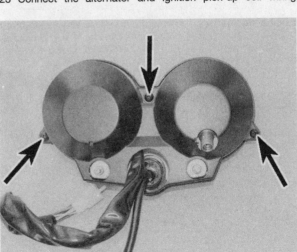

43.2a Bottom cover is secured by three screws

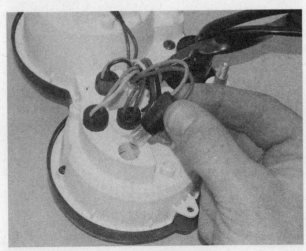

43.2b Unplug the instrument panel bulbholders

44.1a Headlamp bulb removal – all BR models

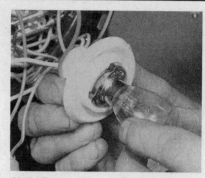

44.1b Ensure bulb locating tangs engage with matching slots in holder

44.1c Pilot lamp bulbholder is a press fit in reflector . . .

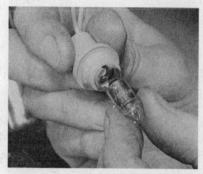

44.1d . . . bulb is of bayonet type – always ensure correct wattage bulb is fitted

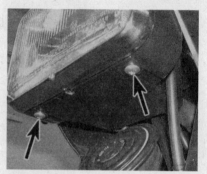

44.3a Remove the two screws (arrows) from the shell to release the headlamp

44.3b Peel back rubber cover to access the bulbholder

44   Headlamp: replacing bulbs and adjusting beam height

Bulb replacement – all BR models, CG125ES-4 and CG125ES-7 models

1 Refer to Chapter 6, Section 6, noting that on BR models the headlamp and pilot lamp bulbholders have been modified slightly as shown in the accompanying photographs.

2 CG125ES-4 and ES-7 models are fitted with a lighting relay. If the headlight fails to work, first check the bulb and headlight fuse – if they are both good, the problem could be a faulty relay. The relay is located on the right-hand side underneath the seat – note that the relay has a four-pin wiring connector. Disconnect the relay and check that there is no continuity between the blue/white and black/brown wire terminals on the relay; now connect the green/red and yellow/red wire terminals to a 12V battery – there should be continuity.

Bulb replacement – CG125-W and CG125M-1 models

3 To access the bulbs, remove the two screws from the base of the headlamp shell and ease the headlamp out of the shell. The headlamp bulb can be reached by peeling back the rubber cover, then manoeuvring the bulbholder against the tension of its two retaining springs to free it from the headlamp. Push the bulb in and turn it anticlockwise to release it from the bulbholder.

4 The pilot lamp bulbholder can be simply pulled out of the headlamp. Push the bulb in and twist it anticlockwise to free it from the bulbholder.

5 When installing new bulbs, use a tissue, rather than your fingers, to handle the glass of the new bulb. Align the pins on the bulb fitting with the slots in the bulbholder. Push the bulb in and

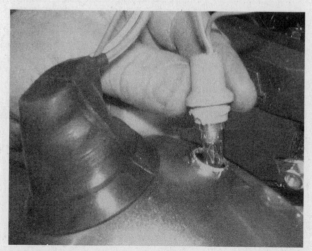

44.4 Pilot lamp bulbholder is a push fit

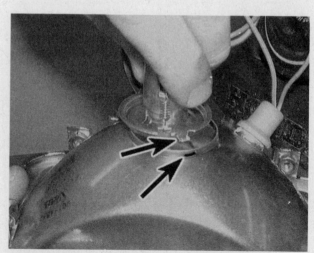

44.5 Note the tab on the bulbholder which engages the slot (arrows)

44.6a The shell is retained by a bolt on each side

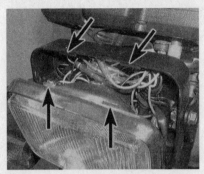

44.6b Engage the lugs at the top of the headlamp (arrows)

44.9 Beam adjustment screw

45.1 Take great care when removing and refitting the tail lamp lens

46.1a Undo the screws with a cranked screwdriver . . .

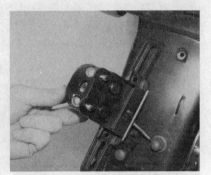

46.1b . . . or displace the assembly to gain access

twist it clockwise. Install the bulbholder back into the headlight and on the headlight bulb refit the rubber cover.

6 To free the headlamp unit completely, leave the bulbs in place and disconnect their wiring at the connectors. Remove the two bolts with spacers, which retain the headlamp shell to the mounting brackets. Feed the wiring through the hole in the back of the shell. Refit in a reverse of the removal procedure. When installing the headlamp in the shell, note that the lugs at the top of the headlamp must engage the slots in the shell.

Beam height adjustment – CG125-W and CG125M-1 models

7 To check the beam setting, position the motorcycle in a straight line facing a brick wall. The motorcycle must be off its

46.2 Lift off the lens cover

stand, upright and with a rider seated. Measure the height from the ground to the centre of the headlamp and mark a horizontal line on the wall at this height. Position the motorcycle 3.8 metres from the wall and draw a vertical line up the wall central to the centreline of the motorcycle.

8 Turn on the lights and switch to dip beam. Check that the beam pattern fails slightly lower than the horizontal line and (in the UK) to the left of the vertical line.

9 To make vertical adjustment, turn the screw set in the centre of the headlamp rim at the bottom edge until the beam height is correct. There is no provision for horizontal adjustment of the beam.

---

45   Tail and stop lamp: replacing bulbs – CG125ES-4 and ES-7 models

---

1 To gain access to the bulb, remove the two screws holding the red plastic lens in position and carefully ease the lens off. The bulb is released by pressing it inwards and turning it anti-clockwise. Note that the locating pins on the bulb are offset so that it can only be installed one way round.

2 When installing the lens, take great care to ensure it is fitted over the top of the reflector inside the tail fairing – it may be necessary to displace the tail fairing to ensure the lens is correctly fitted (see Section 32).

---

46   Licence plate lamp: replacing bulbs – CG125ES-4 and ES-7 models

---

1 If available, use a cranked screwdriver to undo the two lens cover screws on the back of the lamp assembly. Alternatively, undo the two nuts on the underside of the mudguard and displace the lamp assembly and license plate bracket to access the cover screws.

2 Remove the lens cover, then press the bulb inwards and turn it anti-clockwise to remove it.

47.1a Remove the screw from the housing . . .

47.1b . . . then disengage the lens tang . . .

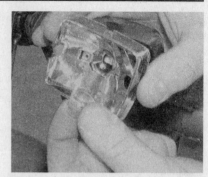

47.1c . . . and remove the bulb

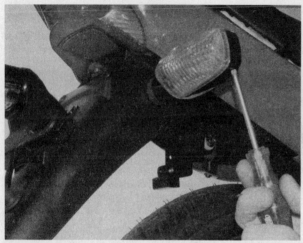

47.3a Remove the screw – CG125ES-4 and ES-7 models

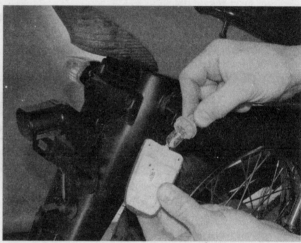

47.3b Turn the bulbholder to remove it

47 Flashing indicator lamps: replacing bulbs – CG125-W, CG125M-1, CG125ES-4 and CG125ES-7 models

CG125-W and CG125M-1 models

1 To access the bulb, remove the single screw from the rear of the indicator housing and unhook the lens from its slot in the housing. Push the bulb in and turn it anticlockwise to free it from the bulbholder.
2 When installing a new bulb, use a paper tissue, rather than your fingers, to handle the glass of the new bulb. Align the pins on the bulb fitting with the slots in the bulbholder. Push the bulb in and twist it clockwise. Engage the tab on the lens with the slot in the housing, then secure the lens with the screw.

CG125ES-4 and ES-7 models

3 To access the bulb, remove the single screw from the underside of the indicator housing and displace the lens. Turn

the bulbholder anti-clockwise to remove it, then pull out the bulb – it is of the capless type. Take care not to damage the fine wire terminals on fitting the new bulb.

48 Flasher unit: location and testing

1 The flasher unit is located on the left-hand side of the motorcycle, to the rear of the battery on all BR models and forward of the battery on CG125-W and CG125M-1 models; remove the left-hand side panel for access. The flasher unit is located on the right-hand side of the motorcycle underneath the seat on CG125ES-4 and ES-7 models – note that on these models, the flasher unit has a three-pin wiring connector, the lighting relay next to it has a four-pin connector.
2 Failure of a single indicator is usually due to a burned out bulb and failure of both indicators on one side can usually be attributed to a faulty indicator switch. If total failure is

48.1a Flasher unit location – BR models

48.1b Flasher unit location – CG125-W and CG125M-1 models

48.1c Flasher unit location – CG125ES-4 and ES-7 models

experienced, and the battery is fully charged and the associated electrical circuits (brake light, horn and neutral light) are functioning correctly, the flasher unit could be at fault.

3 The flasher unit should emit an audible click when in operation. To check the operation of the flasher unit, disconnect its wiring connector and use a short jumper wire to bridge the grey and black or grey and black/blue wire terminals of the connector. Turn the ignition ON (on CG125ES-4 and ES-7 models, start the engine); the indicators on one side should be illuminated (but will not flash) with the indicator switch set in L or R positions. Turn the ignition OFF and disconnect the jumper wire. If the indicator bulbs illuminated during the above test, yet do not work with the flasher unit connected, the flasher unit is confirmed faulty.

49 Fuel level sensor: location and testing – CG125ES-4 and ES-7 models

1 The fuel level sensor is located in the petrol tank. Drain the fuel from the tank, then follow the procedure in Section 12 and remove the tank. Undo the four nuts securing the sensor and lift it out, noting the O-ring. Check the float for damage and that the float arm move smoothly up and down.

2 Reconnect the sensor wiring connector, hold the float in the down (empty) position, and turn the ignition ON. Now raise the float up to the full position and check that the fuel gauge needle moves from E to F. If it does not, disconnect the sensor wiring and test the sensor resistance between the terminals in the wiring connector. Compare the results with the Specifications at the beginning of this Chapter – if they vary greatly, renew the sensor, if they are good it is likely the fuel gauge is faulty.

3 To access the fuel gauge, follow the procedure in Section 33 and dismantle the instrument panel.

50 Clutch switch, neutral switch and diode: location and testing – CG125M-1, CG125ES-4 and CG125ES-7 models

1 The clutch switch, neutral switch and diode are part of the safety circuit which prevents the engine from starting unless the clutch lever is pulled in and the transmission is in neutral. The clutch switch is housed in the clutch lever bracket.

2 To check the switch, disconnect the wiring connectors and test for continuity between the switch terminals – with the lever out, there should be no continuity, with the lever pulled in, there should be continuity.

3 If the switch is good, check for voltage at one of the terminals on the clutch switch wiring connectors with the ignition ON – there will be voltage on one terminal and zero on the other. If voltage is indicated, check the other components in the starter circuit. If no voltage is indicated, or if all components are good, check the wiring between the various components (see the Wiring diagrams at the end of this Chapter).

4 To renew the switch, first remove the clutch lever. Disconnect the wiring connectors from the switch, then push it from the connector end and withdraw it from inside the bracket.

5 The neutral switch is screwed into the left-hand side of the crankcase behind the gearbox sprocket cover. To check the switch, first follow the procedure in Section 9 and remove the cover, then disconnect the wire from the neutral switch terminal. With the transmission in neutral there should be continuity between the switch terminal and earth.

6 If the neutral switch is good but the warning lamp does not come on, check for voltage in the neutral switch wire and check the wire for continuity between the connector, diode and instrument panel (see the Wiring diagrams at the end of this Chapter). Also check the warning lamp bulb and the fuse.

7 The diode is a small block that plugs into the main wiring harness underneath the tail fairing. To check the diode, disconnect the wiring connector and test for continuity between the diode terminals. Now reverse the test probes. The diode should show continuity in one direction only (as indicated by the symbol on the body of the diode). If the diode shows continuity, or no continuity, in both directions, it should be renewed.

51 Starter relay: location and testing – CG125M-1, CG125ES-4 and CG125ES-7 models

1 The starter relay is located on the left-hand side behind the battery. If the starter circuit is faulty, first check the main fuse and, on CG125ES-4 and ES-7 models, the ignition/starter fuse.

2 To check the relay, lift the rubber terminal cover and unscrew the nut securing the starter motor lead. Position the lead well away from the relay terminal. With the ignition switch ON, the transmission in neutral and the clutch switch pulled in, press the starter button. The relay should be heard to click.

3 If the relay doesn't click, switch the ignition OFF and remove the relay – disconnect the battery, then disconnect the relay wiring connector and unscrew the two nuts securing the starter motor and battery leads to the relay.

4 Test the relay as follows. Set a multimeter to the ohms scale and connect it across the relay's starter motor and battery lead terminals. Using a fully-charged 12 volt battery and two jumper wires, connect the positive (+ve) terminal of the battery to the yellow/red wire terminal of the relay, and the negative (-ve) terminal to the green/red wire terminal of the relay. At this point the relay should be heard to click and the multimeter read 0 ohms (continuity). If the relay does not click when voltage is applied and indicates no continuity (infinite resistance) across its terminals, it is faulty and must be renewed.

5 If the relay is good, fit it back on the machine and connect the wiring connector. Check for battery voltage between the yellow/red wire terminal in the connector and earth when the starter button is pressed with the ignition switch ON, the transmission in neutral and the clutch switch pulled in.

52 Starter clutch: check, removal and refitting – CG125M-1, CG125ES-4 and CG125ES-7 models

1 The starter clutch is mounted on the back of the alternator rotor. To check the operation of the starter clutch, remove the

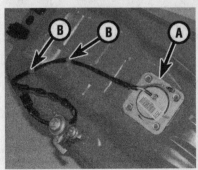

49.1 Location of the fuel level sensor (A) - note the location of the wiring clips (B)

50.1 Clutch switch location

51.1 Starter relay location

52.1 Starter driven gear should rotate freely clockwise

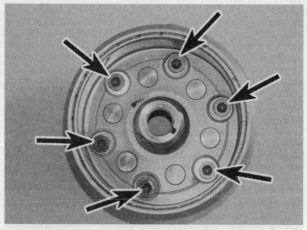

52.2 Starter clutch is secured by six bolts (arrowed)

52.3 Withdraw the driven gear from the starter clutch

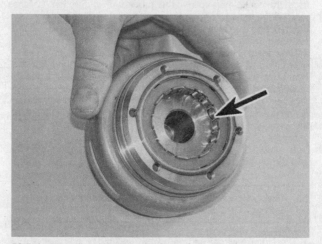

52.5 Inspect the clutch sprags (arrow)

starter reduction gear cover then draw out the gear shaft and reduction gear (see Section 41). The starter idler gear should rotate freely in an anti-clockwise direction but lock in a clockwise direction. Alternatively, remove the left-hand crankcase cover and check that the starter driven gear on the back of the alternator rotor rotates freely in a clockwise direction but locks in an anti-clockwise direction. If not, the starter clutch is faulty and should be removed for inspection.

2 Follow the procedure in Section 41 and remove the alternator rotor. **Note:** *Before removing the alternator rotor, slacken the six starter clutch bolts while holding the rotor centre. If the rotor has already been removed from the bike, hold the rotor with a strap wrench to slacken the bolts.*

3 Withdraw the starter driven gear from the starter clutch. If the gear appears stuck, rotate it anti-clockwise as you withdraw it to free it from the starter clutch.

4 Inspect the starter idler gear and driven gear teeth and renew them as a pair if any teeth are chipped or missing. Check the idler shaft and gear bearing surfaces for signs of wear or damage, and renew if necessary. With the alternator rotor face-down, check that the starter driven gear rotates freely in an anti-clockwise direction and locks against the rotor in a clockwise direction. If it doesn't, the starter clutch should be dismantled. Unscrew the six bolts and remove the clutch assembly from the back of the alternator rotor.

5 Inspect the condition of the clutch sprags and cage inside the clutch assembly; if they are damaged or worn, the assembly should be renewed – individual components are not available.

6 On reassembly, clean the threads of the starter clutch bolts and apply a suitable non-permanent thread locking compound, then tighten the bolts to the specified torque setting. Lubricate the starter clutch assembly with clean engine oil.

53 Starter motor: removal, inspection and refitting – CG125M-1, CG125ES-4 and CG125ES-7 models

1 Disconnect the lead from the starter motor terminal and undo the starter motor mounting bolts. Pull the starter motor out and lift out the mounting bolts. Note the O-ring on the end of the starter motor body.

2 Note the alignment marks between the main housing and the

53.1 Pull the starter motor out

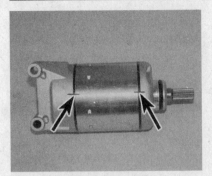

53.2a Note the alignment marks

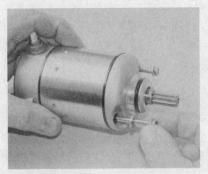

53.2b Remove the two long bolts

53.3a Remove the front cover . . .

53.3b . . . . remove the main housing . . .

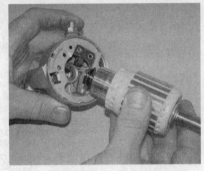

53.3c . . . and remove the rear cover and brushplate assembly

53.4a Remove the terminal nut and washers . . .

front and rear covers, or make your own if they aren't clear. Unscrew the two long bolts, noting how the D-shaped washers locate, and withdraw them from the starter motor. Note the O-rings on the bolts.

3 Remove the front cover, noting the tabbed thrust washer inside the cover, then remove the insulating washer and shims from the front end of the armature shaft, noting the order in which they are fitted. Remove the main housing, noting the cover O-rings. Remove the rear cover and brushplate assembly from the armature commutator, then remove the shims from the rear end of the armature shaft.

4 Noting the order in which they are fitted, unscrew the terminal nut and remove it along with its washer, the insulating washers and O-ring. Withdraw the terminal and brushplate assembly from the rear cover.

5 Lift the brush springs and slide the brushes out from their holders, noting that one brush is attached to the terminal and the other is attached to the brushplate.

6 Check the general condition of all the starter motor components – the parts that are most likely to require attention are the brushes. Measure the length of the brushes and compare the results to this Chapter's Specifications. If either of the brushes is worn beyond the service limit, renew the brush assembly. Inspect the commutator bars on the armature for scoring – the commutator can be cleaned and polished with crocus cloth, but do not use sandpaper or emery paper. After cleaning, wipe away any residue with a cloth soaked in electrical system cleaner.

7 Check for continuity between the commutator bars – continuity (zero resistance) should exist between each bar and all of the others. Also, check for continuity between the

53.4b . . . and remove the brushplate assembly from the cover

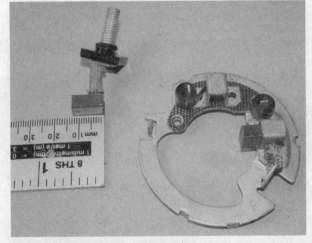

53.6 Measure the starter motor brushes

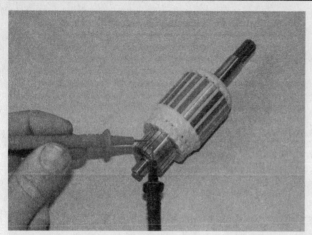

53.7a Continuity should exist between the commutator bars

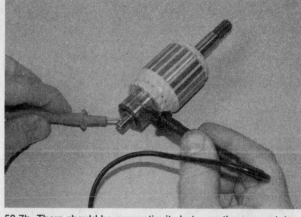

53.7b There should be no continuity between the commutator bars and the armature shaft

commutator bars and the armature shaft – there should be no continuity (infinite resistance) between the commutator and the shaft. If the checks indicate otherwise, the armature is defective.
8 On reassembly, fit the brushplate assembly into the cover, making sure its tab is correctly located in the slot in the cover. Slide the shims onto the rear end of the armature shaft and lubricate the shaft with a smear of grease before fitting it into the rear cover. Check that each brush is correctly located on the commutator.

9 Fit new O-rings onto the main housing and align the marks noted on removal. Slide the shims and then the insulating washer onto the front end of the armature shaft and lubricate the shaft with a smear of grease. Fit the tabbed washer into the cover, install the cover onto the main housing and secure it with the long bolts, making sure the flat edge on each D-washer is correctly fitted against the front cover.
10 When the starter motor is installed in the engine, don't forget to secure the earth lead with the mounting bolt.

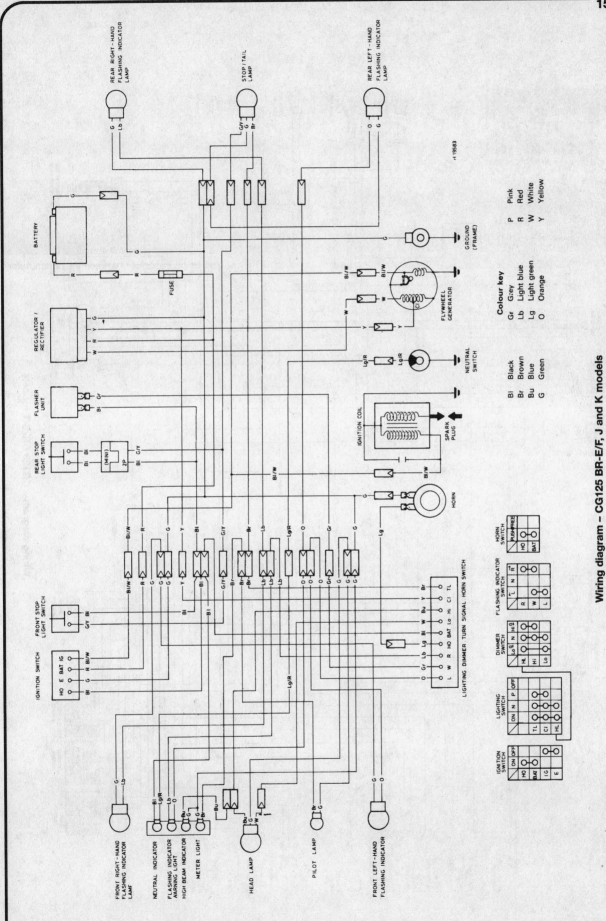

Wiring diagram – CG125 BR-E/F, J and K models

H 19583

Colour key

P	Pink
R	Red
W	White
Y	Yellow
Gr	Grey
Lb	Light blue
Lg	Light green
O	Orange
Bl	Black
Br	Brown
Bu	Blue
G	Green

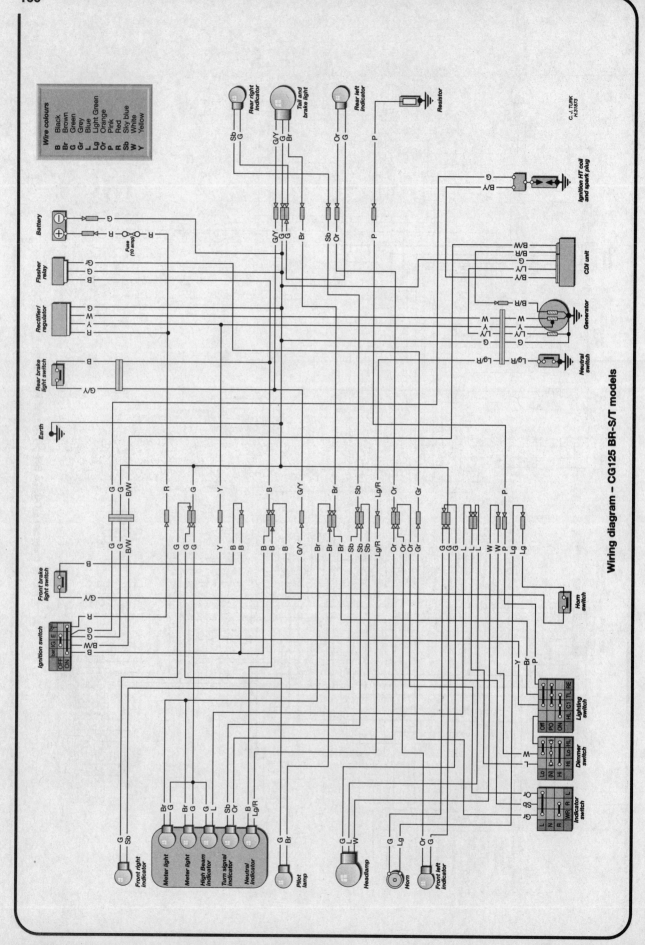

Wiring diagram – CG125 BR-S/T models

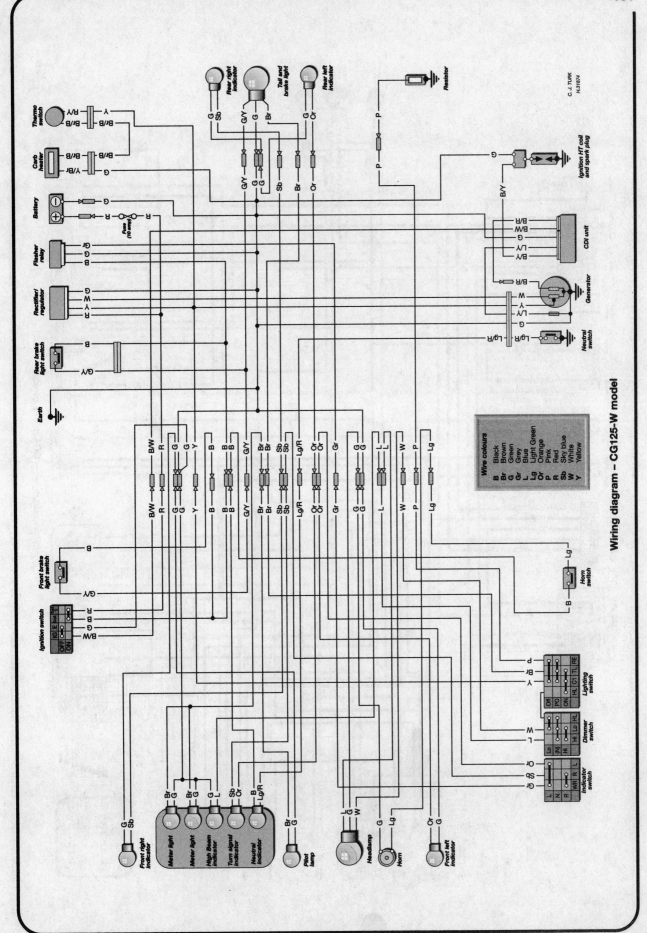

Wiring diagram – CG125-W model

C. J. TURK
H.31874

Wire colours	
B	Black
Br	Brown
G	Green
Gr	Grey
L	Blue
Lg	Light Green
Or	Orange
P	Pink
R	Red
Sb	Sky blue
W	White
Y	Yellow

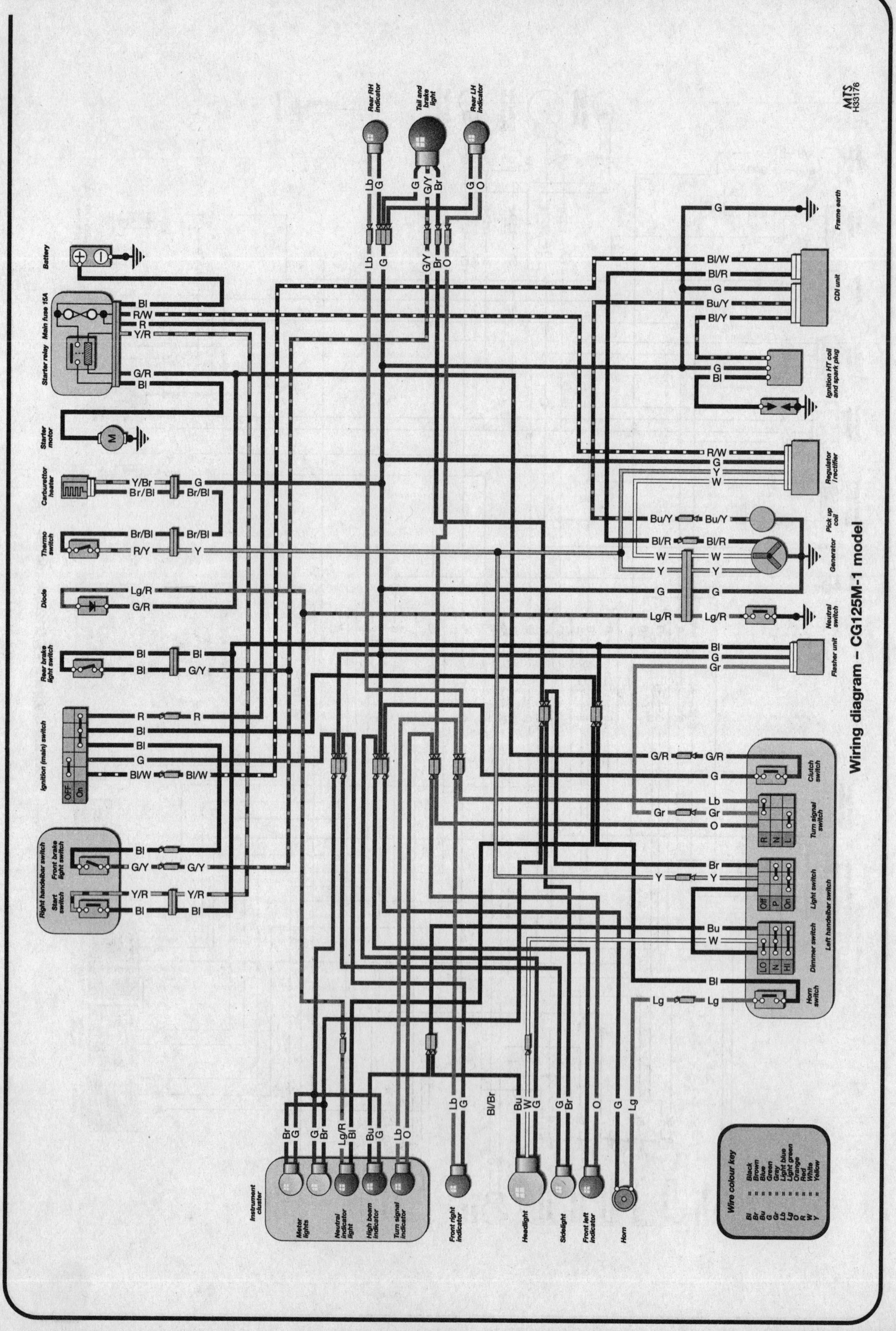

Rear RH indicator

Tail and brake light

Rear LH indicator

Battery

Main fuse 15A

Starter relay

Starter motor

Carburettor heater

Thermo switch

Diode

Rear brake light switch

Ignition (main) switch

Right handlebar switch

Front brake light switch

Start switch

Instrument cluster

Meter lights

Neutral indicator light

High beam indicator

Turn signal indicator

Front right indicator

Headlight

Sidelight

Front left indicator

Horn

Frame earth

CDI unit

Ignition HT coil and spark plug

Regulator / rectifier

Pick up coil

Generator

Neutral switch

Flasher unit

Clutch switch

Turn signal switch

Light switch

Dimmer switch

Horn switch

Left handlebar switch

Wiring diagram – CG125M-1 model

Wire colour key

Bl — Black
Br — Brown
Bu — Blue
Lb — Light blue
Lg — Light green
G — Green
Gr — Grey
O — Orange
R — Red
W — White
Y — Yellow

MTS
H33176

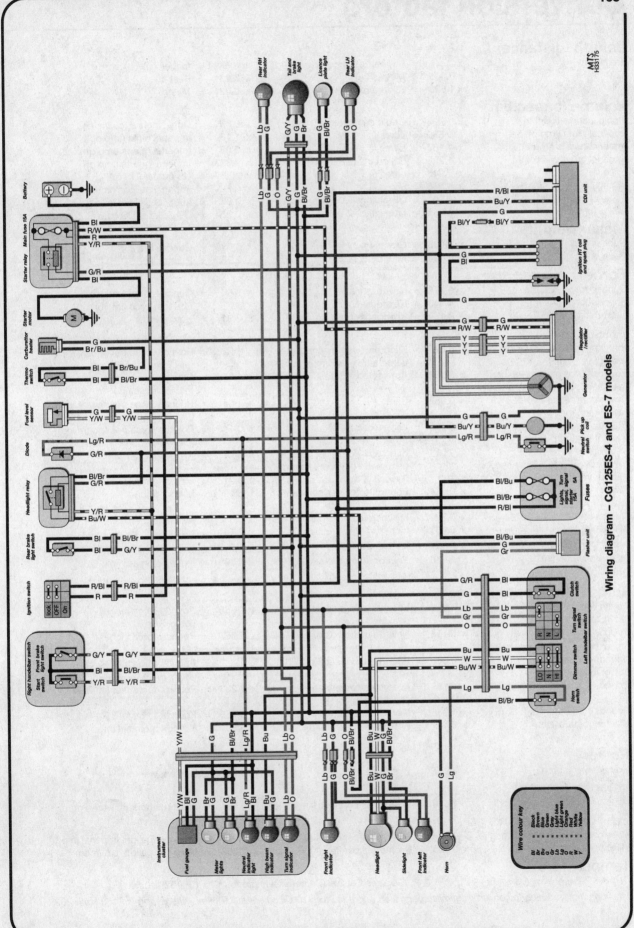

Wiring diagram – CG125ES-4 and ES-7 models

Conversion factors

Length (distance)

Inches (in)	x 25.4	= Millimetres (mm)	x 0.0394	=	Inches (in)
Feet (ft)	x 0.305	= Metres (m)	x 3.281	=	Feet (ft)
Miles	x 1.609	= Kilometres (km)	x 0.621	=	Miles

Volume (capacity)

Cubic inches (cu in; in³)	x 16.387	= Cubic centimetres (cc; cm³)	x 0.061	=	Cubic inches (cu in; in³)
Imperial pints (Imp pt)	x 0.568	= Litres (l)	x 1.76	=	Imperial pints (Imp pt)
Imperial quarts (Imp qt)	x 1.137	= Litres (l)	x 0.88	=	Imperial quarts (Imp qt)
Imperial quarts (Imp qt)	x 1.201	= US quarts (US qt)	x 0.833	=	Imperial quarts (Imp qt)
US quarts (US qt)	x 0.946	= Litres (l)	x 1.057	=	US quarts (US qt)
Imperial gallons (Imp gal)	x 4.546	= Litres (l)	x 0.22	=	Imperial gallons (Imp gal)
Imperial gallons (Imp gal)	x 1.201	= US gallons (US gal)	x 0.833	=	Imperial gallons (Imp gal)
US gallons (US gal)	x 3.785	= Litres (l)	x 0.264	=	US gallons (US gal)

Mass (weight)

Ounces (oz)	x 28.35	= Grams (g)	x 0.035	=	Ounces (oz)
Pounds (lb)	x 0.454	= Kilograms (kg)	x 2.205	=	Pounds (lb)

Force

Ounces-force (ozf; oz)	x 0.278	= Newtons (N)	x 3.6	=	Ounces-force (ozf; oz)
Pounds-force (lbf; lb)	x 4.448	= Newtons (N)	x 0.225	=	Pounds-force (lbf; lb)
Newtons (N)	x 0.1	= Kilograms-force (kgf; kg)	x 9.81	=	Newtons (N)

Pressure

Pounds-force per square inch (psi; lbf/in²; lb/in²)	x 0.070	= Kilograms-force per square centimetre (kgf/cm²; kg/cm²)	x 14.223	=	Pounds-force per square inch (psi; lbf/in²; lb/in²)
Pounds-force per square inch (psi; lbf/in²; lb/in²)	x 0.068	= Atmospheres (atm)	x 14.696	=	Pounds-force per square inch (psi; lbf/in²; lb/in²)
Pounds-force per square inch (psi; lbf/in²; lb/in²)	x 0.069	= Bars	x 14.5	=	Pounds-force per square inch (psi; lbf/in²; lb/in²)
Pounds-force per square inch (psi; lbf/in²; lb/in²)	x 6.895	= Kilopascals (kPa)	x 0.145	=	Pounds-force per square inch (psi; lbf/in²; lb/in²)
Kilopascals (kPa)	x 0.01	= Kilograms-force per square centimetre (kgf/cm²; kg/cm²)	x 98.1	=	Kilopascals (kPa)
Millibar (mbar)	x 100	= Pascals (Pa)	x 0.01	=	Millibar (mbar)
Millibar (mbar)	x 0.0145	= Pounds-force per square inch (psi; lbf/in²; lb/in²)	x 68.947	=	Millibar (mbar)
Millibar (mbar)	x 0.75	= Millimetres of mercury (mmHg)	x 1.333	=	Millibar (mbar)
Millibar (mbar)	x 0.401	= Inches of water (inH₂O)	x 2.491	=	Millibar (mbar)
Millimetres of mercury (mmHg)	x 0.535	= Inches of water (inH₂O)	x 1.868	=	Millimetres of mercury (mmHg)
Inches of water (inH₂O)	x 0.036	= Pounds-force per square inch (psi; lbf/in²; lb/in²)	x 27.68	=	Inches of water (inH₂O)

Torque (moment of force)

Pounds-force inches (lbf in; lb in)	x 1.152	= Kilograms-force centimetre (kgf cm; kg cm)	x 0.868	=	Pounds-force inches (lbf in; lb in)
Pounds-force inches (lbf in; lb in)	x 0.113	= Newton metres (Nm)	x 8.85	=	Pounds-force inches (lbf in; lb in)
Pounds-force inches (lbf in; lb in)	x 0.083	= Pounds-force feet (lbf ft; lb ft)	x 12	=	Pounds-force inches (lbf in; lb in)
Pounds-force feet (lbf ft; lb ft)	x 0.138	= Kilograms-force metres (kgf m; kg m)	x 7.233	=	Pounds-force feet (lbf ft; lb ft)
Pounds-force feet (lbf ft; lb ft)	x 1.356	= Newton metres (Nm)	x 0.738	=	Pounds-force feet (lbf ft; lb ft)
Newton metres (Nm)	x 0.102	= Kilograms-force metres (kgf m; kg m)	x 9.804	=	Newton metres (Nm)

Power

Horsepower (hp)	x 745.7	= Watts (W)	x 0.0013	=	Horsepower (hp)

Velocity (speed)

Miles per hour (miles/hr; mph)	x 1.609	= Kilometres per hour (km/hr; kph)	x 0.621	=	Miles per hour (miles/hr; mph)

Fuel consumption*

Miles per gallon, Imperial (mpg)	x 0.354	= Kilometres per litre (km/l)	x 2.825	=	Miles per gallon, Imperial (mpg)
Miles per gallon, US (mpg)	x 0.425	= Kilometres per litre (km/l)	x 2.352	=	Miles per gallon, US (mpg)

Temperature

Degrees Fahrenheit = (°C x 1.8) + 32   Degrees Celsius (Degrees Centigrade; °C) = (°F - 32) x 0.56

It is common practice to convert from miles per gallon (mpg) to litres/100 kilometres (l/100km), where mpg x l/100 km = 282

Index